THE SUNNY SOUTH

FRONTISPIECE: **Old Cotton Picker**, oil on canvas, 42 x 24 inches, signed lower left: *WAWalker*. Private Collection.

THE SUNNY SOUTH

THE LIFE AND ART OF

WILLIAM AIKEN
WALKER

CYNTHIA SEIBELS

SARALAND PRESS
SPARTANBURG, SOUTH CAROLINA

A Saraland Press Book
509 East Saint John Street
Spartanburg, South Carolina 29302
(803) 583-9847

The Sunny South:
The Life and Art of William Aiken Walker

ISBN 0-9632836-1-8

Developed and produced by Robert M. Hicklin Jr., Inc.

Editor
Lynne Blackman

Assistant Editor
Holly Watters

Design
Anne Morgan Jones

Manufactured in the United States of America
by Quebecor Printing, Kingsport, Tennessee

Table of Contents

FIGURE 1. *Self-portrait of William Aiken Walker,* 1869, photograph colored with oil paints, 6 1/2 x 4 inches, signed and dated on rock: *WAWalker./ 1869.* Printed on cardboard mount: *Photographed by QUINBY & Co./Charleston, S. C.* The Sewell Family Collection, Vidalia, Louisiana.

Foreword

Giving title to a painting is a work of art in itself. The titles of most works are creative at best, confounding at worst. Whether rationally or randomly assigned by artist, client, collector or dealer, these appellations can be a source of great insight, amusement or frustration to the present–day patron. Once named, the art is frequently renamed by subsequent owners or students, thereby adding to the general confusion. This fundamental fact of art–life is nowhere more true than in the works of William Aiken Walker.

Book titles are not much different. In christening this manuscript, we decided early on that life and art pretty well said it all, for this study is as much biography as monograph. We then appended the title, adding THE SUNNY SOUTH in large, capital letters. Appropriately, this is Walker's title for the masterwork reproduced on the book's cover. Moreover, those words sum up Walker's unyielding vision of his homeland.

My work, too, is all about The Sunny South, its people, its culture, its art. The pages you hold in your hand are a testimony to Cynthia Seibels' research and writing. Thanks to her diligence, we believe that many of the missing or misplaced pieces of William Aiken Walker's life are now correctly and expertly assembled here.

A distinct mention must go to the collectors who have cultivated the crop. Jay Altmayer was the first of this century to amass a large and important holding. Jack Warner, Logan Sewell, Billy Morris, and the late George Arden have each pursued Walker with similar fervor. Their respective collections and their willingness to share those treasures with this publication are greatly appreciated.

It should be recalled that each of these gentlemen has relied on the abilities of a number of good dealers to assemble their collections. The late Albert Lieutaud, Ray Samuel, Ray Holsclaw, and Herman Schindler all made immeasurable contributions to Walker scholarship during their lifetimes. Friends like these make it a truly sunny South. It is with this volume that I salute them all.

Robert M. Hicklin, Jr.

Acknowledgements

Thanks and acknowledgement are owed to many persons who lent their time, resources, or expertise to *The Sunny South.* First and foremost, to the book's publisher, Robert M. Hicklin, Jr., who over coffee in New Orleans asked me in May 1988 to write a "little pamphlet," a pamphlet that grew into a volume of nearly three hundred pages accompanied by over one hundred plates. Rob funded the entire project, but most importantly he paid me the honor of inviting me to write my first book.

I am indebted to collectors of Walker's paintings who welcomed my invasion of their homes and offices with tape measure, notebook, pencil, and camera to examine Walker's artistry on the fronts of his canvases, as well as to peer behind cardboard backings for scribbled titles, prices, and other telltale clues to his *modus operandi.*

Particularly, to Jay P. Altmayer, collector, and Walker's biggest fan. Jay was always willing to share his opinions of Walker, and he and his wife Nan gave me free access to the Walker paintings in their beautiful home, while at the same time taking care of my creature comforts as their guest. Jay was also one of my readers, and I appreciate his pure, visceral responses to the manuscript in early and later drafts.

To Jack Warner, Chairman of the Board of Gulf States Paper Corporation, who has assembled the largest collection of Walker paintings in public or private hands. He allowed me uninterrupted hours with the paintings at corporate headquarters and in the Mildred Warner House, which he has lovingly restored, both in Tuscaloosa, Alabama. And to Charles Hilburn, his right-hand man, who escorted me about Tuscaloosa, supplied photographs, and was ready, willing, and able to answer my every query. Finally to the marvelously organized Pat Chism of Gulf States Paper who set me and my editorial staff straight on dimensions, titles, dates, signatures, and other vital details in the final months of manuscript preparation.

To Mr. and Mrs. Logan Sewell of Vidalia, Louisiana, who have assembled a gem of a Walker collection. Not only are their paintings some of the artist's best, but they own the most complete set of lithographs after Walker's paintings. Mr. Sewell was also a reader, for which I am grateful.

To Bill Monroe of New Orleans, whose ancestors personally knew Walker, and who, from their bequests augmented with purchases made at local auctions, has assembled a singular collection of Walker's still life, landscape, and portraiture.

To Tina Rathborne and Cocie Rathborne, whose grandmother became enamored of Walker's work in the 1940s and purchased many paintings in New Orleans and New York which became the basis of their collections.

To Mrs. Patricia Arden of New York City, for granting me access to a portion of the Walker paintings collected by her late husband Mr. George Arden.

To Roger Ogden of New Orleans, whose carefully chosen Walkers enrich his outstanding collection of Louisiana painting, and to his assistants Ann Ogden and Kenneth Barnes, who actually showed me the paintings on one of my research trips to the Crescent City.

To the late David Morton of LaGrange, Kentucky, who was so fond of his Walker painting, *The Sunny South*, that he would not consider parting with it for any sum of money. After Mr. Morton's death, Rob Hicklin was able to acquire it, and thus it lends its title to the book.

To Gregg John Hall, great-great-grandson of Walker's friend, William Henry Gregg, for sharing family history in a delightful and forthcoming way and for protecting and ultimately releasing to the market one of Walker's masterpieces, *Blackberry Winter.*

To many others who either brought their paintings to my attention or took time out from busy lives to talk about the artist and their love for his work, including Robert L. Moore, Jr., M.D.; Mr. and Mrs. Donald Bush; William S. Morris III; Remak Ramsey; Theresa Thompson; Mrs. Virgil Cooper; James Wallis; Mrs. Judy Vane; the late Ray Samuel; and the late W. E. Groves.

To Walker's family members, especially his grandnieces Mrs. Julia Walker Bradley and Mrs. Josephine Walker Martin, who freely shared with me their fond memories of "Uncle Willie." The hours I spent with these sisters were the most pleasant of all my Walker research. They passed away within a month of each other shortly after I had interviewed them, and it is in fond memory of them that this book is written. To Mrs. Henry C. Heins, Jr. who in the summer of 1988 took time from a frantic schedule of managing children and grandchildren to share her knowledge of the Walker family genealogy and to show me Walker's diary, sketchbooks, poetry, and other papers then in her mother's estate. She has remained my constant contact with the Walker family and has been a source of unfailing interest and encouragement. To Mrs. Edward Hall Walker, who ladened me with modern clippings from Charleston newspapers pertaining to Walker and shared her enthusiasm for his work. To Mr. and Mrs. Philip L. Walker, who fed me at their home, showed me their Walker paintings, and pointed me in the direction of others.

To other friends made along the way including Robert G. Barnes; the distinguished Charleston art historian Anna Wells Rutledge, whose grandfather not only knew Walker, but also commissioned a painting from him; Gail Rothrock Trozzo, a relative of the Pacettis, who shared with me letters, drawings and paintings by Walker still in her family; and Frank Mann of Louisville, who placed before me fourteen letters written by William Aiken Walker and led me to the home of David Morton, where hung *The Sunny South*, the two happiest surprises of my research.

I would also like to thank the many art world professionals who brought paintings to my attention, including Maureen O'Brien and Alicia Longwell of the Parrish Art Museum, Southampton, New York; Angela Mack, formerly of the Gibbes Museum of Art, Charleston; Lise C. Swensson of the South Carolina State Museum, Columbia; Bert Harter of the Louisiana State Museum, New Orleans; Joseph Cotton, Director of the Old Court House Museum, Vicksburg, Mississippi; Tom Savage, Curator of the Historic Charleston Foundation; Phyllis Peet, consultant to the High Museum of Art, Atlanta; Margie S. Laughlin of the Museum of Fine Arts, St. Petersburg; the Vose family, proprietors of Vose Galleries, Boston; and the following persons, all of New York City: Evelyn Tompkins of Sotheby's; Elaine Banks of William Doyle Galleries; John Driscoll, President of Babcock Galleries; Michael Horvath of Spanierman Galleries; and my old friend and former colleague Gerold Wunderlich, President of Gerold Wunderlich and Company.

To my field researchers, the late Ruth Williams Cupp of Charleston and Jane Chapin of Galveston, Texas, and my research assistants in New York City, Carol A. Joseph, Shana Olson, and Anna Gabriel.

To Alfred Harrison of the North Point Gallery in San Francisco for a wealth of information on art in Charleston during the War Between the States, and for his opinion of the date of the event depicted in Walker's painting *Bombardment of Fort Sumter*, an opinion which I accept.

To Mary Jane Kinsman of Louisville's Filson Club and George Yater of Louisville for correctly identifying the location of Walker's Louisville studio. To independent scholar Bruce Chambers for his knowledge of liberty cap iconography.

To Ann Caneer, Director, Ponce de Leon Lighthouse Preservation Association, for bringing to my attention the photographs of Walker and Dr. C. Lewis Diehl. And to Dan Bell, Historic Resources Coordinator, South Carolina State Parks, for his knowledge of Old Dorchester.

To the many personnel in historical and art institutions who generously provided research assistance, including Steven Hoffius of the South Carolina Historical Society, Charleston; the librarians of the Research Division of the New York Public Library, the Print Room of the New York Historical Society, and the Frick Art Reference Library, all in New York City; the librarians of the Maryland Historical Society, Baltimore and the Louisville Public Library; Nettie Oliver of the Filson Club in Louisville; Sherrill Redmon, Archivist of the University of Louisville; Lise Darst of the Rosenberg Library in Galveston, Texas; Charles E. Brown of the Mercantile Library, St. Louis; the curatorial staff and manuscripts division of the Historic New Orleans Collection; the New Orleans Public Library; Jackie Fretwell of the Saint Augustine Historical Society; and the Humanities and Manuscripts Divisions of the Howard Tilton Memorial Library at Tulane University, New Orleans.

To John Fowler, author of the forthcoming Walker *catalogue raisonné*, who was always free with information he had gathered, leads to others, and his own insights from working with Walker material over many years.

To Rob Hicklin's highly professional staff, Kim Tuck and Holly Watters, who supplied on a moment's notice color transparencies, dimensions of paintings, insight into the mysteries of word processing, rides to and from the Greenville-Spartanburg airport, and plenty of hickory-smoked barbecue when I was in town. Holly deserves a special place in heaven for her work in the past year alone, taking hundreds of corrections and changes over the telephone, and freeing me from the task of securing photographs and permissions-to-reproduce from owners of Walker paintings.

I owe special thanks to Miles Chappell, art historian and my professor at the College of William and Mary, who painstakingly read—with unstinting use of a sharp, red pencil—the second draft of the manuscript.

Winnie Walsh, my first editor, encouraged me to find direction and purpose to the huge amount of facts I eagerly assembled. She is largely responsible for the book having the form it does and for it being readable.

Editor Lynne Blackman, who bravely plunged into the manuscript in its final draft, employed her way with words to polish the text. Alone and with Holly she has burned the midnight and weekend oil over the past three years, reading and re-reading, checking and re-checking all the "picayune little details," to use her words, that make up a book. Lynne has been a joy. There is no question that if I had it to do over again, I would want to do it with her.

Designer Anne Jones worked her magic to present the manuscript and plates in the handsome form you have before you. My gratitude is immense for her imagination, skill, sharp eyes, and good judgement.

Finally I wish to thank my terrific friends and loved ones, especially my husband John Kolp, who over the past six-plus years has remained supportive, interested, and full of suggestions.

Cynthia Seibels
New York City
July 13, 1994

Introduction

Mention the name William Aiken Walker to a collector of American art and he or she is likely to tell you that Walker painted slaves. No statement could be further from the truth. Yes, Walker painted the sentimental likenesses of grizzled, elderly black field hands and the plantations they worked, and yes, he realized fame and fortune in his lifetime thereby. But it is important to note that he only began to paint black laborers sixteen years after the Emancipation Proclamation had freed them from the bondage of slavery. Who were these people and why was Walker fascinated by them, fascinated to the point of obsession? And why did he begin to paint them long after slavery was outlawed—and outmoded—in the United States?

By the year 1880 and at the age of forty-one, Walker had made a career and a name for himself as a painter of still lifes, landscapes, portraits, and genre scenes. These subjects were mainstream types in American art, types that had earned him critical acclaim and a comfortable living, types he suddenly abandoned for subject matter with a strongly regional flavor.

From his fledgling efforts at the age of eleven to his robust sketches at the age of eighty-one, Walker's choice of subject matter fixes him as a paragon of taste in art of the South. He lived in various cities throughout the region over his lifetime, and always his art was reflective of what the contemporary, local market demanded. The paintings of his youth done in urbane, ante-bellum Charleston differ markedly from those he executed in the industrial metropolis of Baltimore following the War Between the States. Similarly, those painted in and of the cotton fields of the post-Reconstruction South portray a totally different life than those of his later years painted in resort communities of the New South as it entered the twentieth century. Art for art's sake was not a credo by which William Aiken Walker operated. Totally self-reliant for his livelihood, Walker painted what would sell.

The destruction and re-creation of the South shaped the life and career of William Aiken Walker. He was an ordinary man who survived an extraordinary experience, and out of that experience he drew the energy and the subjects for his life's work. He recorded the outward reality of what he saw, motivated by the inner reality of what he knew from a bygone era.

This book is arranged chronologically because it is as much a biography of William Aiken Walker as it is an analysis of his art. The fortunes and misfortunes of Walker's life are presented in the context of the most pivotal period in the history of the South. His days are played out against the backdrop of the major events of the time, particularly the adaptations Walker was forced to make as one living in the South before, during, and following the War Between the States. The extensive moving about he did during the unsettled period of Reconstruction is detailed. The simultaneous rebound of Walker's personal circumstances and the region's economy at the end of Reconstruction is also discussed.

Sources used in reconstructing his biography include: the Walker family genealogy; church and cemetery records; public documents, such as Walker's death certificate, passport application, estate inventory, and property deeds of his family; city directories; personal letters; and a journal. Where dated, paintings and drawings have been a tremendous aid in tracing Walker's whereabouts throughout his life. The memories of family members who knew Walker were helpful, entertaining, and primarily useful as leads to works of art and other, certifiable sources of information. Anecdotal information has been kept to a minimum. Walker was generally well-liked and by all accounts a colorful, eccentric character. As such, a great deal of extraordinary stories about him abound. These can no longer be heard first-hand from persons acquainted with Walker. At best today they are second and third generation tales, and their telling has been limited for the sake of sound scholarship.

The eve of the twentieth century marks the start of a particularly rewarding period of Walker's life for the biographer, because more information survives from Walker himself than from any previous period. Walker's only existing letters, which date from April 1899 through February 1914, are informative as to his itinerary during those years, his personal likes and dislikes, his health, and most importantly, his working methods and the type of subject matter that interested him. The works of art themselves from this period are helpful, too, for Walker was more inclined to date paintings and drawings at this time, making possible an extended stylistic analysis. Walker's earliest known drawings date to 1899. Some include color notes, and they are excellent tools for analyzing his methodology. In *plein aire* landscapes and still lifes he exhibits a realism and spontaneity which is often lacking in genre scenes done earlier in his career. His still lifes reveal that he was capable of meticulously copying any natural object with all the skill of a trained botanist or zoologist, and indeed, the fact that he inscribed many renderings of fish with their proper scientific names suggests that he was at least a serious student of scientific classification.

Every type of painting that Walker undertook is discussed: still lifes, portraits, genre, land- and seascapes, and animal subjects; paintings on canvas, academy board, brass plates, and over photographs, as well as sketches in pencil and pen-and-ink, have their place herein. The works are analyzed as to style and content, and the sources of Walker's inspiration are discussed. Walker seems to have been an imaginative imitator, adapting the themes of other artists to his own purposes and rendering them in a unique manner. He was astute in his choices, and this resulted in a remarkably successful career.

The critical reception that Walker's paintings encountered in the press from his earliest efforts well through the 1890s is presented, as well as how these reviews encouraged or discouraged some of his choices. Popular reaction is deduced from evidence of his market, analyzing the numbers of each type of painting that Walker produced and the prices he charged for them. Original purchasers of his paintings whenever known and their reasons for patronizing him are discussed, further enhancing an understanding of his diverse audience.

The study of the history of American art is a phenomenon of our time. It took the pioneering efforts of artists like Elie Nadelman and Sam Halpert, beginning in the 1920s, to discover the beauty inherent in the paintings and sculptures of the untrained or folk artists. Historians such as Charles Coleman Sellers, a descendant of the Peale family whose curiosity was whetted by the art of his ancestors, added to these early efforts. Beginning as it did in the Northeast, the study of American art for decades centered on the study of artists who trained in the New York, Philadelphia, and Boston academies, all modeled upon European examples, and those same artists who at some time in their youth sought additional training in Paris, Rome, Düsseldorf, and other continental art centers. We now know that from the mid-nineteenth century, if not earlier, regional schools of art were cropping up all across the United States.

Painting in the South, offering the first encyclopedic study of art created from Maryland to Florida, from the Atlantic seaboard to Texas, was published by the Virginia Museum of Fine Arts (Richmond, Virginia) in 1983. In that volume brief histories of individual artists with one or two illustrations of their work were examined within the context of historical periods. The reader did not get so much an impression of what was occurring in particular localities as he did an awareness of what was happening in the region as a whole. Yet *Painting in the South* has proved to be a springboard for further detailed study. Since then a study of Louisiana landscape painting has been published, as well as monographs on Charleston portraitist Henrietta Johnston, Kentucky limner William Edward West, and others.

It is hoped that this in-depth review of the life and art of William Aiken Walker, who was every inch an artist of the South, may be a useful tool for continued study of the art of the South, a region whose unique contribution to American art has only recently begun to be appreciated.

CHAPTER

ONE

Early Years

FIGURE 2. ***Ducks and Woodcocks***, 1866, oil on canvas, 24 x 18 inches, signed and dated lower left: *WAWalker. 1866.* Collection of Jay P. Altmayer.

William Aiken Walker was born and raised in Charleston, South Carolina, and though he pursued an itinerant existence for most of his adult life, he always considered Charleston his home. When Walker's life began, the city of Charleston was in transition. A rapidly growing railroad system laid claim to the port, transforming the genteelly agrarian, ante-bellum seat of society into a booming industrial center. Walker's early art career reflects the duality of Charleston's past and Charleston's future. While easel paintings were commissioned from him by the landed aristocracy, he also produced colored photographs to cater to the demands of an expanding, urban middle class.

Charleston has been called "the most Southern of Southern cities."[1] Certainly in the militant defense of slavery by its ante-bellum planters, as the site of the first act of secession from the United States that led to the War Between the States, and as the place where the first shots of that war were fired, Charleston qualifies for the distinction. Throughout the colonial period, Charleston had been the only significant cosmopolitan center in the South. Charleston was a mecca of trade, politics, education, religion, and the arts from its very founding in the seventeenth century. The city had close commercial ties with England and the Continent—ties that were stronger than the bonds between Charleston and her colonial sister cities to the north. As an international trade center, she attracted immigrants and visitors of many nationalities, especially English, French, Scotch-Irish, and German. As the capital of South Carolina until 1790, members of the legislature met within her walls on a regular basis, not only to pass laws but also to exchange ideas and socialize. Charleston also became a learning center, home to teaching academies, private libraries, and scholarly societies. And she had an amazingly diverse religious composition for an English colony, with large communities of Catholics, Lutherans, and Jews in addition to the Episcopal majority.

Historically, the dominant element in Charleston politics, society, and commerce was the wealthy, landed elite, predominantly of English lineage, who owned plantations of hundreds of acres in the surrounding tidewater and on the sea islands that buffered the Carolina coast from the Atlantic Ocean. As a group, these planter aristocrats valued tradition, duty, education, and religion. Plantations were passed down from father to son, generation after generation. Familial and regional loyalties were intense and to be defended at all costs. Education was intended to cultivate the thinking processes and to foster the art of communication. A high premium was placed upon good manners and the ability to engage in polite conversation. Religion was fervently practiced and applied to every aspect of life. Naturally, a Christian rationale was found to support the moral rightness of slavery.

These South Carolinians maintained a dual existence, spending the fall and spring months on their estates overseeing the planting and harvesting of cash crops by black slaves. In contrast, they enjoyed the summer and part of the winter, popularly known as the *season*, in Charleston, where they sold their crops and ogled the latest fashions from abroad. Some stayed with their well-to-do city cousins or in fine hotels. Many had second homes in Charleston, mansions surrounded by beautiful gardens filled with fruit trees and tropical, flowering plants. For months at a time, they would entertain one another with sumptuous dinners and balls, and attend the theatre, concerts, lectures, and horse races. Artists from the Northeast flocked to Charleston during the season to fulfill the planters' requests for portraits of themselves and their families, their race horses, hunting dogs, and their stately homes.

Aristocratic and proud, these planters lived lavishly, whether in the country or in Charleston, and it was this conspicuous lifestyle that gave rise to the myth of the Old South. Aptly described by Messrs. Wilson and Ferris as "a literary and cultural construct" developed by the 1830s, this fancy evoked images of "kindly old marster with his mint julep, happy darkies singing in the fields, coquettish belles wooed by slender gallants."[2] It was embodied in novels such as John Pendleton Kennedy's *Swallow Barn, or A Sojourn in the Old Dominion* (1832) and *Horse-Shoe Robinson* (1835), as well as Eliza Ann Dupuy's *The Planter's Daughter: A Tale of Louisiana* (1857).

From the colonial period through the first half of the nineteenth century, Charleston was a major center of trans-Atlantic trade. In 1816 the value of Charleston's exports totaled nearly eleven million dollars, second only to the amount exported from New York. Rice, cotton, and, until about 1790, indigo were the leading cash crops raised in the lowcountry, the coastal area of South Carolina, of which Charleston was the heart. Rice grown in the swampy mainland remained economically viable well into the nineteenth century. A particularly fine grade of long staple cotton known as sea-island cotton was developed along the coasts of Beaufort, Colleton, and Charleston districts. Until about 1800, when this type of cotton gave way to the heartier short staple variety grown in the upcountry regions of the state, South Carolina's economy was in the hands of a relatively small group of lowcountry planters.

Cultivation of cotton, indigo, and rice were extremely labor-intensive before the advent of the machine age. Thus the lowcountry planter's largest investment and asset was manpower: the black slaves that he could purchase on an open market and whose lives he controlled. The ruling elite instituted radical measures to insure continuance of the slave trade and to protect themselves and their property from slave uprisings. To prevent the fomenting of rebellion, South Carolina slaves were forbidden to learn to read and write, and by city ordinance black sailors had to be incarcerated for the period that their ships were docked at Charleston. Anyone come to town to preach abolition was promptly made aware of the personal, bodily danger to which he or she was liable.

In 1818 short staple cotton hit an ante-bellum high of thirty-five cents per pound, but one year later overproduction resulted in a worldwide collapse of the cotton market. There followed a series of booms and busts for the Charleston economy. Demand for Carolina rice rose in Europe in the 1830s, resulting in a period of prosperity for the entire city. Construction increased. The Charleston Hotel, an imposing columned mass in the Greek Revival style, opened in March of 1838, burned one month later, and was promptly reconstructed and reopened the following July. City Hall received a facelift. Government officials authorized the planting of gardens and the laying of serpentine walkways at White Point in the creation of the Battery, Charleston's beautiful waterfront promenade.

But rice alone could not sustain the economy. Another depression struck the cotton market in 1839. In 1844 the price of short staple cotton reached its ante-bellum low, selling for five cents per pound. To make matters worse, politically powerful lowcountry planters made it difficult for the upcountry product to be traded in the city. Although a canal connecting the Cooper and Santee river systems brought a good deal of short staple cotton to Charleston, the upcountry growing region was continually extending farther and farther west, and an expanded railway system was required to get upstate cotton to Charleston market. In order to protect their stately homes from the noise and dirt of belching steam engines, wealthy Charlestonians prevented railroad lines from going directly to the city's wharves. As a result, the rail lines stopped just outside the city limits, and cotton had to be carried by wagon to dockside at exorbitant charges. It became cheaper and more efficient for upcountry planters to send their cotton by rail to New York, Baltimore, Philadelphia, or even faraway Boston. By the end of the 1840s, these cities handled sixty percent of South Carolina's exports.

In the mid-1840s some of these trade barriers were removed. The railroad was permitted to extend fully to dockside, and steam-powered engines previously consigned to the city's periphery were allowed south of Line Street. Foundries and machine shops serving the railroads developed rapidly. By 1850 Charleston was the third largest manufacturing center in the South after Richmond and New Orleans.

An important element of the Charleston economy were those merchants whose livelihoods were directly dependent upon the trade of cotton, the cotton factors. A factor acted as a planter's agent, selling his crop on the world market, arranging for its shipment, securing supplies to be used in the work of the plantation, buying and selling slaves, and performing other essential services in town on behalf of the planter whose property and residence might have been located several days' journey from Charleston. The factor would often lend the planter money against the proceeds of a future harvest, charging the current rate of interest, which usually hovered around eight percent, a substantial return for his efforts.[3] Although dependent upon the factor for his financial success, the lowcountry planter traditionally did not consider this trader his equal. Those involved in international trade were most likely to be immigrants and were looked down upon by the native-born, landed aristocracy. Until 1820 only one of the twenty-one trading houses in Charleston was owned or managed by native Carolinians.

The population of Charleston County numbered nearly 83,000 persons in 1840. The white population was predominantly of English origin with significant percentages of the citizenry claiming French or Scotch-Irish ancestry. The Scotch-Irish had begun to emigrate to Charleston at the end of the seventeenth century. The majority of these immigrants were humble, hard-working people who sought an opportunity to improve their lot in life. One Scotch-Irish success story concerns William Aiken, Sr., who arrived in Charleston from County Antrim, Ireland in 1806 and built a substantial fortune as a merchant. A man of many callings, he served in the South Carolina legislature and was a founder and the first president of the South Carolina Canal and Railroad Company. At his premature death in a hunting accident in 1831, Aiken was proclaimed one of the wealthiest men in the state. His only son and namesake, who inherited a vast fortune as well as considerable business responsibilities, took more of an interest in agriculture than commerce and created an exemplary rice plantation on Jehossee Island near Charleston.

Another successful Scotch-Irish immigrant was John Falls Walker, who was born on December 14, 1798 and left County Armagh for Charleston as a young man. He was naturalized as an American citizen in Charleston on October 14, 1822.[4] John Falls Walker may have arrived with letters of introduction to his compatriot William Aiken, Sr. It is also possible that he became a close friend to William Aiken, Jr. (1806-1887), who was more nearly his contemporary. In either case, it seems that Walker named his youngest son, William Aiken Walker, for one of these men.[5]

John Walker settled down quickly. He married Elizabeth Mylne Flint (baptized November 13, 1801), the daughter of Jane Mylne and Joseph Flint of Charleston. The couple lived in Elizabeth's childhood home at 23 State Street with her widowed mother and two sisters. The house was situated on a quiet avenue not far from the Cooper River's bustling wharves. Their first child, a daughter, was born on October 5, 1823. She died at the age of five in the autumn of 1828. On February 20, 1829, Elizabeth Walker died from complications giving birth to a son, George William Walker. John Walker continued to live with his female in-laws, certainly a necessary arrangement, considering his newborn son, but also apparently a happy one. By April of 1832, he had married his late wife's sister, Mary Elizabeth Flint (born 1795 or 1796).[6]

By this time John Walker was well established. In Charleston directories he appears as a cotton factor under his own name. His office was located on Boyce's Wharf, at the tip of Charleston, where East Bay Street curves to meet the Battery. Lying at the point where the waters of the Cooper River flow into Charleston Harbor, Boyce's Wharf was a prime location for trade.

Despite fluctuations in the cotton market, the late 1820s and early thirties were generally a time of prosperity for Walker. In 1829 he was able to purchase the Flint house on State Street from his mother-in-law.[7] Three years later, he bought a house and adjoining property at 306 East Bay Street, a few blocks uptown.[8] The lot was quite large, ample enough for the cultivation of a formal garden in the Charleston style with boxwood hedges, fruit trees, palmettos, and fragrant flowering plants. He owned three slaves and employed one free woman of color in his home.[9] He was a man of considerable means and responsibilities.

The Walkers' extended, multi-generational household was typical of family living arrangements at mid-century. John Walker's sister-in-law Sarah lived with the family at least until 1830, and his mother-in-law continued to live with them after the move in 1832 to the house on East Bay. In fact, in the will Walker wrote some years later, he stipulated that in the event of his death, his mother-in-law should continue to live with his wife and children and be supported by them.

John and Mary Flint Walker had their first child in 1833. He was named Joseph Flint Walker in memory of his maternal grandfather.[10] Six years later their second and last child was born. William Aiken Walker came into the world on March 11, 1839, the road of life smoothed for him by his father's success.[11]

John Walker died in June of 1841 and was buried in the yard of St. Philip's Episcopal Church beside the graves of his first wife and only daughter. His death was expected, for he drew up his last will and testament a month or so before he died. Stress may have contributed to his demise, for the cotton market was in the midst of its severest ante-bellum depression.

In his will John Walker named his children, George William, Joseph Flint, and two-year-old William Aiken, as heirs and stipulated that his "estate real and personal" be kept together for their education and maintenance, and for the care of their mother and grandmother until his eldest son George should attain the age of twenty-four.[12]

There was money enough to give little William the education befitting a son of Charleston's prosperous merchant class.[13] Affluent families, such as the Walkers, were expected to bear the expense of educating their children. Whereas planters hired tutors who lived on the plantation, city dwellers sent their children to schools run by churches and learned societies. College attendance was rare, and for one's son (but never a daughter) to study at a university was viewed as a sign of exceptional prosperity in ante-bellum South Carolina. There is no evidence to suggest that William Aiken Walker attended college, yet he did receive a fine, albeit atypical, education for a young man of Charleston.[14]

In Southern male academies of the ante-bellum period, the curriculum had its foundation in the classics. Latin and Greek, rhetoric, philosophy, and mathematics were to be mastered. Modern languages, music, art, and versification were what a contemporary teacher described as "the ornamentals."[15] They were commonly taught to young ladies, not to young men. Letters, songs, and poems that Walker wrote as an adult attest to his ability to speak and write fluently in both French and Spanish, and suggest that he possessed a smattering, if not a command, of Swedish and German. He also turned out to be a gifted composer, lyricist, and piano player. These qualities as well as his early exposure to techniques of painting and drawing suggest that his education was typical of what was taught not in the male academies, but rather in the *female* schools. Perhaps the emphasis given to these subjects in Walker's education was a result of his growing up in a household dominated by women, who would have been likely to place a premium on such areas of learning.

It is apparent that Walker had studied art by the age of eleven. In the first annual fair of the South Carolina Institute held in 1850, he exhibited an oil painting which elicited mention in the press. There was no art school in Charleston when William was growing up, but he may have received art instruction either as part of his academic curriculum or in a private setting. Local artists offered small classes in their homes or studios, and numerous itinerant artists who visited Charleston advertised art instruction in addition to filling orders for portraits or landscapes. Artist and author Thomas Addison Richards (1820-1900) taught in Charleston in the 1840s. In 1848 and 1849 a Mr. and Mrs. Delauney were there—he teaching painting, drawing, and ancient and modern languages and she teaching English. Another teaching couple, Mr. and Mrs. Henry Bounetheau (she, the former Julia Clarkson Dupre of Charleston), advertised in 1855 and 1856 that they offered "classes in Drawing and Oil Painting . . . for the youth of both sexes."[16] Walker could have studied with any of these individuals or with Charles Fraser, to whose work some of Walker's early efforts bear a strong resemblance.

Artists had long found a healthy market for their work in Charleston. Henrietta Johnston (1674-1729), who arrived in the colonial city in 1708 from England, painted portraits in pastel of Charleston's leading citizens until her death. The Philadelphia-born portraitist Henry Benbridge (1743-1812), visiting Charleston for the first time in 1772, decided to make his home there. For some fifteen years he painted the portraits of prominent South Carolinians, as well as history paintings and the type of group portraiture known as the conversation piece that came into vogue in the late eighteenth century. South Carolina native Charles Fraser (1782-1860) enjoyed a busy career that spanned four decades in Charleston, painting portrait miniatures, oil portraits, landscapes, and game still lifes. The visiting artist too was well received in Charleston. Between 1818 and 1821 Samuel Finley Breese Morse (1791-1872) spent the winter season in Charleston, where he was inundated with orders for portraits. Planter John Ashe Alston paid Morse $800 for a full-length portrait of his daughter Sally, a fee higher by hundreds of dollars than the artist could have expected to receive in his native Massachusetts.

Beyond abundant private patronage, Charlestonians supported the fine arts on a civic level as well. To commemorate the visit of President James Monroe to their city in 1819, the Common Council of Charleston commissioned Morse to paint a life-size portrait of the Chief Executive. It was placed in City Hall, where it may be seen to this day. In 1850 the city requested a portrait of the recently deceased Carolina lawmaker John C. Calhoun from the brush of George Peter Alexander Healy (1813-1894)

of Chicago. Healy found such a good market in Charleston that in April of 1861, unthreatened by South Carolina's secession from the Union and the subsequent military build-up, he was there, "engaged in painting a number of portraits."[17]

In the days before photography, the demand for portraiture in Charleston, as throughout the United States, far exceeded the call for any other type of painting. Portraits documented life's many rites of passage: a young woman's engagement; a child's christening; a gentleman's election to a fraternal organization; or the attainment of a military or civic honor. Portraits even commemorated the dead, artists being called out of their beds in the middle of the night by grieving relatives to sketch the visage of a newly deceased family member. The amateur Charleston sculptor and painter John Stevens Cogdell (1778-1847) provided this service, modeling busts in clay from dead subjects.

As the nineteenth century unfolded, landscapes became increasingly popular, particularly scenes of familiar, nearby subjects. Charles Fraser's American landscapes, including a view of Haddrell's Point near Charleston, earned him his first recognition in the Charleston press in 1816.[18] A decade and a half later, the mysterious artist who signed his canvases "S. Bernard" found enough beauty on the Charleston waterfront to paint two panoramic views of the city from Charleston Harbor and one view along the Battery.[19] (See figure 3.) Thomas Addison Richards was one of the earliest exponents of the Southern landscape. With his brother William Carey Richards as editor, he brought out a slim volume in 1842 titled *Georgia Illustrated* that offered the reader remarkable images of the natural wonders of that state. When Richards established himself in Charleston the following year, a local magazine exhorted the public to commission "home views" from his brush.[20]

Game pictures were popular with Charleston's planter aristocrats for whom hunting was a prime social and recreational activity. The result of a memorable day's shoot—piles of hares, quail, teals, and partridges—immortalized on canvas, hung above many a Charleston sideboard in the first half of the century. In 1823 John Stevens Cogdell, in writing from Charleston to a friend, praised the work of a Mr. Shields, noting "his partridges were living within the frame—his ducks were ready to be picked & his Hawks were ready to fly—if you waved your hat in the room."[21] Charles Fraser

FIGURE 3. **S. BERNARD** (active circa 1830). ***View along the East Battery, Charleston***, 1831, oil on canvas, 23 3/4 x 35 1/4 inches, signed and dated lower right: *S. Bernard Px/1831*. The Mabel Brady Garvan Collection, Yale University Art Gallery, New Haven, Connecticut (1932.282).

filled many commissions for still life paintings pertaining to the hunt and to fishing. His *Dog and Birds*, depicting a spaniel proudly guarding his catch of dove and quail, was commissioned by Charles Alston and hung in Fairfield, Alston's plantation home on the Waccamaw River. More commonly Fraser painted game birds hanging by their feet against wood paneling in trompe l'oeil fashion. (See figure 4.) *The Fraser Gallery*, an exhibition of the artist's work organized three years before his death, featured a number of such works. Also included were two fish still lifes, *Fish Crevalle and Sheepshead Suspended* (lent by Mr. W. C. Gatewood) and *Fish, Sheepshead* (lent by Dr. R. W. Gibbes).[22]

Unfortunately for the artists of Charleston, there were no art galleries in the city where they could regularly display and sell their work. Many stores displayed paintings in their street-front windows, such as Courtenay's, Thayer's, and Roorbachs's book shops; Baker's, Caulier's, and Harper's apothecaries; and the studios of gilders and framers such as Messrs. Current, Jones, Barelli, and Torre. Certain civic and social institutions would often make their halls available for exhibitions, including the College of Charleston, the St. Andrew's Society, the Charleston Library Society, and Apprentice's Hall. The latter frequently opened its rooms to one-man and group shows, and the press cited its "praise-worthy efforts" in this regard.[23] Despite such community support of the arts and artists, however, the professional art dealer was non-existent in ante-bellum Charleston.

The success of efforts by Charleston artists to organize formal associations for the display and promotion of their work fluctuated with the economic swings of the first half of the nineteenth century. The South Carolina Academy of Fine Arts held its first exhibition of the work of "native artists" in 1816. Thereafter it annually mounted a display of paintings, statuary, and engravings contributed by local artists, as well as American and European works lent by local collectors. Typically a visitor to the academy's galleries could view portraits by George Romney, Sir Joshua Reynolds, Sir Henry Raeburn, and other artists of the British school; paintings by Americans Benjamin West, Gilbert Stuart, John Wesley Jarvis, and Charles Fraser; and works attributed to (but most likely copied after) European masters such as Corregio, Rubens, and Wovermann. With the downturn in the economy during the early 1830s, the

FIGURE 4. CHARLES FRASER (1782-1860). *Still Life—Duck and Partridges*, circa 1840, oil on canvas, 24 x 20 1/8 inches. The Greenville County Museum of Art, Greenville, South Carolina.

FIGURE 5. ***Still Life with Virginia Partridges***, 1858, oil on panel, 18 1/2 x 14 1/4 inches, signed and dated lower left: *WAWalker. Dec 21 1858.* Robert M. Hicklin Jr., Inc., Spartanburg, South Carolina.

academy failed. In 1835 it disbanded and sold its building to pay off debts. Following the demise of the South Carolina Academy of Fine Arts, the Academy of Arts and Design opened in 1837, but lasted only one year.

The most promising of the successive art organizations in the ante-bellum period was the Carolina Art Association, which was organized in the spring of 1858. It opened a gallery where it sponsored the display in 1859 of Emanuel Leutze's *Jasper Rescuing the Flag at Fort Moultrie*, a Charleston scene from the American Revolution. The twelve paintings which the association had assembled as the nucleus of a permanent collection were destroyed in the Great Fire that swept through Charleston in 1861. The Carolina Art Association was not revived again until 1895.

Local artists enjoyed a boon in 1849 with the organization of the South Carolina Institute. Chartered for the purpose of promoting "Art, Mechanical Ingenuity, and Industry," the institute proposed to sponsor a fair each year where the latest products of agriculture, industry, and the arts produced in the state would be displayed. The first fair opened in November 1850 and featured jams, jellies, pumps, and rice machines as well as drawings, statuary, oil paintings, miniatures, and the products of the various new photographic processes. The first reference to William Aiken Walker as a practicing artist is found in connection with this fair. Though Walker's work went unlisted in the catalogue to the fair's exhibits, a reporter for the *Charleston Courier* acknowledged seeing oil paintings by "Master W. Walker . . . of this city" among the exhibits.[24]

William Aiken Walker's earliest known surviving painting is a game still life depicting Virginia partridges. Dated December 21, 1858 it is remarkably similar to Charles Fraser's *Still Life—Duck and Partridges*. (See figures 4 and 5.) Walker's work incorporates the small ledge and dark recess that Fraser favored, attesting to the young artist's admiration of his predecessor. The following year Walker portrayed live animals in at least two paintings. One is a commissioned piece which shows that his young talent had earned him a patron. *Dog 'Wasp'* (figure 6) was solicited by Francis James Porcher (1821-1872), a Charleston merchant who collected paintings

FIGURE 7. **Bulls Defending a Cow**, 1859, oil on canvas, 18 x 26 inches, initialed and dated lower left: *WAW 1859*. The Sewell Family Collection, Vidalia, Louisiana.

For a young artist such as Walker, making copies not only provided an income, but the act was excellent training for the eye and the hand. In nineteenth century art academies, students repeatedly made sketches of casts taken from classical Greek and Roman statuary. Those aspiring artists who had the opportunity to study abroad copied paintings by the Old Masters that hung in the galleries of Europe. In 1858 Walker placed on public display a copy he had made, probably from an engraving, of a painting by the English artist John Frederick Herring. The *Charleston Mercury* reported on June 12, 1858:

A YOUNG ARTIST: Yesterday we were shown the painting of one of our young city artists, at Messrs. Courtenay and Co.'s store. The painting is a copy of one of Herring's farmyard scenes. The young artist is WM. A. WALKER, son of the late JOHN FALLS WALKER. By a close attention to the working up of color, yet a judicious toning and blending, our young artist may, in a little time, give us a picture equal in painting to his very excellent drawing.[28]

Though Walker's copy is lost today, a look at Herring's oeuvre suggests that the picture might have featured a barnyard populated with any combination of horses, cows, sheep, dogs, cats, or chickens, and their respective young.

An 1859 game still life also found favor with the press:

That rising young artist, whose works we have heretofore noticed in the *Mercury*, and who modestly places an anagram signature at the corner of his canvas, symbolizing the initials W.A.W., has recently hung at Messrs. Courtenay's bookstore, the last and best specimen of his easel. It is a game study showing a few ducks suspended against a wall, and would be considered flattering to older artists. It will gratify the attention of every lover of art.[29]

Game and fish still lifes occupied Walker's talent from 1858 through 1866. (See figures 2, 5, and 8.) In his paintings, freshly caught birds or fish are invariably dis-

FIGURE 8. ***Dollarfish and Sheepshead***, 1866, oil on canvas, 21 x 17 inches, signed and dated lower left: *WAWalker. 1866*. Collection of Jay P. Altmayer.

The artist Charles Fraser painted at least two still lifes that featured sheepshead. Since their present location is unknown, we can only conjecture that they may have been models for Walker's painting. Certainly the shallow picture space of this still life by Walker, the wood panel background, and the vertical arrangement of the fish have parallels in Fraser's known paintings of game birds.

played against the warm brown of a wood-paneled wall in a decidedly trompe l'oeil effect. They hang suspended by a bit of twine or blue or pink ribbon from a nail driven into the panel. Fish are hung singly or in pairs; birds are paired or bunched in groups of three sometimes with other game, their variegated plumage bringing a wealth of color and texture to the canvas. Walker's antecedents are to be found in the work of Dutch still life painters of the seventeenth century, notably that of Carl Fabritius (1622-1654). However, Walker found his immediate inspiration in the work of fellow Charlestonian Charles Fraser.

There is no documentation to prove that Walker was a student of Fraser's, and the difference in their ages makes a student-teacher relationship unlikely. Fraser was fifty-one years older than Walker. A Charleston belle described the elder artist as "growing old, wears spectacles and looks cross" in 1836, three years before Walker was born.[30] But the striking similarity in Fraser's and Walker's treatment of game suggests that Walker was well acquainted and much impressed with Mr. Fraser's work.

Walker was born at the dawn of a new era in American art preferences. In 1839, the year of his birth, the French government had released the rights to the invention of the daguerreotype process, and all over the United States artists turned to photography. The advent of the daguerreotype spelled the beginning of the end for the dominance of the portrait painter, or limner. The daguerreotype was made of a silvered glass treated with iodine to be light sensitive when developed in the presence of mercury vapor. Because of its fragility the daguerreotype often was placed in a case made of embossed leather lined with velvet. The vogue for daguerreotypes hit Charleston in the early 1840s. Not only were people anxious to have their own likenesses taken by the new "lightning process," but they also bought images of public figures, such as the actress Jenny Lind and South Carolina Senator John C. Calhoun. Photography supplemented the work of even the best portrait studios. Charleston artist Christian Mayr (circa 1805-1851) advertised in 1841 that, in addition to portrait and historical painting, he "executes whole length likenesses in Daguerreotype."[31] He was no exception. Photography had not yet become a special-

FIGURE 9. ***Portrait of a Young Lady***, circa 1865, photograph colored with oil paints, 4 x 2 3/8 inches, signed lower right: *WAWalker./Artist.* Printed on verso with photographer's name and address: *J. E. McLees,/Artist,/1310 Chestnut Street,/Philadelphia.* Verso also bears a three-cent stamp of the Internal Revenue Service that is canceled with the date: *Sept. 19 1865.* The Sewell Family Collection, Vidalia, Louisiana.

Note that the back of the photograph bears the name and address of a Philadelphia photographer. The subject more than likely was a Charleston belle who posed for the photograph on a visit to Philadelphia and subsequently asked Walker to color it. There is no evidence of Walker having lived or worked in Philadelphia.

ized art unto itself. Rather it was the painters, and particularly portrait painters, who mastered and practiced the new mechanical process. In 1848 another Charleston artist, John McDonald (active 1848-1851) advertised daguerreotypes "of superior beauty and excellence . . . and when required will be colored up to nature surpassing the beautiful style of Miniature Painting."[32]

By the 1850s photographs were printed on paper in an early process that was known as callotype. These were sometimes colored with oil paints. Owing to the opacity of the medium, the resulting oilettes, as they were called, had the appearance of miniature paintings. Walker is known to have colored photos made by the Quinby Gallery, Charleston's leading photography studio at the time. Two painted photos, both dated 1860, once belonged to the Carolina Art Association, but are lost today. A self-portrait dated 1869 (figure 1) reveals his developing skill. Walker may have discovered, like Mayr, that for an artist to make a decent living he had to master not only the techniques of painting and drawing, but of photography, or at least the technique of coloring photographs, as well. There is abundant evidence from Walker's life that he consistently colored photographs until about 1880. Whether he made the photographs that he colored cannot be proved. In any case, his early experience as a colorist gave him a decided predilection for rendering fine detail in his oil paintings. The act of coloring a lip or a brow on a face less than one inch high requires keen powers of concentration and remarkable manual dexterity. Throughout Walker's painting oeuvre it was the details—not the broad effects—that fascinated him and over which he labored. His early work with photography was in large part responsible for this trait. (See figure 9.)

In ante-bellum Charleston a young artist could effectively steep him- or herself in the tradition of Western art dominated by portraiture, landscape, still life, and animal painting. The works of Charles Fraser, Samuel F. B. Morse, George P. A. Healy, and other of America's leading artists, as well as masters of the English and Continental schools, graced the walls of Charleston's finer homes and public buildings. Opportunities to study privately with local or visiting artists were frequently available. William Aiken Walker was fortunate to have been born in this city and into a family who nurtured his developing artistic interest. Having won the attention of Charleston's art community and the local press while still a young man, William Aiken Walker's career was off to a promising start.

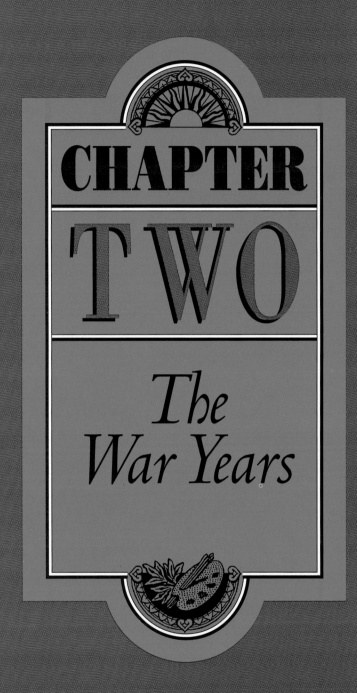

CHAPTER

TWO

The
War Years

FIGURE 10. *Circular Church in Ruins,* 1868, oil on canvas, 19 1/2 x 15 1/2 inches. Private Collection.

The year 1861 inaugurated a dark period in William Aiken Walker's life. Like other young men of Charleston, Walker was called to service by the Confederate Army early in the War Between the States. Discharged for reasons that are unclear, he continued to serve the Confederacy in a civilian capacity. He lived out the war in Charleston, in which the hopes of the Confederacy lay, but which was gradually beaten down by fire, bombardment, and economic privation. Artistic patronage having ceased early on in the war, Walker abandoned the still life and animal painting upon which he had begun to build a fine reputation and turned instead to the portrayal of dismal current events. He suffered the death of persons close to him. In a rare group of writings from his pen that date to this period, he pours out his grief over these losses. Moreover, between the lines one can read the shattered hopes and dreams of a young man whose reality was drastically changed by events beyond his control.

Charleston was the birthplace of the Confederate States of America, and it was the location of the first shots fired in the War Between the States. As such it was the object of much vitriolic hatred in the North, where the press routinely referred to it as the "hotbed of the rebellion." South Carolina was the first state to call a convention to consider secession from the United States. And, after meeting at Institute Hall in Charleston where state delegates signed the Articles of Secession on December 20, 1860, South Carolina also became the first state to officially withdraw from the Union. On order of Governor F. W. Pickens, South Carolina militia units occupied Castle Pinckney and Fort Moultrie, defensive locations in Charleston Harbor, on December 27, 1860. Three days later the United States Arsenal at Charleston was captured.

Charleston was also the first area to claim Confederate President Jefferson Davis' attention. He appointed the brilliant engineer and artillery expert, Brigadier General Pierre G. T. Beauregard, commander of Confederate troops at Charleston. Beauregard immediately set about strengthening defenses around Charleston Harbor. His goal was to build a circle of fire around Fort Sumter and bring the federal garrison there, commanded by Major Robert Anderson, to its knees. Beauregard began shelling Fort Sumter on April 12, 1861. Thirty-four hours later Anderson surrendered. Fort

Sumter remained in Southern hands for nearly four years, and as long as it did, it remained a symbol of faith for all Southerners—and especially for Charlestonians—in the ultimate triumph of the Confederate cause.

South Carolina men had rushed to enlist as soon as the Articles of Secession were signed. From the wealthiest to the humblest, all were seized by war fever. Military service had long been an integral part of every male South Carolinian's life. Men between the ages of sixteen and sixty were liable for service in the state militia at any time, and companies were required by law to drill once every quarter. State militia service was the right thing to do, for the readiness to defend one's home and people was essential to the chivalrous Southern ethos. South Carolina men fulfilled their duty in style. During the peaceful years between the Mexican War and the War Between the States, militia companies took on the appearance of social clubs. Charleston's Irish Volunteers and the Charleston Rifle Company, for instance, owned halls that featured bowling alleys and gymnastic facilities. Many companies adopted festive, brightly colored uniforms, and their meetings provided members an opportunity to indulge the peculiarly masculine delight in dressing in costume and parading.

Walker too was quick to respond to the call of duty and to aid in the defense of all that was familiar and dear to him. As a member of Charleston's Palmetto Guard, a militia company headed by Captain George B. Cuthbert, he was stationed at the Point Batteries on Morris Island from March 11 to May 1, 1861. On the latter day the regiment was called into the service of the Confederate Army and ordered to Richmond to report to Colonel J. B. Kershaw, officer in charge of the Second Palmetto Regiment of South Carolina Volunteers. Walker left Charleston with his company on May 9 and, journeying by train, arrived in Richmond two days later. He was assigned to Camp Davis, and his name appears on the first company muster-in roll taken at the camp on May 22.[1] Walker was conscripted as a private, and a private he remained for the four months that he served in the Confederate Army. His discharge was signed at Richmond on August 31, 1861 for reason of "surgeon certificate of disability."[2] There is no record of his having been wounded. He may have feigned an illness, a common practice among soldiers, or he may have fallen victim to camp fever, otherwise known as dysentery, or to typhoid. Unsanitary conditions in the camps, on both the Union and Confederate sides, felled more soldiers throughout the war than did combat injuries.

Walker left Richmond with twenty-two dollars in his pocket, his army pay for the months of July and August. He returned to Charleston in September 1861 and lived in the home of his brother and sister-in-law, Joseph and Emma Mazyck Walker, with whom his mother also lived.[3] Although he never reenlisted after discharge, Walker did work in a civilian capacity as a draughtsman for the Confederate Engineers Corps at Charleston. Surviving is a *Map of Charleston and Its Defences* [*sic*] drawn under Walker's supervision by Lieutenant John Ross Key. Dated November 28, 1863, it shows the city of Charleston and Charleston Harbor together with all surrounding forts, batteries, and underwater defenses laid by the Confederates.[4]

Walker found his hometown little changed in his absence. Confidence soared. Confederates held the key defensive points around the harbor, including Forts Sumter, Johnson, and Moultrie. Walker missed the intense celebration that had thrilled the city after the decisive Confederate victory at Bull Run, but he found his fellow Charlestonians in continued high spirits, buoyed by their conviction of a Confederate victory.

Three months later, however, the tide began to turn. What Union military strategists could not win by direct naval attack, they were determined to take slowly by economic starvation. The United States Navy imposed a blockade at the entrance to Charleston Harbor in December 1861. With the exception of a few deft blockade runners, the majority of ocean-going cargo ships could not break through. Cotton and rice rotted on the city's wharves. Conversely, shoes, clothing, and other necessities that South Carolina industries were not equipped to produce were unable to enter the city. In time the local economy was at a standstill.

To add to Charleston's woes, fire devastated a major portion of the city on the night of December 11, 1861, leaving hundreds of families homeless. Its cause is unknown, but its place of origin is believed to have been the woodworking shop of William P. Russell, which stood at the foot of Hasell Street, only five blocks from Walker's boyhood home. The blaze spread rapidly, for there were few able-bodied men in Charleston to fight it. Those Confederate soldiers stationed on the islands ringing Charleston Harbor watched helplessly as the fire raced west, toward the heart of the city, then south toward the sea, destroying five hundred residences, five churches, and an untold number of commercial buildings. Gutted were the Circular Congregational Church on Meeting Street, the Roman Catholic Cathedral of St. John and St. Finbar, Institute Hall, where the Articles of Secession had been signed a year earlier, and the gallery of the Carolina Art Association. With all of Charleston's resources dedicated to building up the city's defenses, clearing of the fire's debris and reconstruction did not commence until after the war. In the summer of 1863, a full eighteen months after the fire, a British visitor observed that the "portion of the city destroyed by the great fire presents the appearance of a vast wilderness in the very center of the town, no attempt having been made towards rebuilding it; this desert space looks like the Pompeians [*sic*] ruins, and extends . . . for a mile in length by half a mile in width."[5]

In 1868 Walker immortalized the effects of the fire in two oil paintings, *Circular Church in Ruins* and *St. Finbar's Roman Catholic Cathedral*, in which both houses of worship are shown as shells of masonry, their roofs and interiors lost. (See figures 10 and 11.) Painted after the war but before the churches' reconstruction, the paintings are Walker's memorials to the years of tribulation Charleston suffered. *St. Finbar's Roman Catholic Cathedral* is drawn with a controlled hand that delineates the mortar between each course of stone, each upright member of the surrounding iron fence, and each pebble in the foreground. Walker did not shroud the background in a gray or pearly haze, an effect employed by contemporary academic painters. Rather, objects near and far are colored with similar intensity and drawn with equal precision. This painstaking attention to detail suggests a literal approach to the subject that is often characteristic of the self-taught artist. In Walker's case this approach was reinforced by his work with photographic images. Compositionally, Walker's painting possesses qualities that are suggestive of cityscapes by seventeenth century Dutch artists Jan van der Heyden and Gerrit Berckheyde, notably a low horizon and a spacious, open arrangement of buildings, compared to which the human figure is dwarfed.

FIGURE 11. *St. Finbar's Roman Catholic Cathedral*, 1868, oil on paper mounted on masonite, 11 3/4 x 18 3/4 inches, signed and dated lower left: *WAWalker. 1868.* The Carolina Art Association/ Gibbes Museum of Art, Charleston, South Carolina.

Walker was not the only artist working in Charleston during the war years. There were the artist-correspondents, like Frank Vizetelly (1830-1883) of the *Illustrated London News*, assigned to document the war front. Soldiers and sailors on both sides of the conflict—professional artists in civilian life—were frequently ordered by their superior officers to make "official" visual records of equipment, fortifications, and military action. Finally there were the native artists, like Walker, who had grown up in Charleston, and for whatever reason, remained at home. One of the latter was John B. Irving, Jr. (1826-1877), the son of a local doctor, who had studied at the art academy in Düsseldorf in the 1850s and returned to open his Charleston studio three years before fighting erupted. During the war Irving painted a view of Camp Gaillard on Morris Island for Francis J. Porcher, the same patron who had commissioned the portrait of his dog Wasp from Walker in 1859.[6] Other local artists included Mr. A. Grinevald, who early in 1861 painted *A View of the Harbor* as fortifications were being rapidly constructed, and Lawrence L. Cohen (born circa 1836), who had the honor of designing the first Confederate flag at the request of Charleston's Lafayette Artillery.[7]

The young Philadelphian Xanthus Smith (1839-1929) served in the United States Navy as captain's clerk aboard the USS *Wabash*. While the *Wabash* took part in the Charleston blockade between September 1862 and July 1863, Smith made numerous sketches in pencil and oil of his ship and others in the blockading squadron. After the war many of these served as models for easel paintings which he sold to naval officers who had been at Charleston.

Lieutenant John Ross Key (1832-1920), who worked with Walker in the Confederate Engineer Corps, was a Marylander by birth who had studied in the art academies of Munich and Paris. His official duties included mapping the Charleston area, but in his free time he painted. One of his paintings, entitled *Siege of Charleston*, was displayed in a Charleston shop and offered at raffle in April 1864.[8]

The largest number of paintings of wartime Charleston to have survived as a group were created by Confederate Ordnance Sergeant Conrad Wise Chapman (1842-1910). Chapman was raised in Italy where he studied art with his father, the expatriate Virginian John Gadsby Chapman (1808-1889). Passionate in his support of the Confederate cause, Conrad Chapman came to America and enlisted in the 46th Regiment, Virginia Volunteers. When the regiment was posted to Charleston, his commanding officer Brigadier General Henry A. Wise recommended the young artist to General Beauregard, who had decided to have the defense of Charleston fully documented. Between September 1863 and March 1864, Chapman sketched the fortifications in Charleston Harbor. From those eyewitness drawings, Chapman and his father in Rome completed thirty-one brilliant oil paintings which today are in the collection of the Museum of the Confederacy in Richmond, Virginia.[9]

In August of 1863, Charleston city proper became the target of Yankee shelling. It was the bold, if not duty-bound, artist who bravely shuttled between islands and the peninsula on which the city lay to record events as they unfolded. Sketches or photographs were the most common media for on-the-spot work, but where time, safety, and materials allowed, artists would, in the relative comfort of their studios or barracks, render these rapidly made visual notes into finished easel paintings. The public display of such paintings by Walker, Irving, Key, and others proclaimed Charleston's greatness and heightened public confidence.

Walker was very much in the mainstream artistically as a paint brush recorder of current events in Charleston. He was an eyewitness to the Union ironclad attack on Fort Sumter of April 7, 1863, an event which he immortalized in a painting years later. (See figure 57.) Walker sketched the action in Charleston Harbor on that day from a position on the Battery. In 1886 he recreated his original sketch (now lost) in an easel painting, which most probably resulted from a commission by a Charleston patron. A drawing in watercolor (Collection of the Historic Charleston Foundation, Charleston, South Carolina) that is contemporary to the oil serves as its key, identifying the location of forts, defensive batteries, monitors, Confederate ironclads, and ships.

Fort Sumter had been pounded several times by United States ships prior to April 7, 1863, but the ironclad bombardment of that day for the first time caused Charlestonians to doubt the strength of Confederate fortifications and to fear for their homes and their lives. One eyewitness account recalled, "all the ladies began to move out of Charleston on the morning after the repulse of the Monitors, the impression being that the serious attack was about to begin."[10] When the monitors suddenly withdrew, leaving Fort Sumter in Confederate hands, optimism in Charleston reached new heights.

In 1864 Walker used the same April 7, 1863 bombardment of Fort Sumter to decorate a playing card (figure 12). On the card, Walker recorded twelve figures surveying the action in the waters of Charleston Harbor. Fort Sumter, with its Confederate colors flying high, is in the distance at center. Fort Moultrie on Sullivans Island is to the left; the Confederate ship *Juno* passes in front of the island. These details Walker painted onto a surface measuring a mere 3 1/4 x 2 inches, a further example of his fondness for the minutiae of appearance and his keen ability to delineate it.

The playing card is one in a deck of fifty-two; fifteen other cards of the deck were also decorated by Walker. For kings, he limned the bust-length portraits of four Confederate leaders: President Jefferson Davis, General Robert E. Lee, General Pierre G. T. Beauregard, and the late General Thomas Jonathan "Stonewall" Jackson. The likenesses of Beauregard, Davis, and Jackson were based upon widely circulated pre-war photographs, while that of Lee was taken from the wood engraving published in the *Southern Illustrated News*, October 17, 1863, in which Lee was depicted, for the first time, as bearded. [11]

The deck's queens are anonymous females, each wearing some piece of Confederate military attire. The queen of hearts also wears a liberty cap. Walker would have been well familiar with the device, for it appeared in the state flag of South Carolina and in flags of many Confederate regiments.

Jacks are represented by black male servants or white Confederate soldiers. In a double visual pun, Walker has represented the jack of spades as a black man, and he has placed in the man's left hand a spade for digging. Blacks conscripted into the Confederate army were assigned the most odious tasks, such as grave and latrine digging. The figure is sockless and wears a shabby, patched coat that is too large for him. This miniature rendering is an early indicator of Walker's perception of blacks, whom he would portray, similarly attired and engaged in menial labor, in hundreds of paintings after 1880.

FIGURE 12. Set of Sixteen Decorated Playing Cards, 1864, oil, ink, and watercolor on playing card, 3 1/4 x 2 inches each, ace of spades is signed and dated: *W.A. Walker/Charleston, S.C. Sep. 1864.* Collection of Jay P. Altmayer.

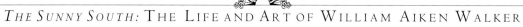

FIGURE 13. JOHN ROSS KEY (1837-1920). *The Bombardment of Fort Sumter*, 1865, oil on canvas, 29 x 69 inches. The Greenville County Museum of Art, Greenville, South Carolina.

Another war-related picture by Walker was a view of the crumbled walls of Fort Sumter as seen from Fort Johnson. Publicly displayed in October 1864, it attracted the following notice in Charleston's daily newspaper:

THE RUINS OF FORT SUMTER. A very faithful representation of the ruins of Fort Sumter, as seen from Fort Johnson, painted by Mr. Wm. A. Walker, of the Engineer Corps, is now on exhibition at Dr. Aimar's Drug Store, corner of King and Vanderhorst streets.[12]

From August 1863 through September 18, 1864, Fort Sumter weathered three major and eight minor bombardments which reduced its brick walls to rubble, yet failed to bring about its surrender. The fort remained invincible until General William Tecumseh Sherman's march through South Carolina in February 1865 forced its abandonment.

Though Walker's Fort Sumter painting is now lost, it may be compared to other known examples. James Island, on which Fort Johnson stood, remained in Confederate hands until the fall of Charleston. This fact, combined with its proximity to Fort Sumter and the outer islands guarding Charleston Harbor, made it a favored vantage point for artists of Confederate sympathy throughout the war. Frank Vizetelly had positioned himself there when he sketched Fort Sumter—its walls still solid— eighteen months prior to the display of Walker's painting. The engraving made after Vizetelly's drawing appeared as an illustration in the April 4, 1863 issue of the *Illustrated London News*. John Ross Key took a position on James Island overlooking Fort Johnson when he painted *The Bombardment of Fort Sumter* (figure 13). When displayed in Baltimore and New York after the war, Key's broadly topographical painting garnered positive reviews for its accuracy and attention to detail.[13]

Walker's half-brother George William Walker was killed at the Battle of Gaines' Mills in Virginia on June 27, 1862. His mother Mary Elizabeth Walker died less than a year later, on June 19, 1863, at the age of sixty-seven. She was buried in the cemetery of St. Philip's Church, where the remains of her husband rested. The twenty-four-year-old William expressed his grief over her death in a sweet, sentimental poem, "To Mother in Heaven."

Mother above from yon star-lighted dome,
Smile on thy children and bless our sad home.
To heaven thy spirit has taken its flight,
Our home is in darkness where once all was light!
Mother, dear Mother, each night in our prayers,
We murmur thy name in sadness and tears,
Thy spirit is wafted to kingdoms of bliss,
And left me dear Mother without a last kiss!

Mother, dear Mother, the old cushioned chair
Is empty, no longer its rocking we hear;
The little ones creeping up sadly at night
Stand round it awaiting thy "kiss" and "good-night!"
Softly we whisper and tell them on high
Thou'rt roaming with Angels far thro' the blue sky;
Gently we kiss them and lay them to sleep,
Mother, dear Mother, thy watch o'er them keep!

Mother, dear Mother! we call but alas!
No answer comes back, save a sigh from the past!
And the cold wintry as it sweeps o'er the plain,
Strikes a chill to our hearts with its moaning refrain!
But Mother, a light shining bright thro' the years
Of the future, is brightning our path full of cares:
Tis the beacon of Faith lighting up the dark shore,
We follow it Mother to meet thee once more![14]

The verses sound florid to twentieth century ears, but a close reading reveals a great deal about Walker. We cannot doubt that he deeply felt his mother's loss. That the family was very close is also indicated, for Walker, in using *we* writes for all his

FIGURE 14. Front cover of "Mes Pensées," 1866. "Mes Pensées" is a composition book containing poetry handwritten by Walker in the mid-1860s, 1902, and 1908. Front cover is decorated in oil, ink, pencil, and gouache on cardboard, 9 x 6 3/4 inches. The Carolina Art Association/Gibbes Museum of Art, Charleston, South Carolina.

mother's survivors. This group of mourners included not only himself, who at the time was living in his brother Joseph's home, but also Joseph, Joseph's wife Emma, and their three children, all under the age of six. The poem too suggests that Walker had a sensitive, emotional nature.

In addition to these painful losses, there may have been a tragedy of a romantic sort in Walker's life during the war years. A book entitled "Mes Pensées," in which he penned "To Mother in Heaven," contains twenty-three other poems (figure 14). While five poems at the back are humorous verses written when Walker was in his sixties, the other nineteen seem to have all been written in Charleston by 1866, according to Walker's handwritten imprint on the book's front cover. Dedicated to a mysterious "Belle Ange," most of the early poems are in English, with three in French and three in Spanish. Written in a sentimental style similar to the verse quoted herein, they describe the joy of newfound love and the anguish of unrequited affection. Included are two poems about moonlit voyages—a romantic subject to begin with but especially so to a Charlestonian in the days of naval blockade—in which Walker writes of gliding over the waves with his bride-to-be.

We do not know what affair Walker had in his youth, whether there was a "Belle Ange" whom he courted or whether he worshiped some lovely creature from afar, too bound to his family or too shy to express himself except in the safety of a handwritten book. Since the book descended in the Walker family until it was given to the Gibbes Museum of Art, we may conclude it never was given to the object of his affection. Walker never married, although he was often heard, when in his seventies and eighties, to fondly mention his "dear wife who was to have been."[15]

It is tempting to read the "Mes Pensées" poems as poignant, autobiographical confessions, but what is more relevant in these verses, completed with one year's hindsight on the terrible war years, is that they reveal in William Aiken Walker a sense of loss. Perhaps a thwarted love affair was part of that loss, but more generally, the poems may be seen as symbolic of a dark period in Walker's life, a mirror to his feelings of despair. It will be two years—1868—before there is again any record of William Aiken Walker, two years to which no paintings can be assigned, two years in which, we must assume, he strove to find his bearings in a world profoundly changed from the one he once knew. One has only to recall his paintings of the ruins of Fort Sumter, the ruins of the Cathedral of St. John and St. Finbar, and the ruins of the Circular Congregational Church, as well as his verse, to realize that from 1864 until 1868, William Aiken Walker's artistic expressions centered on destruction and loss. To overcome the loss and to find a means of supporting himself, Walker chose to take leave of his home and family and seek a new existence.

CHAPTER THREE

Reconstruction

FIGURE 15. *Gathering Herbs,* 1871, oil on canvas, 12 1/4 x 9 1/8 inches, signed and dated lower left: *WAWalker.1871.* Collection of Mr. and Mrs. Quincy Scarborough, Fayetteville, North Carolina.

The period immediately following the War Between the States is an undocumented time in William Aiken Walker's life, as it was in the lives of many Southerners hard hit by the war. We can only speculate as to Walker's activities from 1866 until 1868, by which time he had settled in Baltimore, Maryland. But Baltimore proved to be only the first of four Southern cities in which Walker would try to establish himself during the tumultuous years known as Reconstruction.

During the decade 1867-1877, a Republican administration in Washington, D.C. dictated to the Southern states how they were to elect state and Congressional representatives, fully involving the newly emancipated blacks in the governmental process. While considered a bleak period by Southern whites who tried to rebuild ruined fortunes, it was a time that brought new opportunities to Southern blacks. Guaranteed to them for the first time were the rights to an education and to participation in government. Southern whites were threatened by these changes, which disrupted a social and economic order that had been in place for over two hundred years. Individuals feared for their personal safety, while agricultural interests were concerned that the once dependable labor force of enslaved blacks would be dissipated as black families abandoned the plantations for cities or new land to the north and west. Further, in the first months of Reconstruction many white planters and farmers were in doubt as to whether they would even own land to cultivate by their own labor. In scattered areas throughout the South, particularly the Carolina coastal region, United States Army officers parceled out abandoned estates in forty-acre lots and gave them to the freedmen. For Southerners of both races it was a period of enormous adjustment.

From August 1863 until February 1865, Charleston suffered a bombardment lasting 587 days. Finally on February 17, 1865, with federal troops led by General William Tecumseh Sherman closing in from Savannah, able-bodied Charlestonians made for the railway station or mounted carriages, carts, horses, or donkeys—whatever conveyance they could come by—and fled the city. On that evening the Stars and Bars were hauled down from above Fort Sumter, and Confederate soldiers manning the fort slipped away across the quiet waters of Charleston Harbor. The next morning the city was in federal hands.

A mere three months later, Whitelaw Reid visited what he called "the city of desolation."[1] Black soldiers patrolled the streets. The few Charlestonians who had remained behind—the old, the very young, the sick, and the handicapped—presented a sorry sight, their complexions pale and sallow from want of a healthy diet. Restaurants and clubs were closed. The only patrons to be seen in the few taverns that remained open were Yankee officers. Once a prominent landmark, the Charleston racecourse showed signs of hard wear as a Confederate prison. Behind the grandstands stretched row upon row of crude graves, where Yankees who had died in captivity lay buried. The aristocratic Carolina planters had vanished; their grand homes on the Battery and East Bay Street were, at the close of the war, quarters to federal officers.

Charleston was decimated. A thriving trade center of nearly 40,000 inhabitants before the war, the city proper had shriveled to a population of less than 20,000 by the summer of 1865.[2] Outsiders streamed in once Yankee occupation began, but they were people who came in desperation—innocents seeking protection and scavengers greedy for abandoned treasures.

After the fall of Charleston in early 1865, Walker may have taken refuge in Cheraw, South Carolina, joining his brother Joseph who had removed there in late 1863 or in 1864.[3] But by 1866 Walker was back in Charleston.[4] Whether Joseph's Charleston home on Rutledge Street survived the extensive looting of the city; whether it was occupied by Yankee troops; whether Walker may have been engaged in restoring the house for the family's return are open questions. That he could have supported himself as an artist in the ruined city is unlikely.

By the autumn of 1868, Walker was established as an "artist and teacher of languages" in Baltimore.[5] He encountered a strikingly different world from his native Charleston in this modern, industrial city. Baltimore's population in 1868 was approaching a quarter of a million, more than five times the size of pre-war Charleston. Far from having suffered privations during the war, Baltimore's early occupation by the federals actually infused money into the city, for her manufactories were fully engaged in the war effort.

Baltimore was rich, and this prosperity allowed the arts to flourish. Major art collections formed at mid-century remain the nucleus of two of the city's leading museums today, the Walters Art Gallery and the Peabody Institute. Before the war, William T. Walters had patronized American artists of the Hudson River school such as John Kensett (1816-1872), Asher B. Durand (1796-1886), and Frederic Edwin Church (1826-1900), and he had commissioned drawings of Plains Indians and the Rocky Mountains from the Baltimore painter Alfred Jacob Miller (1810-1874). After the war, his collecting continued unabated, though he began to show a preference for works by contemporary European artists. He increasingly made purchases of the latest products of the Munich and French schools, while remaining a loyal patron of Baltimore's still life painter Andrew John Henry Way (1826-1888).

The Peabody Institute was built and presented as a gift to the people of Baltimore by the wealthy merchant and banker George Peabody. On October 25, 1866, the Peabody opened its doors to the public. Housed in a plain white marble building of the Grecian style at the corner of Charles Street and Mount Vernon Place, it maintained a reference library, lecture hall, conservatory of music, and an art gallery. It quickly became a pleasant gathering place for the community at large and particularly for local artists.

Artists fared well in Baltimore in the mid-1800s and immediately after the war. A few, such as Way, who returned there from his studies in Florence in 1854, painted in Baltimore throughout the conflict. John Ross Key, Walker's colleague from the Engineers Corps in Charleston and a Baltimore native, re-established himself there after his Confederate service. Francis Mayer (1827-1899), Arthur Quartley (1839-1886), and Allen Redwood (1844-1922) had also opened studios in Baltimore by the end of the 1860s.

Walker took rooms at 16 1/2 North Charles Street, between Lexington and Fayette streets, right in the heart of the city. In the immediate neighborhood were daguerreotype studios, upholstery workshops, a china shop, stationers, the studios of other artists, and—something that Walker had never encountered in Charleston—commercial art galleries. Only two doors from Walker's studio was the gallery of Butler and Perrigo, which occasionally displayed his work.

Walker was a welcome addition to Baltimore's artistic community. He became a member of the Wednesday Club, a group of artists, musicians, and actors—mostly amateurs and all men—who came from the upper crust of Baltimore society.[6] Members included music patron Wilkins Glenn, portraitist John R. Robertson, and Dr. A. J. Volck, a dentist, cartoonist, and designer in silver. They assembled at eight o'clock each Wednesday to enjoy a musical or dramatic performance staged by their own members. Supper followed at ten o'clock and was faithfully accompanied by numerous toasts. Later the gentlemen joined in what they called "the Circus," a madcap, spontaneous series of farcical performances and song, which they would invariably conclude with a rousing rendition of Verdi's "Anvil Chorus" from *Il Trovatore*, accompanied by the beating of coal shovels, andirons, tea kettles, or whatever was handy. Robertson's undated drawing entitled *Anvil Chorus at Sutro's* depicts Walker seated at the piano, his left arm extended in the act of conducting his gentlemen friends.[7]

The Wednesday Club traced its origins to weekly gatherings that began in 1858 in the home of music dealer Otto Sutro. After some years the club was formally organized and permanent rooms were found at 20 North Charles Street, a building owned by club vice-president Wilkins Glenn. Here also, in 1871 and 1872, Walker maintained a studio.[8]

Late in 1869 Walker began his only known journeys outside the Southern states. He visited New York City in the fall of that year where he joined the employ of Charles D. Fredericks and Co., photographers, before sailing for Cuba to work in the company's Havana studio as a colorist.[9] Whether he was in New York a month, a week, or a few days is unclear, but this visit was probably the only one he ever made to the art capital of the United States. This is an important omission in Walker's career. Many artists that Walker knew had established themselves in New York. John B. Irving, Jr., a Charleston native ten years Walker's senior, had settled in the city after the war. Irving opened his studio in the Tenth Street Studio Building where Frederic Edwin Church, Sanford Gifford (1823-1880), William Jacob Hays (1830-1875), and other of America's leading painters were then practicing. By 1869, John

Ross Key, who had gone from Charleston to Baltimore in the spring of 1865, was also living in New York.

That Walker never availed himself of the opportunity to study at the National Academy of Design in that city or privately with any of New York's many distinguished artists reveals his unique and practical approach to art and work. For Walker, art was a vocation, a profession that did not require academic training, but rather relied on natural skill. Furthermore, it was a vocation best pursued in the familiar environs of the South.

Walker did stay in New York long enough to see shows at Booth's Theater and the Academy of Music. He may very well have seen *Il Trovatore*, with which he had pleasant associations through his Wednesday Club membership, for it played at the Academy in early December, and he probably took in *King Henry IV, Part I*, which was then at Booth's. Later, addressing his journal at Havana, he compared that city's Grand Teatro Tacon to the New York houses noting, "The Teatro is very pretty, but not as fine as 'Booths' or Ac. of Music N. Y."

Walker's two-month Cuban stay is the only period of his life that is meticulously documented by a surviving journal.[10] The diary begins with a description of his departure by steamship from New York City and ends abruptly two months later, when, dispirited and exhausted, Walker contemplated returning home.

Walker boarded the *Eagle*, a ship of the American Mail Steamship Company under the command of Capt. M. R. Greene, in New York on Thursday, December 9, 1869. It seems he enjoyed a lively, genial passage. In his journal he described the voyage as "very pleasant, nice set of passengers, pleasant weather & beautiful moonlight [*sic*] nights." He entertained his shipmates, he wrote, with "soirees on board with aid of the Piano."

The *Eagle* pushed through the Narrows of New York Harbor for a course far out to sea. After five full days she lay off Moro Castel at the entrance to Havana Harbor. On the morning of December 15, she was permitted to enter the harbor, and there Walker found "vessels of all nations." He went ashore at 10:30 in the morning and headed straight for the "Gallery of C. D. Fredricks y Davis, Calle de la Habana 108, where," he writes, "I got fixed and to work before dinner."

Cuba was very accessible to Americans at that time and was a popular vacation spot. A booming tourist business generated a demand for souvenir pictures; consequently, the need for colorists to enliven those images followed. Walker worked feverishly, putting in as much as nine to ten hours each day and often painting six days each week. By January 1, he had painted forty-seven photos and had netted $137.95. The monetary rewards were good enough, but he found his work uninspiring. Repeatedly he noted in his journal, "worked hard all day," or "same routine," or "nothing interesting." Only after he had been employed with the photos for about six weeks did he indulge himself in an artistic diversion, writing on January 29, "very little to paint today. Made a sketch in oil of Habana St. from my studio window," one of only two references in the Cuban diary to an original work of art.

Walker was not at a loss for amusement in the evenings and on his free days. The exotic tropical country appealed to his sense of adventure. He made day trips to colorful, out-of-the-way villages, played billiards, attended a cockfight, went to the opera, strolled in the evening, enjoyed a fat Havana cigar now and then, and indulged his fondness for good coffee and fine chocolates. His companions in these varied pursuits were a Mr. W. K. Collins of New York, whose acquaintance Walker had made on board the *Eagle*, and, less frequently, a Mr. Kerr and a Mr. Bailey. Walker makes no mention of these gentlemen working to offset the expense of their Cuban stays; therefore, it may be assumed that they were financially secure, particularly Collins, who stayed at the Santa Isabel, Havana's most elegant hotel.

On Sunday, January 16, after a full day of sightseeing, Walker "went to Sta. Isabel & sat on Balcony of Collins room enjoying the splendid view of the Bahia by moonlight smoking fine Habanas. At 10 went to the 'Dominica' [Havana's world-renowned cafe and a gathering spot for foreigners as well as natives]. . . . Spent a most charming day, enjoyed the sea breeze very much, quite a relief to get out of my studio for a day." The very next day he "went out in a small boat sailing on the Bay by moonlight with Collins. Very lovely. Played Billiards, took refrescos at Dominica & went to bed." Another outing he described thus:

CHAPTER THREE

Reconstruction

FIGURE 15. *Gathering Herbs,* 1871, oil on canvas, 12 1/4 x 9 1/8 inches, signed and dated lower left: *WAWalker.1871.* Collection of Mr. and Mrs. Quincy Scarborough, Fayetteville, North Carolina.

Had a very pleasant drive of a league to Cojima which is a very pretty spot on the seashore about 15 houses including the Fonda. The old stone castle of C. [Cojima] is built on the rocks overhanging the ocean, pretty beach nearby where we gathered shells. Good bathing. Spent two hours very agreeably & returned to Guanabacoa where we took Rail cars for Regla. . . . Took ferryboat back to Habana & dined at 4 P.M. with Kerr at Fonda 'El Oriental.'

A recurring complaint of Walker's throughout his time in Cuba was of feeling unwell, and particularly of having headaches. A day in the country left him feeling tired but good; yet, a day in the studio often gave him cause for complaint. He wrote on Saturday, January 8, "Quite sick from over-work," and the following day, "Rose at 8 am. Still very sick, headache." On Wednesday, January 19, he noted, "Hard work. Same routine. . . . Quite sick all day, worn out & headache. Climate & work very bad for me." Walker surmised that the climate had an ill effect on his health, and it is possible that he suffered in Cuba's tropical environment from disease. However, it must also be noted that by working in a photography studio, Walker was exposed to highly toxic chemicals used in the development process. It was uncommon for a colorist to complain of feeling ill, so it is possible that Walker was involved in more than just the coloring process.

Walker left Havana in February of 1870, but where he went from there is a mystery. His last journal entry, written in Havana on Saturday, February 12, states simply, "Busy. Collins called. Spoke of going home, think I will go too. Warm again. Unwell." He might have taken a steamer with his friend Collins back to New York, or he could have booked passage to Charleston to visit his family, or to Baltimore to resume his life there. (Havana had direct, weekly steamboat connections to all three cities.) It is also possible that Walker went to Europe at this time. An article appearing in a Baltimore newspaper in the spring of 1871, which will be quoted later, alludes to such a trip, but neither paintings of European subjects nor additional corroborating evidence has come to light. In any event, for the remainder of 1870, Walker's life is undocumented; only in 1871 is there evidence for his having picked up the brush again in Baltimore.

Interest was keen among the art promoters of Baltimore to find buyers for the work of local artists. In the spring of 1871, the gallery of Perrigo and Kohl (successor to Butler and Perrigo) mounted its first annual Baltimore exhibition. The display remained up for a few days and was followed by a dispersal of the pictures at public auction. So important were the twin events of exhibition and sale that nearly every newspaper in the city saw that both were covered. One reviewer wrote, "The exhibition of paintings now in progress at the gallery of Messrs. Perrigo & Kohl, at the corner of Fayette and Charles streets, promises to be the initiative step towards an annual display of the fruits of the labor of the artists in Baltimore." This writer singled out Walker's two contributions for particular praise:

> Mr. Walker, a native of South Carolina, but who has enjoyed the benefits of a lengthy sojourn in the galleries of Europe, contributes to the exhibition two original pictures, and although the paintings are small, they attract a large share of the attention of visitors to the gallery. One picture represents a colored boy, of 1859, trudging across a plantation. He is clad in the cast-off garments of his master, and presents a sorry figure. The other picture is entitled "One of the Attractions of the Seashore," representing a miss seated upon a rock and indulging in a love-lorn gaze over the broad expanse of ocean. The drawings of Mr. Walker possess an exquisite sense of harmony. In gradations and variety he carefully studies nature. Feeling is conspicuous in his work, and in the making up of his landscape world he condenses so the grand elements of the natural that one feels his ideal while recognizing the truthfulness of the actual scenery.[11]

The present location of these paintings is unknown. The "colored boy," the article tells us, was painted in 1859 when Walker was in Charleston. His attire and his association with the plantation suggests that this painting was closely related to the subjects that Walker would paint after 1880. In the picture of the young lady at the seashore, who indulges "in a love-lorn gaze" over the waves, it seems that Walker depicted on canvas the same feelings about which he had written in the poems to

"Belle Ange." These poems, which told of ocean voyages, parted lovers, and promised reunions, were written in Charleston in the mid-1860s; therefore, it is likely that the painting was made there at the same time.

It is curious that Walker should submit to this important show and sale two pictures that he had painted long before adopting Baltimore as his home and, furthermore, pictures that were undervalued relative to the work that other artists contributed. (The average price fetched for each picture at the auction was about $39, yet Walker's *A Native of South Carolina* earned only $16 on April 25, the first night of the sale, going to a Mr. Orndorf, and *One of the Attractions of the Seashore* earned $18 when purchased the following evening by W. W. Remington.)[12] This suggests that Walker did not have a body of current work in his studio. Walker's listing as "artist" in the city directory may have referred not so much to the fact that he was a painter of original works of art as it did to his activity as a colorist of photographs, a skill which had made his Cuban sojourn possible. Walker's painted photographs have turned up with increasing frequency in recent years, and most are datable to the 1860s and 1870s. Though he painted on canvas and artist's board, photographs, which were more quickly executed, could have provided a steadier flow of income. Perhaps, for a time in Baltimore, Walker's original paintings were strictly his avocation. He could afford to paint them only after he had established a reliable clientele for his photography business.

In 1871 Walker's artistic imagination was captivated by the industrious boys who made their living on Baltimore's streets. Street persons were a subject that had appealed to local artists for over a decade. In 1858 Thomas Waterman Wood (1823-1903), during his two-year Baltimore tenure, had painted a series of small character studies of local street peddlers, including *Baltimore News Vendor*, *Market Woman*, and *The Apple Vendor* (figure 16), all created at the request of his Baltimore patron John C. Brune.[13] The newsboy had been a much explored theme in other Northeastern cities since the 1840s. Depictions included *The Newsboy* (1841) by Henry Inman (1801-1846) of New York, *Buffalo Newsboy* (1853) by Thomas LeClear (1818-1882), and *Newsboy Selling 'New York Herald'* (figure 17) by James Henry Cafferty (1819-1869), to cite a few. Artists who painted street urchins did so in a particularly

FIGURE 16. THOMAS WATERMAN WOOD (1823-1903). *The Apple Vendor,* 1858, oil on canvas, 18 1/2 x 14 1/2 inches, signed and dated lower right: *T. W. Wood./ 1858.* Private Collection.

FIGURE 17. JAMES HENRY CAFFERTY (1819-1869). *Newsboy Selling 'New York Herald,'* 1857, oil on canvas, 16 x 12 inches, signed and dated lower right: *J. H. Cafferty 1857.* Collection of Mr. and Mrs. Walter H. Rubin.

endearing manner, glossing over their poverty and homeless condition by rendering them well-scrubbed, ruddy-cheeked, and cherubic.

Walker painted at least three similar subjects. His earliest is of a newsboy and dates to 1871. The anonymous model for *Newsboy Selling the Baltimore Sun* (figure 18) stands on a city sidewalk, bundled against the cold. He offers the viewer a paper with his right hand while his left he keeps tucked inside a pants pocket. Under his

FIGURE 18. *Newsboy Selling the Baltimore Sun,* 1871, oil on academy board, 11 1/4 x 7 1/2 inches, signed and dated lower left: *WAWalker. 1871.* The High Museum of Art, Atlanta, Georgia; Gift of Mr. and Mrs. George E. Missbach (74.7).

left arm he holds his supply of papers. The boy, while clean, is not in any way beautified as was the wont of other painters of the genre. Walker offers a straightforward depiction of what was then a type in Baltimore and other Eastern cities.

Walker's other known street character of this period, a boy musician, was painted in 1872. Entitled *A Few Bars' Rest* (location unknown), it shows a young fiddler collapsed from exhaustion on the steps of a Baltimore brownstone. The picture was exhibited soon after its completion, earning high praise for its creator.

A Superb Painting./There is now on exhibition at the establishment of Judge & Dawson, 96 North Charles street, an oil painting that cannot fail in arresting the attention of every lover of true art. It is denominated "A Few Bars Rest," [*sic*] and represents a wearied boy, asleep upon the stoop of a building, and a violin beside him tells the story of the picture. The lad, a street musician, has become fatigued with his tramp, and has sought "a few bars rest" upon the stoop. The position of the boy is life like, and his countenance denotes that he is enjoying a delicious "nap." The coloring of the picture is so exquisitely rendered and the surroundings to the main subject so artistically blended, that the painting stamps Mr. Walker one of the most gifted artists now in Baltimore, and who in a very short time must stand at the head of his beautiful profession.[14]

Far from being ashamed of the existence of these poor creatures on their streets, Baltimore residents felt pride in the resourcefulness of these boys, who exemplified the enterprising spirit that infused the entire city. Too, they were examples of how well Baltimore looked after its unfortunates. A description of the city of Baltimore published in 1873 proudly lists over thirty institutions for the relief of the poor, many for children.

Another picture Walker painted in this vein, the now lost *Homeless Boy*, was submitted to the Industrial Exposition in Louisville, Kentucky in the fall of 1872. In Louisville Walker encountered a harsher critic who apparently was unmoved by the sentimentality of the theme.

THE HOMELESS BOY,/by W. A. Walker, of Baltimore, and "Home Again" by the same artist, are well wrought, though some defects are apparent. The boy's foot is out of proportion, and his hand is not well made. The grass springing through the crevices of the pavement about a spot which has other indications of being constantly frequented by street passengers is rather forced and need not have been resorted to for the purpose of producing the impression that it was spring or summer. The face of the homeless little wanderer, the position of his body, and the raggedness and poverty of his general appearance are, however, deserving of more than usual praise, and go far to redeem the imperfections of the work.[15]

Unbeknownst to this reviewer, Walker had recently settled in Louisville, where he found a great demand for portraits. Walker joined the mass exodus of artists who fled Baltimore each summer in order to travel, sketch, and gather material to be used in easel paintings when the winter season confined them to their studios. When Walker left in the summer of 1872 and failed to return that fall, his absence was noticed, a testament to the fine reputation he had established in Baltimore. The *Capital* reported in October:

Our Studios have hardly yet begun to resume their usual activity. Many of the artists still remain away; some are at the sea-side; some among the mountains, while others are far away on the plains and the Pacific slopes. . . . Redwood and Walker, Jones and Rhinehart, Key and Connelley, Volck and Sauerwein, still remain away, and their inspiration is sadly missed among their fellow workers here. . . .William A. Walker, known as a musician and composer almost as well as an artist, and hardly less as a *literateur*, has been drifting around with pen and pencil all summer, and now has settled down in Kentucky for a few months. He has opened a studio corner of Fourth and Greene [*sic*] Streets, Louisville, where he is busily at work filling a large number of orders, principally of portraits.[16]

Perhaps Walker's failure to return to Baltimore was due to a depression in the art market. In the mid-1870s hardly any Baltimore artists were experiencing the success that they had at the start of the decade. The Maryland Academy of Art held a festive exhibition in December 1871 in which Baltimore's leading artists, including Walker, participated.[17] The academy had been organized only eighteen months earlier to promote the appreciation of the fine arts in Baltimore. Its founding was inspired by the awareness "of a growing interest in art, that it was [a] propitious moment for the formation of this academy." In the classical, academic tradition of art instruction as offered in the nineteenth century, casts of "nearly all the masterpieces of antiquity" were ordered from abroad.[18] But two years later, these casts and other works belonging to the academy were removed and transferred to the Peabody Institute, and the academy was dissolved.

Sales of works of art also began to decline. The annual sale of pictures by Baltimore artists, held for the third time in the spring of 1873, was described as "a shabby affair."[19] The decline accelerated throughout the seventies, prompting a sympathetic observer to write in 1881:

> Our best art talent, failing of encouragement at home, has, with few exceptions, drifted away to other cities but especially to New York. Two of those who continue among us—Mayer and Way, both medalists of the Centennial Exhibition—find a better market for their works in other cities than their own.[20]

By contrast, Louisville was undergoing rapid economic growth. The city was located in the middle of the richest tobacco belt in the South, and manufactories were developing at a rapid pace. At the time of Walker's arrival in the summer of 1872, Louisville was bustling with preparations for its first major exposition of art and industry. A large hall had been specially designed and built for the Louisville Industrial Exposition, which opened to the public on September 3. It was a showcase for the latest products of Kentucky agriculture, manufacture, and design, featuring

FIGURE 19. *Fourth St. Looking South from Junction of Green St.*, line engraving. Reproduced in *Illustrated Louisville, Kentucky's Metropolis* (Chicago: Acme Publishing Company, 1891). The Filson Club, Louisville, Kentucky.

The building on the southwest corner of Fourth and Green streets (at right in the engraving) was called the McDowell Block. It was constructed two to three years before Walker occupied a studio there in the fall of 1872. The building on the opposite corner (at left in the engraving) was the Louisville Opera House. Green is now known as Liberty Street.

---

fine Kentucky-grown tobacco, machinery, furniture, pistols, and fishing tackle. In the ladies' section, wax flower arrangements, embroideries, and other home crafts were exhibited. In the art section were displays of contemporary sculptures and paintings by American and European artists.

What is significant about the Louisville Industrial Exposition regarding the study of Southern art is the enthusiasm with which the city's press responded to works by

Southern artists, an indication of an emergent, regional cultural identity. In their promotional efforts, the Exposition's organizers went to great lengths to attract the notice and business of neighboring Southerners. The South and North Alabama Railroad was completed about the time of the Exposition, putting Louisville into easy, direct connection with the Alabama cotton belt, as well as the port cities of the Gulf Coast. To celebrate this event, Louisville's mayor invited a delegation from Alabama, headed by the governor of that state, to attend the fair. The delegates were given a gala reception at the House of Refuge, a local orphanage for boys, followed by a special tour of the Exposition, and a champagne luncheon in the Exposition Building. One of the city's daily papers reported the activities, prefaced by the following words:

The completion of the South & North Alabama Railroad has brought us in easy reach of the rich mineral resources of Northern Alabama, her vast and productive cotton fields in the central portion of the State, and her seaport, which looks out upon the blue waves of the Gulf of Mexico. It has brought us nearer the rich products of Georgia, and nearer the sea port of Florida, which upon its beautiful and capacious harbor, holds a future bright with possibilities; and above all, Louisville, a Southern city, is brought into closer relations with Southern business men, and as an emporium of trade can look forward with confidence to rapid and large accessions of trade from these districts. It was proper, therefore, for the representatives of our municipal interests, the Mayor, the General Council, and the Board of Trade to crown the day of the arrival of our Southern guests. . . .[21]

The art critic for the *Daily Louisville Commercial* responded to the broad, regional outlook of the Exposition's promoters by calling attention in one review to the work of Southern artists. In a short article that appeared after the close of the Exposition, the reporter cited the work of Baltimore artist Andrew John Henry Way, the sculptor Edward Valentine (1838-1930) of Richmond, and William A. Walker of Charleston. He praised Way's oysters ("and almost every one remembers the juicy and appetizing oysters in a little lunch picture in the west gallery"), but reserved more enthusiastic compliments for Walker, writing, "There was also in the gallery a very superior picture of a setter, painted by Major [*sic*] Wm. A. Walker, of South Carolina, the property of General S. W. Ferguson, of Mississippi. The picture is entitled, 'On the Lookout,' and is a remarkably fine one." The reviewer expressed the hope that all three artists would participate in Louisville's second annual industrial exposition, already planned for the following year. "We may say that Baltimore will be well represented at our next Exposition in art matters. We hope so, and trust that we shall have a finer gallery in which to display pictures."[22] This reviewer's hope as well as his apology suggest that Louisville was not as advanced in the fine arts as some of her residents might have liked. Perhaps this is the very reason that Walker was attracted to Louisville. Seeing the market for American talent like his own declining in Baltimore, he remained in Louisville, which seemed to offer great opportunity.

It is logical to assume that Louisville's rapid growth and prosperity put more disposable income in the pockets of her citizenry and increased the demand for portraiture and for decorative paintings to hang on parlor walls. We may imagine that this was Walker's conclusion upon his arrival in Louisville. He found far fewer artists practicing there, nine to be exact, as compared to Baltimore's thirty-five in 1870. The Louisville artists were: Alexander Conn (op. 1863-1872), five members of the Maltby family, Plumer Prescott (1833-1881), William Ver Bryck (1823-1899), and H. H. Cross (1837-1918).

Walker took a studio in what was the equivalent of a center for the arts, the McDowell building on the southwest corner of Fourth and Green (the latter now Liberty) streets, opposite Louisville's Opera House (figure 19). Portraitists Prescott and Ver Bryck also had studios in this building, as did the photographer Henry D. Stowe.[23] The location was prime. Main, Market, Jefferson, and Green streets were filled with what a contemporary described as large, handsome shops and warehouses, while the numbered cross streets were lined with mansions and manicured yards.[24] This same writer was impressed by the city's "miles of elegant streets, its smooth pavements, its fine hospitals and churches, its mammoth hotels and pretty theaters,

FIGURE 20. **Boy with Goat**, 1872, 11 x 8 inches, oil on academy board, signed and dated lower left: *WAWalker. 1872*. The Morris Museum of Art, Augusta, Georgia.

its bustling 'Exposition' and its brilliant society. . . ."[25] Surely Walker took part in this vibrant cultural life during the months that he was there. The nearby Opera House, which booked a continual stream of dramatic and operatic road companies, must have attracted his regular patronage.

The only images that survive from Walker's Louisville period are two painted photographs. One represents a little girl seated on the bank of a stream, while the other, a self-portrait, shows Walker in the studio painstakingly painting a brace of game in the manner of Charles Fraser. Perhaps the promise of clients that the booming city held forth in the autumn of 1872 was never fulfilled to Walker's satisfaction. A reason for this could be that collectors' preferences in Louisville, as in Baltimore, were shifting to the new paintings coming out of France and Germany. The attention paid by the *Daily Louisville Commercial* to works by Southern artists, as previously discussed, was countered by the view championed in the pages of the *Courier-Journal*, where paintings by Jean Leon Gerome, Ernest Meissonnier, and Oswold Achenbach elicited descriptions such as "a triumph," "superb," and "exquisite work." In contrast, the *Courier-Journal* effectively damned the work of American artists with faint praise.

> We come now to speak of some productions by our native artists in the Exposition; and every one will admit that in general they merit a favorable criticism. The imperfections incident to works wrought under those disadvantages which almost always surround an American artist are apparent, but they are, nevertheless, creditable, and their authors well worthy of commendation.[26]

It will be recalled that the *Courier-Journal* was the same paper which had printed the harsh critique of Walker's *Homeless Boy* quoted earlier. The foregoing represents, while not exactly a hostile attitude, certainly one that an artist would not find encouraging.

By 1874 Walker had established himself in Galveston, Texas, a tropical port on Galveston Bay surrounded by thirty-one miles of glistening, white beaches. Galveston's business district had a quaint look to it, with its many long piers and jetties running out into the water, giving the city an appearance similar to Walker's native Charleston.

Walker took rooms in a building at the corner of Market and 21st streets.[27] There were only three other artists in Galveston at this time, including the portraitist C. Hofrichter, who had studio space in the same building as Walker. It would seem that, here again, Walker arrived in a young city with the hope of filling an artistic void.

After the War Between the States, the merchants of Galveston worked energetically to make their city the premier port for the export of Texas cotton. Many farmers had moved across the Mississippi River after the war. Much of the land in the tidewater was depleted from the growing of cotton, and as a result, a mix of people came to Texas to begin anew or to begin for the first time. These new Texans included young planters who had lost everything except the resourcefulness to start over again in a strange land, small farmers from the Piedmont, and newly emancipated blacks seeking their first farm land. The land at the head of Galveston Bay was excellent for cultivating the valuable long staple cotton that had been grown on the sea islands of South Carolina before the war. By 1873 Galveston annually dispatched some 350,000 bales of cotton—which comprised two-thirds of the state's production—to Liverpool, London, Bremen, and Hamburg. The city could not construct wharves quickly enough to keep up with the booming cotton trade. Stevedores would go knee-deep into the waters of Galveston Bay with their mule-driven carts to load or unload the many schooners unable to dock.

So impressed was Walker with Galveston's expansive harbor that he painted the city as seen from the bay, his only painting to have emerged so far from his two or more years in Galveston. In scale and composition Walker's *View of Galveston Harbor* (figure 21) is in the tradition of eighteenth century Anglo-American panorama painting. The style is generally characterized by a distant view of a city looking over an expanse of open water that fills the foreground of the picture plane. The city itself is seen on the horizon; the position, silhouette, and detail of each building is precisely rendered. The skyline, including soaring church steeples, is dwarfed by the interposition between artist and city of the towering masts of ocean-going vessels under full sail. Walker was familiar with such views, for many had been painted of his hometown, and many of those paintings were highly accessible as engraved reproductions. These models included the eighteenth century prints after views by Bishop Roberts (died 1739) and Thomas Mellish; *The City of Charleston, So. Carolina* (circa 1835), an aquatint engraving by William Keenan (born circa 1710) of Charleston after a drawing by Charles Vignoles; and *Charleston Harbour, S.C.,* published as an engraving by T. Addison Richards in his magazine *Orion.* S. Bernard, artist of *View along the East Battery, Charleston* (figure 3), had also painted two panoramic views of the city from the water in 1831.

A broad, sweeping panorama, Walker's *View of Galveston Harbor* earned praise for its accuracy and attention to detail. In an article appearing years later in the *Galveston Daily News,* the painting was described at great length. The writer of the article obviously was certain that Walker's painting was an accurate portrayal of Galveston at an earlier time. To the left of center in Walker's picture may be seen two side-wheel steamers, the *Clinton* and the *Mary,* passenger boats that worked between Galveston and New Orleans. Just about at the center of the picture is the *City of Waco* of the Mallory Line, which plied the waters between Galveston and New York.[28] Of the three barks at right, the first was the *Samuel G. Glover* and the second, the *Sarah Douglass,* both used in transporting cotton to England. Just above the bowsprit of the *Douglass* is the steeple of St. John's Methodist Church, constructed in 1871. Last but not least, Walker placed himself in the painting. In the right foreground is a small boat rowed by two men with the artist as helmsman facing them.[29]

Upon its completion in the autumn of 1874, Walker immediately set about promoting his latest work. On October 28, the *Galveston Daily News* ran the following notice:

Port of Galveston

The *News* acknowledges the receipt from Mr. W. A. Walker, artist, of a handsome photograph of his painting of the "Port of Galveston, Texas. 1874."

The picture gives a clear and accurate view of the shipping, shows the leading features of the bay front and embraces every kind of vessel, from the fisher's punt to the stately ocean steamship.

Walker placed the painting on view in Mason's bookshop at the corner of Center and Market streets in Galveston. He received at least one offer of purchase from

FIGURE 21. *View of Galveston Harbor,* 1874, oil on canvas, 29 x 63 inches, signed and dated lower left on barrel: *WAWalker. 1874.* Courtesy of the Rosenberg Library, Galveston, Texas.

Charles Fowler of Galveston, but he and Fowler could not agree on a price. The painting subsequently hung in Rose's Galveston photography studio until purchased by R. D. Bowen of Paris, Texas.[30]

In 1876 Walker travelled to San Antonio, then a largely Mexican town of six to seven thousand inhabitants. There he painted the imposing ruins of the San Jose Mission (figure 22). This magnificent church, erected by the Spanish in 1768 in their efforts to Christianize the Indians, was noted for the heavily carved Baroque facade of its western portal and the single bell tower at its western end. It was a popular subject with artists. Seth Eastman (1808-1875), as a lieutenant posted to San Antonio, sketched the mission in 1848. Thirty years later Thomas Allen (1849-1924) made drawings of the famous western portal.

Walker's painting has its antecedents in his *Circular Church in Ruins* (figure 10) and *St. Finbar's Roman Catholic Cathedral,* (figure 11), which he painted as hulks looming hauntingly over war-damaged Charleston. For sheer size—the canvas measures 23 1/4 x 35 inches—*San Jose Mission* surpassed these earlier efforts in monumentality. The expansive quality of the sky and the flatness of the land enhance the mission's dominance of the picture plane, while the figures at left serve as points of reference to the towering proportions of the mission complex. The low horizon, characteristic of eighteenth century Dutch landscapes and city views, also lends grandeur to the structure, allowing the bell tower to stretch to more than half the height of the picture plane.

During the mid-1870s Walker maintained close ties to Baltimore and may even have harbored the intention of returning there when times became more propitious for artists. In turn, memories of Walker and his work lingered long in Baltimore, where in 1879 or 1880 it was reported in one of the local newspapers:

Mr. W. A. Walker, formerly of this city, but who for the last six or seven years has been leading a nomadic life throughout the Southern States, writes from Augusta, Ga., that his health has been very precarious for a long time

FIGURE 22. **San Jose Mission**, 1876, oil on canvas, 23 1/4 x 35 inches, signed and dated lower left on rock: *WAWalker./1876.* Courtesy of the Witte Museum and the San Antonio Museum Association, San Antonio, Texas.

past, and that he yearns to get back to the home of his adoption. He has sent on a pair of pictures named respectively 'The Banquet' and 'The Banquet Interrupted.' Both possess considerable merit and would be popular as chromos. They are to been seen at Bendann's art store, 127 W. Baltimore street.[31]

Walker lived in Augusta for two years, 1879 through 1880. He possibly worked in partnership with J. Usher, a local photographer, with whom he shared a studio address.[32] Augusta was a thriving commercial center in the late 1870s. Spared by General William T. Sherman on his rapacious run through Georgia, the local economy quickly recovered, thanks to booming textile mills. As farmers abandoned the exhausted coastal plain for the richer soil of Texas and the Carolina Piedmont, Augusta found itself strategically positioned for growth and prosperity. Situated on the Savannah River, Augusta had the water power necessary for the operation of cotton mills. Six such mills were erected in Augusta in the 1870s, and by 1891 the Georgia city was referred to as "the Lowell of the South." The opening of banks and other businesses naturally followed. Walker opened an account at the Planters Savings and Loan of Augusta that he maintained until he died. This is not surprising. Augusta, lying one day's journey by rail from Charleston, would have been a logical stopover point for him in travelling between Charleston, where he retained close family ties, and New Orleans, where he would reside for much of the 1880s.

Walker's Augusta paintings, *The Banquet* and *The Banquet Interrupted*, are unfortunately lost. It is generally believed that these works were tabletop still lifes featuring a combination of cheese, bread, fruit, or other unattended comestibles to which mice help themselves, rather than genre paintings of persons seated in an elegant dining room. Walker did at least three still lifes with mice in the 1870s. *A Free Lunch* (figure 23) is known by the lithograph made after it by Currier and Ives. *Still Life with Cheese, Bottle and Mouse* (1876; Collection of Malcolm W. Monroe, New Orleans, Louisiana) and *Old Shoe with Mice* (1879; Louisiana State Museum, New Orleans, Louisiana) are two other paintings of this type.

Mention of *The Banquet* and *The Banquet Interrupted* in the Baltimore newspaper is important, for it offers insight into Walker's marketing techniques. Walker by no

FIGURE 23. Currier & Ives, lithographers. After William Aiken Walker. *A Free Lunch*, 1872, lithograph, 11 1/4 x 14 inches, signed and dated on the stone lower left: *WAWalker. 1872.* The Library of Congress, Washington, D.C.

means abandoned his clientele when he moved from one city to another; rather, he sent fresh work to art dealers or shopkeepers for them to display and sell on his behalf. Bendann's in Baltimore is but one example. Later in Walker's life there is evidence of a long distance marketing relationship with Robert A. Rowlinski of Savannah, Georgia. A friend of Walker's, Rowlinski would sell Walker's paintings from a stand in the lobby of a Savannah hotel. He took care of all the duties that an art dealer would, ensuring that the pictures were attractively framed and put under glass for their protection.[33]

Other of Walker's paintings from the late 1870s and early 1880s reveal that he traveled quite a lot on the Mississippi River during that time. *Poker Game* (figure 24), a radical departure from the single-figure genre scenes he had painted in Baltimore, depicts five men playing cards. It is a rare attempt by Walker to portray an interior space; usually he posed figures either outdoors or before a blank wall. Four men play cards, while a fifth looks on. The seated man in shirtsleeves who faces the viewer triumphantly holds up a full house. The man seated at right, with hat shoved back and a cigar stuck in his mouth, is a caricature of the country rube, a type in American folklore who was always duped. (This type also appears in pictures of horse trading by William Sidney Mount.[34]) The men are journeying down river to New Orleans, as indicated by the destination inscribed on the large crate in the corner of the cabin.

Here Walker reveals himself as the consummate literalist. With his technical skill he gives the modern viewer a rare look into a riverboat cabin of the late nineteenth century. The Gothic tracery of the arch supporting the cabin ceiling is similar to that in *Interior of the Steamboat Princess* (1861; Anglo-American Art Museum, Louisiana State University, Baton Rouge, Louisiana), a painting by Adrien Persac (active 1857-1872). It was a design element typical of Mississippi riverboats of the period. We see that wood stoves were placed in sandboxes as a fire safety precaution; chairs were sturdy and splay-legged, unlikely to tip should the river turn rough. Walker carefully recorded details of decoration: the pretty, though not overly complicated, pattern of stained glass on the doors leading from the cabin; and the lightly stained wood of the cabin walls and floor, each board drawn with precision. It is this forthright quality that infuses all of Walker's paintings and makes them such cherished visual documents of a bygone time.

It will be recalled that Walker already had a client on the Mississippi River, General Samuel Wragg Ferguson, who had lent Walker's *On the Lookout* to the Louisville Exposition in 1872. A Charleston native, Ferguson had attended the United States Military Academy at West Point and served the Confederacy as aide to General Beauregard at Charleston before attaining the rank of Brigadier General at the age of twenty-seven. After the war he studied law at Charleston and was admitted to the South Carolina bar. Through his marriage to Catherine Lee, he came into possession of Ditchley, a cotton plantation on Deer Creek near Greenville, Mississippi. The couple also maintained a home at the corner of Broad and Central streets in Greenville.

FIGURE 24. **Poker Game**, 1880, oil on cardboard, 7 x 10 inches, signed and dated lower left: *WAWalker. 1880.* Inscribed on crate at left: *J. B. W/New Orlea. . ./La.* (There is a trace of another inscription at center left. It is incomplete.) Collection of Jay P. Altmayer.

In 1882 Walker painted the General's daughter, Miss Percy Ferguson (figure 25). The canvas is alive with detail, Walker having taken care to delineate each eyelet of Percy's Sunday-best lace dress with care and placing her in the midst of a wild, natural setting, where ivy, lichen, and thin-bladed grasses are precisely drawn and richly colored. For all the intricate detailing of her surroundings, the subject's face, by contrast, is unanimated, and her body, with a forearm resting atop a stone pedestal, appears stiffly posed. Her wide-eyed, fixed expression and stance suggest a demeanor that Walker would have a subject assume in the photography studio, where one had to stand unmoving, unblinking, and barely breathing for several seconds. It

FIGURE 25. ***Portrait of Miss Percy Ferguson, Greenville, Mississippi***, 1882, oil on canvas, 50 x 30 inches, signed and dated lower left on rock: *WAWalker. 1882.* Collection of Helen S. Martin.

FIGURE 26. *Banana Peddler of Greenville, Mississippi*, circa 1883, oil on academy board, 6 1/2 x 4 1/2 inches, signed lower left: *WAWalker.* Collection of Jay P. Altmayer.

A note on the back of the picture reads, "Banana Peddler, as he appears daily on the streets of Greenville, Mississippi. Presented by Rev. Joseph Bogen Feby 1883 see letter on back of picture." The letter on the back of the picture reads:

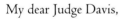

Greenville, Miss.
January 26/83.

Hon. C. F. Davis
Keokuk, Iowa.

My dear Judge Davis,

Please accept the enclosed as a token of friendship from one who admires you as man of honor and integrity. The picture reproduces a banana-peddlar [*sic*], a fellow who walks the streets of Greenville. He is a curious specimen of humanity, and a type of Southern life. The painting was done by an artist-friend of mine, & I think it is perfect. I hope it will please you, and though small in value will be accepted as given, in a spirit of friendship.

My family and myself send our best regards and well wishes to you and you. . . .

Cordially
Jos. Bogen

PS. Please remember us to Dr. Shaffer and his family.

is therefore quite likely that Walker painted the portrait from a photograph, rather than from a sketch, which would have had a more spontaneous quality.

Also in Greenville, Walker painted one of the town's eccentric street characters, the banana peddler. Whereas in Baltimore he had been fascinated by the orphan boys who made their living on the city streets, here he drew a grown man viewed as a "local type," resulting in a work that exemplifies Walker's increasing tendency toward caricature. The *Banana Peddler of Greenville, Mississippi* is not so much a portrait—

FIGURE 27. *Portrait of Lottie Mitchell*, 1880, oil on canvas, 7 7/16 x 6 3/4 inches, signed and dated lower left: *WAWalker. 1880.* Image courtesy of the Historic New Orleans Collection, New Orleans, Louisiana (1953.135).

attempting to capture and convey a particular countenance—as it is a genre painting, in which clothing, accouterments, and objects of the subject's stock in trade at once identify his role in the marketplace and his rank in society. Soon Walker would apply these criteria to renderings of black individuals, subjects that would occupy him for the remainder of his career.

Another of Walker's favorite stopovers on the river was Vicksburg, Mississippi. There he became a friend to the Mitchell family, and in 1880 painted a portrait of their ten-year-old daughter Charlotte (figure 27). The subject is framed by Walker's favored green foliage background, which he used as early as 1872 in *Boy with Goat* (figure 20). Her dress is brilliantly colored with stripes of pink and white, exemplifying Walker's love for surface detail. Facial features are drawn with a firm, solid line. Deep shadows on both sides of the nose lend it three-dimensionality. As in the portrait of Percy Ferguson, the subject's features are arranged in a fixed expression, which lends her a sobriety beyond her years. Lottie, as she was known to friends and family, would be a lifelong friend of Walker's. She never married, and after her father's death she ran a boarding house and tea room in New Orleans' Garden District to support herself and her mother.[35] New Orleans hearsay has it that Walker was a guest in her boarding house during his time in that city. He certainly could have dined frequently at her table, but by Walker's own account, he boarded in the home of a Creole woman in the French Quarter. A surviving token of his friendship with Lottie Mitchell is a miniature oil painting of a beach scene that he inscribed, "Christmas Greetings with best wishes to Lottie, from your old friend Wm. A. Walker. 1906." (See figure 79A.)

Another Vicksburg acquaintance was Austin A. Trescott, whose portrait Walker made in the form of a painted photograph (figure 28). Trescott is pictured with the flag of his Confederate regiment. Though the portrait is undated, it may very well have been painted in 1880 during the same visit to Vicksburg on which Walker painted the young Lottie Mitchell. Trescott's portrait is a Confederate subject, after all, and it was right around 1880 that Southerners of Walker's generation began to take a keen interest in the War Between the States, an interest which had a perceptible impact upon contemporary art.

A private in the Volunteer Southrons, Company A, 21st Mississippi Regiment, A. A. Trescott was born in Ohio in February 1837. He was clerking in a Vicksburg store when the War Between the States began, and he promptly enlisted with the Confederate forces. His regiment served in some of the fiercest battles of the war, including Malvern Hill, Fredericksburg, Gettysburg, the Wilderness, Petersburg, and Cedar Creek. The regimental flag shown in the portrait was secreted away from Appomattox and hangs today in the Old Court House Museum in Vicksburg. The

FIGURE 28. *Portrait of A. A. Trescott, Member Volunteer Southrons, 21st Mississippi Regiment,* circa 1880, photograph colored with oil paints, 7 1/4 x 5 inches (sight), signed lower left: *WAWalker.* Inscribed on flag held by subject: *21st REGT/MISS/VOLS.* The Old Court House Museum Collection, Vicksburg, Mississippi.

photograph was probably taken in a studio, and Walker added the landscape background with regimental tents to lend the finished portrait a wartime identity.[36]

Walker's art from the late 1870s and early 1880s offers evidence that he regularly visited Charleston and maintained close ties there. In 1879 he painted *Oysters at the Charleston Hotel* (figure 30), so identified by the initials *CH* on the rim of the plate.

Figure 29. *Portrait of Kate Wilson Smith*, 1876, oil on canvas, 17 1/4 x 14 1/4 inches, signed and dated lower left: *WAWalker. 1876.* Private Collection.

Kate Wilson was born in Vicksburg, Mississippi on August 2, 1855, the daughter of Irish immigrants. On April 14, 1874 she and Murray Forbes Smith were married at Vicksburg's Church of the Holy Trinity. The couple resided in Vicksburg and had a plantation home at Greenville, Mississippi. Although the portrait was painted two years after her marriage, Mrs. Smith posed for Walker in her wedding gown. The setting is her house in Vicksburg. The portrait is owned by the subject's great-granddaughter.

FIGURE 30. ***Oysters at the Charleston Hotel***, 1879, oil on canvas, 17 7/8 x 21 3/4 inches, signed and dated lower center: *WAWalker. 1879.* The Warner Collection of Gulf States Paper Corporation, Tuscaloosa, Alabama.

Oysters on a plate is a motif that originated in Dutch still life painting of the seventeenth century. One of the first artists to portray the subject was Willem Claesz (1594-circa 1679). Andrew John Henry Way (1826-1888), Baltimore's leading still life practitioner during Walker's years in that city, often chose oysters as his theme. Way's oysters perhaps were the source of Walker's inspiration.

FIGURE 31. ***Ruins of the Church at Old Dorchester***, 1880, oil on canvas mounted on board, 12 x 7 1/2 inches, signed and dated lower right: *WAWalker./1880*. Robert M. Hicklin Jr., Inc., Spartanburg, South Carolina.

Old Dorchester, located on the Ashley River twenty-four miles from Charleston, South Carolina, was founded in the late 1690s by settlers from Massachusetts. After destruction by the British during the American Revolution, Old Dorchester and the fort adjacent to it were abandoned, its structures of brick and stone left to human scavengers and encroaching vegetation. As early as the 1840s, this ghost town was a lure to local artists seeking romantic subject matter. The tower was added in 1751 to the Episcopal Church of St. George, which was originally built in 1719-1720.

One year later he painted the remains of the church tower at Old Dorchester (figure 31), continuing the theme of church ruins which he had explored earlier. And in 1881, as will be discussed in the following chapter, Walker was commissioned by a Charleston cotton merchant to paint a panoramic view of a flourishing cotton plantation. Soon such scenes of the South's Cotton Kingdom would thrust William Aiken Walker into national prominence.

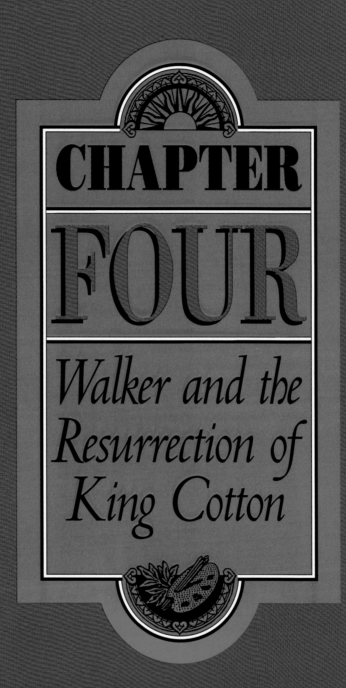

CHAPTER FOUR

Walker and the Resurrection of King Cotton

FIGURE 32. ***Plantation Economy in the Old South***, circa 1881, oil on canvas, 22 x 42 inches, signed lower left: *WAWalker*. The Warner Collection of Gulf States Paper Corporation, Tuscaloosa, Alabama.

ometime in the early 1880s, Walker settled into a routine of itinerancy that he would follow for the rest of his life. He divided his time between the cool Blue Ridge Mountains of North Carolina, Florida's Atlantic coast, and until 1897, New Orleans, Louisiana, then the South's cultural capital. He relieved the lengthy journeys between one place and another with visits to his family in Charleston and to planter friends scattered throughout the Deep South. The distinguished Mr. Walker gained a following wherever he went. His natty mode of dress and gregarious nature attracted the attention of passersby on street corners where he sometimes erected his easel, while his quick wit and gift for storytelling made him continually welcome in the homes of friends and family members. In this era following Reconstruction, Walker specialized in painting subjects that conformed to a national consensus on life in the South. He shrewdly produced large quantities of these paintings—many in an assembly line fashion—at a variety of prices. With them, his reputation soared.

These paintings are the foundation on which Walker's fame is built. They are paintings of blacks at work or at rest; blacks picking cotton; blacks carting cotton to market; blacks selling garden produce; blacks dozing on New Orleans' levee; blacks with cotton baskets atop their heads or at their sides; blacks pausing briefly from their labors with cotton clinging to the frayed edges of their tattered clothes; blacks resting at their cabins; blacks proudly displaying their 'possum catch. He painted two known rice fields and one sugar cane plantation, but for the most part, Walker's concern was the Cotton Kingdom, newly resurrected, and what he perceived to be the black man and woman's rightful place in it. Many an artist painted the black before Walker did, and other artists who were his contemporaries dallied with the subject. But William Aiken Walker is the first American artist to have made the depiction of the South's blacks a specialty. The subject dominated his oeuvre from 1881 until 1893, and even then he could not completely abandon it. His total production has yet to be counted, but his souvenir-size portraits of black field hands and their miserable cabins, which remained a mainstay of his income into the twentieth century, number in the hundreds, and there are believed to be many more hidden away in the proverbial attics of old Southern homes. So successful were these paintings that in 1908 the *Galveston Daily News* reported that his plantation scenes and pictures of "old negroes in the cotton fields . . . have brought him fame and quite a nice fortune."[1]

Fame and fortune came to Walker soon after he established himself in New Orleans and became involved in its lively art world. The Crescent City may have captured Walker's attention as early as 1873 or 1874 if he travelled by steamboat from Louisville to Galveston, for New Orleans would have been the connecting point between these cities. As wild, exciting, and alluring as Galveston and San Antonio were in the mid-1870s, Walker decided, after several years in the Lone Star State, that the Southwest was not for him. The refinement of life in older parts of the South better suited his temperament. Too, it is probable that he found it difficult to earn a livelihood in Texas where a broad base of art patronage was not yet established. Galveston's population in 1870 numbered 14,000, making it the largest city in the state. Had Walker gone to Texas with no greater ambition than to make and color photographic portraits, he would have found a limited market. Similarly, although Augusta was booming at the time of Walker's arrival in 1879, its lack of an art gallery must have been discouraging.

New Orleans, by comparison, was a large, cosmopolitan center. In 1880 its population numbered 216,000, which included the native-born as well as immigrants from Italy, France, England, Ireland, Spain, and Germany. It was a city known for its multiple cultural identities, one in which Walker could navigate easily with his command of languages. Paintings, statuary, photographs, and prints lined the walls of a number of commercial art galleries and were regularly reviewed in the press. Like the Charleston of his childhood, so New Orleans was in the late nineteenth century an international shipping center. Culturally diverse and alive, Walker must have found New Orleans tremendously appealing.

Long before the War Between the States, New Orleans had supplanted Charleston as the South's leading export center of cotton. Following the War of 1812, the city's economy entered an era of significant growth. The rich, loamy soil of the

FIGURE 33A & 33B. ***Little Girl on a Donkey with Black Escort***, circa 1880, a photograph and a photograph colored in oil paints, 8 1/4 x 5 1/8 inches each. The painted version is signed at lower right: *WAWalker*. Private Collection.

This illustration offers a before and after view of a photograph that Walker colored with oil paints. Here one can see that his motive was not only to add color to the photographed image, but to actually embellish the composition. The elaborate wrought iron in the photographs suggests that their setting was New Orleans.

valleys of the Mississippi, Red, Ouachita, and Tenses rivers were found to be most suitable for the growing of short staple cotton, and as in Galveston, planters from eastern parts of the South flocked to the fertile area. Meanwhile, land south and west of New Orleans was ideal for the growing of sugar cane, a market that had begun to boom toward the close of the eighteenth century, thanks to new refinery techniques that made large scale production viable. Louisiana's extended system of natural waterways allowed cheap steamboat transportation of agricultural products to market at New Orleans. By 1840 New Orleans was second only to New York in the value of its exports.

Although the Louisiana economy suffered a severe setback during and immediately after the War Between the States, by the early 1880s it had rallied. The channel at the mouth of the Mississippi River had been deepened to allow for passage of the large ocean-going steamers of the day, and work was undertaken to repair and reconstruct the levee along the Mississippi at New Orleans. Railroad expansion followed. By 1880 five trunk lines served New Orleans, and three years later the city was linked to California. The improved facilities in both river and rail transportation enabled the city to regain its commercial prominence.

New Orleans had a large and thriving community of artists in the latter half of the nineteenth century, and in particular a distinctive school of landscape painting. The vast majority of the successful artists practicing there were European-born, and they brought with them painting techniques taught in the continental academies. These painters turned to the local countryside in seeking subjects for their brush. Consequently, the works of French-born Richard Clague, the Spaniard Andres Molinary, and the Norwegian native William Buck were filled with the swamp and bayou, the cypress tree, and Spanish moss of southern Louisiana. Charles Giroux (born circa 1828), who came to New Orleans from his native France in the late 1860s, found picturesque subject matter in the cotton fields and rural black life of the Mississippi Delta.[2] The works of these renowned artists, as well as paintings by those of lesser talent, picture the hazy, languorous landscape along the river's shore, the lone cabin of a trapper or fisherman adding local color.

It is only natural for communities to take an interest in the activities and accomplishments of their talented citizenry, and this is perhaps especially true in regard to artists. In the Charleston newspapers, Walker's early paintings had been graciously noted when he was but eleven years old. Similarly, in the Baltimore press, exhibitions and auctions of paintings by Baltimore artists were conscientiously reported for days, so that not one of their works could escape the connoisseur's attention. Indeed, this was the case throughout the United States in the nineteenth century, and for this reason art historians undertaking research will go almost immediately to the newspapers of a city in which a particular artist resided to gather information on what he or she produced and how contemporary critics responded to it.

In the South, a regional awareness of the work of Southern artists and of Southern subject matter had begun to manifest itself in the late ante-bellum period. It was a regionalism that transcended city limits and state lines, a chauvinistic attitude that had its roots in Southern history and heritage. It was a spirit that flourished in New Orleans. In reviewing *The Song of the Cotton Plantation* (location unknown) by New Orleans artist John Antrobus (1837-1907) that was on view at the St. Charles Hotel in January 1859, the *New Orleans Daily Crescent* had this to say:

> This is the first of a series of twelve pictures representing Southern life and nature which Mr. Antrobus intends to paint, and he was impelled to the immense undertaking by the determination to vindicate the claims of the scenery of the South to the consideration of artists. Hitherto it has formed no portion of the subjects of the brush, and the general idea was, that there is nothing in the South worth painting. Artists roam the country of the North, turning out pictures of its scenes and scenery by the hundred yearly, but none come to glean the treasures with which the grand and beautiful country of the South and its peculiar life abound. This picture will enlist admiring attention wherever it goes, both because of its intrinsic merits and because the subject is a novelty in the sphere of high art, though it represents a scene in which all feel an interest, both those to whom such are familiar, and those who have heard and desire to know of them.[3]

Eleven years later, the New Orleans press went to every length to support the attempt of local painter Everett B. D. Julio (1843-1879) to sell by subscription his new painting, *The Last Meeting of Lee and Jackson* (1869; The Museum of the Confederacy, Richmond, Virginia). When engravings of it were distributed to subscribers throughout the South, it became a veritable icon of the Lost Cause. The artist was proclaimed a genius, and the painting hailed as his masterpiece.

Particularly after the federal mandates of Reconstruction were lifted and Southern states returned to home rule, Southern identity in works of art was embraced. New Orleans artists capitalized on this regionalistic spirit in 1880 when a group of them united to form the Southern Art Union, a chartered organization of amateur and professional artists. The members held their first meetings at the St. Charles Hotel before obtaining permanent space on the second and third floors of a building at 203 Canal Street, where the organization opened its doors to the public for the first time in May of 1881. The purposes of the Southern Art Union were to establish a permanent gallery space where works by Southern artists might be viewed and sold at any time; to maintain a museum to which "paintings, crayons and engravings" in private collections might be loaned for viewing by the general public; and to operate a circulating library and a school of design. Its founders hoped that in its first year the Union would attract three to four hundred members, so the burden of creating paintings, drawings, bronzes, etc. for exhibition would not fall on too few. The *Daily States,* reporting on their progress, noted:

> Foreseeing the inability of home artists to occupy the art gallery space, the artists from any of the Southern States will be entitled to membership and to fill the gap that will undoubtedly still remain. . . . [The Southern Art Union] will provide itself with one or more large halls, arranged especially as to light, and possessing great wall space. In this will be placed the works of Southern artists, which will, of course, be given the choice of position.

Further, works on loan to the museum were to be reflective of collections

> owned in this city or in any Southern city. . . .There are a great many of these works of art in this city, some few of them being of immense value in the art world, and all these gathered together, added to what local and Southern talent is continually producing, will make as fine a collection as can be shown in any city of the United States.[4]

Although the formation of the Southern Art Union represented the first attempt by the artists of New Orleans to come together for the mutual promotion and sale of their work, as well as that of their colleagues throughout the South, other venues were open to them in the post-war years. There were a number of commercial establishments in New Orleans which displayed the work of local artists. Frank Wagener of Germany began in 1866 to import and deal in lithographs, prints, oil paintings, and picture frames. He took an active role in promoting the work of the New Orleans artists, hosting exhibitions on their behalf in his shop. A charter member of the Southern Art Union, Wagener was on the hanging committee for its first exhibition in May 1881.[5]

Theodore Lilienthal, New Orleans' leading photographer in the mid-1880s, similarly set aside space in his studio in which local artists could exhibit. He had come to New Orleans from Germany in 1854, and in the early years operated his photography business from a small space at 121 Poydras. He obtained the exclusive license in Louisiana and Mississippi to the patented Lambertype process, and by 1880 his enterprise had expanded to occupy four floors in the Touro building on Canal Street. A portion thereof was a gallery for the exhibition of his photographs, and between 1883 and 1886, he invited local painters and sculptors to exhibit there from time to time.[6]

The dealer who became most involved with New Orleans artists was Frederic William E. Seebold, who annually sponsored an exhibition of the work of local talent in his gallery. A native of Hanover, Germany, Seebold arrived in New Orleans about 1861. After service in the Confederate Army, he opened a shop on Canal Street where he dealt in prints, paintings, and artist's supplies. He befriended just about every New Orleans artist, often entertaining them in his home, and his gallery became a gathering place for writers and musicians as well. He was revered as an art friend, patron, and dealer until his death in 1921.[7] By the mid-1880s Seebold's gallery was considered to be the "headquarters" of art in New Orleans.[8]

It is not certain when Walker began to make New Orleans his winter home, but he may have done some work there as early as the winter of 1875-1876. "Fine Collection of Pictures for Sale" reads a headline in the *New Orleans Republican* on February 22, 1876, the article proclaiming, "one of the finest collections of oil paintings, engravings and chromos ever placed on exhibition in this city, is now open to the public at No. 100 Canal street, and the Mesers. [*sic*] Montgomery, auctioneers, will begin their sale tomorrow night. . . . Several other fine pieces are from the studio of Mr. W. A. Walker." It would seem from this casual mention of Walker's studio that he had already established himself in New Orleans and was a familiar figure in the local art community. By 1883 Walker was regularly spending part of his year in New Orleans. He lived in "a large, comfortable room in an old French house" on St. Louis Street between Royal and Bourbon in the *Vieux Carre*, New Orleans' French Quarter.[9]

In that year, four paintings by Walker were included in the "Collection of Paintings by Leading New Orleans Artists" mounted in Lilienthal's Art Gallery. They were titled *Street Arab, Happy Family, Cotton Field,* and *Deer Creek.*[10] Though none of these titles have been linked to pictures that are identified today, the first is presumed to have been inspired by the Turkish guise that some New Orleans vendors, outfitted in silks and fez, adopted to sell trinkets on the street. *Deer Creek* likely was a view of the cotton fields and cotton gin that stood on the bank of Deer Creek at Ditchley Plantation, the Mississippi property of Walker's friend Samuel Ferguson. *Cotton Field* was priced at seventy-five dollars and the remaining three at fifty dollars each, a significant increase from the fifteen and eighteen dollars his pictures had earned at auction in Baltimore.

In the summer of 1883, Walker and Charles Giroux together placed their pictures in the shop of Samuel T. Blessing, a dealer in pictures and picture frames, before going off on their summer journeys. A reviewer for the *Times-Democrat* in making his rounds of the shops displaying art that summer, was particularly struck by what he saw of the two painters' works.

> At Blessing's, on Canal street, are several paintings that possess merit of a high order. In the window are three landscapes by C. Giroux—scenes on the Teche, that in some respects are very superior. . . .One, the objective, is a cabin near the banks of the river; a large number of chickens are scattered here and there, and on the edge of the bayou are several cows. Low lines of marsh and cypress swamps interspersed with an occasional pine, gives a charming effect to the Arcadian scene.
>
> A picture by Walker, called 'Rattle Snake Bayou, Mississippi,' is full of freshness and force. It is one of the first in a new field of painting. It represents plantation life, not coarse and vulgar, as some in attempting to portray have made signal failures and debased their artistic talent, but a real spirited

FIGURE 34. ***Big B Cotton Plantation***, 1881, oil on canvas, 25 x 40 inches, signed and dated lower right: *WAWalker. 1881.* Collection of Jay P. Altmayer.

This painting was commissioned by Stephen Minot Weld (1842-1920), who during the War Between the States was Colonel, 56th Massachusetts Volunteers. After the war Weld was involved in the cotton business, first as a mill owner and later as a broker. He gave the painting to his son Philip Balch Weld (born 1887), a principal in the cotton firm W. M. Weld & Co. of Boston. For years, the painting hung in the company office at 89 State Street, Boston. After liquidation of W. M. Weld in 1938, Weld's widow gave the painting to H. A. Peterson, who had joined the firm in 1926. In 1956, Peterson gave the painting to Howard Troutman of Bates Manufacturing Company of Lewiston, Maine. It was purchased by the present owner in the mid-1960s.

picture full of life, industry and progress. The scene represents the cotton season. The center is a cotton field, rich in all the glories of the white fleecy staple. Several very natural groups of 'cotton pickers' are engaged in gathering the staple. In the near foreground is a wagon loaded with bales of cotton and drawn by three mules. On the wagon are two men, veritable types of the plantation negroes. The great clods of mud clinging to the wheels of the wagon and two 'car dogs' lighting in the rear are very natural. Back of the cotton field is the gin-house and several small dwellings. At one side are a row of cabins, before which are little 'pickaninnies' engaged in youthful sports. An old 'mammy' is deeply interested in watching the children. On the opposite side the field is shut in by a dense undergrowth, mild and luxuriant with the splendors of our Southern clime, made all the more brilliant with the gorgeous dress that nature assumes when the year is dying.[11]

This is the first critical response to a subject that is quintessentially associated with William Aiken Walker. In this style Walker combined elements of landscape and genre painting to render vivid visual reminders of life, labor, architecture, and topography on cotton plantations of the Old South. Six large plantation scenes are known today: *Big B Cotton Plantation* (figure 34); *The Sunny South* (figure 35); *The Cotton Plantation* (figure 37); *A Cotton Plantation on the Mississippi* (lithograph after the painting, figure 36); *Plantation Economy in the Old South* (figure 32), and *Blackberry Winter* (figure 39). They are painted on canvases that range in size from approximately 21 x 36 to 30 x 50 inches, placing them among the most monumental paintings of Walker's career. Two are known to have been painted to fulfill commissions. Walker received one hundred dollars from Edward L. Wells for *The Cotton Plantation* (figure 37), said to represent a plantation near Augusta, Georgia. It hung in the offices of Lesesne and Wells, a cotton brokerage firm in Charleston, and subsequently descended in the Wells family until it was sold to Kennedy Galleries in 1968.[12]

Big B Cotton Plantation (figure 34) was commissioned in 1881 by Stephen Minot Weld, a cotton broker of Boston, Massachusetts. Like the others, it represents cotton picking season in the Deep South, which extended from late August to early

FIGURE 35. **The Sunny South**, 1881, oil on canvas, 22 1/8 x 36 1/8 inches, signed and dated lower left: *WAWalker. 1881*. Collection of Dr. and Mrs. Ron Lawson, Memphis, Tennessee.

FIGURE 36. Currier & Ives, lithographers. After William Aiken Walker. *A Cotton Plantation on the Mississippi*, 1884, lithograph printed in colors, 21 x 30 inches, signed and dated on the stone, lower left: *WAWalker. 1883*. The Library of Congress, Washington, D.C.

The painting after which this lithograph was made was painted by Walker in 1883. Previously in the collection of Mrs. Whitney Porter, the painting is presently owned by the Gilcrease Museum, Tulsa, Oklahoma.

FIGURE 37. *The Cotton Plantation*, 1881, oil on canvas, 21 1/2 x 35 inches, signed and dated lower right: *WAWalker. 1881.* Private Collection.

January. Black women, each uniquely attired in colorful costume, are shown at center picking the bolls. The cotton goes into burlap sacks that the women wear suspended from their shoulders. As the sacks are filled, they are emptied into large baskets, which in turn are emptied into the blue wagon, seen at far right, as it comes around. The driver will transport the cotton to the gin house, the building with the tall smokestack, where it will be seeded, compressed, and bound into bales—all part of the ginning process. The wagon in the left foreground carries the finished bales to the steamboat, which will then convey them to New Orleans. There the cotton will undergo a further compression process before being loaded onto an ocean-going vessel for shipment to a Northern or foreign mill. A wagon that has just been unloaded of its bales is seen coming up from the riverbank. Four women in the right foreground pause in their work to converse. Two of them balance the typical two-handled cotton baskets on their heads, while the little boy seated on a burro at far right mimics his elders by balancing a stick on his head.

As closely as he observed the human activity, Walker also described the natural environment and the physical plant of the plantation. On the opposite side of the road from the gin house is a three-story dwelling—the "big house," as the planter's home was called—along with its dependencies, including an icehouse, smokehouse, and stable. The branches and leaves of each cotton plant edging the road are precisely drawn and carefully colored. Walker here built up paint on the canvas as a means of rendering texture. Loading his brush with white paint, he would apply the tip of it to the canvas, leaving a thick, ridged mark that convincingly portrays the deep, soft mass of a cotton boll. His sky, by contrast, is thinly painted. Using the side of his brush in short, sweeping strokes, Walker created a blue expanse of an appropriately limpid appearance. The clouds, also laid down with a loose hand, seem to swirl and dash across the canvas.

The scene has great depth, thanks to Walker's competent handling of the principle of vanishing point perspective. The rows of cotton, the road perpendicular to the picture plane, and the angle at which the houses are aligned in relation to the road converge to lead the eye to a point just to the right of center, where the plantation gate opens onto the loading area and, as implied by the waiting steamboat, the world market beyond.

Walker painted *Big B Cotton Plantation* eighteen years after the signing of the Emancipation Proclamation. What is important about the timing of this major work in Walker's oeuvre is that, contrary to previous scholarly belief, it was not painted during the days of slavery. Its inspiration was retrospective in origin. It has to do with what writer Joel Chandler Harris called "the old timey Negro, the plantation type," for it represents the lowly field hand of the past and his place in the once-great Cotton Kingdom.

To understand what motivated this painting and others like it, and the reason for their combined critical success, one must first understand the effect that the

FIGURE 38. **J. A. PALMER**, photographer (op. 1870s). ***Cotton Field,*** stereograph, 3 15/16 x 7 inches. Printed on cardboard mount: *No. 171 Characteristic Southern Scenes. Cotton Field. Photographed by J. A. Palmer, Aiken, S.C.* Photograph Collection; Miriam and Ira D. Wallach Division of Art, Prints and Photographs; The New York Public Library; Astor, Lenox, and Tilden Foundations.

failure of Reconstruction had on a gentleman of Walker's background and station. In the South Carolina lowcountry where Walker had grown up, the plantation system was virtually eliminated by the War Between the States. Many Carolina planters never returned to their homes after the war; some of those who did were to be seen tending a grocery or driving a cart.[13] A Northern visitor observed, "I do not believe that the ruin of the French nobility at the first revolution was more complete than that of the proud, rich, and cultivated aristocracy of the lowcountry of South Carolina."[14]

Lowcountry land had long been exhausted by the growing of cotton, and after the war and the emancipation of slaves, the planters' cheap, dependable labor force disappeared. In those cases where abandoned plantation property was not consumed by creeping vegetation, it was parceled out by Reconstructionists in forty-acre lots to the former slaves. Some freedmen made valiant efforts to cultivate cotton as a cash crop, but the vast majority pursued a subsistence existence, raising enough chickens, hogs, and vegetables to feed their families, with perhaps a little left over to sell at market in Charleston. The once rich Southland of Walker's childhood had from 1865 through the 1870s the appearance of a land ravaged by famine.

By contrast, the Deep South and the West made rapid economic comebacks. Northern investors poured capital into Louisiana sugar and rice plantations, while cotton continued to flourish in the rich soils of east Texas, the Mississippi Delta, and the Georgia foothills. Young, able-bodied blacks of the Carolinas migrated westward, hearing that work was to be found there. They were compensated in a variety of ways. Some worked for wages, relocating seasonally as different crops required attention. Others participated in sharecropping; though they owned no land, they were entitled to a portion of the crop that they raised on a plantation.

Where the plantation system survived—in Louisiana and Mississippi, and in tobacco growing areas of Virginia, for instance—the outward appearance of plantation labor was little changed from pre-war days. A visitor to a Virginia tobacco plantation made this observation in 1885:

> The negroes are still the chief laborers in the fields and artisans in the workshops; and, excepting that they are no longer chattels that can be sold at will, their lives move in the same grooves as under the old order of things. Their occupations and amusements are the same. As yet there has been no increase in the physical comforts of their situation, and but little change in their general character; but this is the first period of transformation, when it is difficult to detect and to follow the modifications that are really taking place.[15]

What this writer describes with journalistic detachment is an accurate, unromantic picture of contemporary plantation life. Similarly, we may imagine Walker happening onto any of a number of plantations in Louisiana, Mississippi, and Georgia after 1880 and recording similar scenes in sketchbooks or on film. These images took him back to the safety and sentimentality of his youth, to the prosperity and peace of Carolina plantation life, a way of life cherished by anyone growing up in ante-bellum Charleston. In depicting the vision of this life as manifested on plantations of the Deep South after 1880, Walker was recording what in whites' minds

FIGURE 39. *Blackberry Winter,* 1884, oil on canvas, 30 x 50 inches, signed and dated lower left: *WAWalker. 1884.* The Warner Collection of Gulf States Paper Corporation, Tuscaloosa, Alabama.

   Blackberry Winter was owned by William Henry Gregg of St. Louis, Missouri, Walker's host on Florida fishing voyages at the turn of the century. Gregg gave the picture to his daughter and son-in-law Mr. and Mrs. Charles Melville Hays (nee Clara Jennings Gregg) sometime after 1896, the year in which Hays became manager of the Grand Trunk Pacific Railway Company of Canada and the couple settled in Montreal. Hays died at sea April 14, 1912 in the *Titanic* disaster. Mrs. Hays retained the painting until her death in 1955. It subsequently was owned by the Hays' grandson who, in turn, bequeathed it to his grandson who owned it until 1994.

   The arresting, frontal pose of man and mule in *Blackberry Winter* is unique in Walker's work. Rather than inviting the viewer to casually observe repeated, everyday activities as do the paintings *The Sunny South* and *The Cotton Plantation,* for example, the confrontational stance assumed by the primary figures poses a barrier to the enjoyment of the placid scene that may be glimpsed behind them.

was a truth that could brook no change: that whites controlled the land and the capital, and that blacks did the work. Moreover, as artist and interpreter, Walker was presenting scenes of his world—the white world of the Old South—made right again. He would focus on these bits of personal paradise with such intensity that for seven years his oeuvre admitted almost no other subject but the cotton field and the men and women of burden who brought it to bear.

Though Walker's obsession with the theme may have been singular, his subject was not without precedent. The Southern plantation and the slave appear in illustrations and paintings dating from the late ante-bellum period. "The Rice Lands of the South," an article published in *Harper's New Monthly Magazine,* November 1859, is liberally illustrated by its author Thomas Addison Richards with landscape and genre views that depict coastal Carolina and Georgia in idyllic, pastoral terms. Black women plant rice attired in dresses that show off their slender arms and shapely calves. Their slim waists are emphasized, as are their dainty, slippered feet. Some wear wide-brimmed straw hats to protect themselves from the heat of the sun. They bend with ease to their hoes, each a picture of femininity and grace. Richards' article also offers a view of a planter's house, a vignette depicting a row of five identical cabins titled *The Negro Quarters,* and a close-up view of a black family gathered in front of one of these simple structures—a subject Walker would also treat—titled *Negroes at Home.* Richards emphasizes the beauty of each subject, softly framing his scenes with moss-clad trees. In his portrayals of black slaves at work he renders well-clothed figures that move lithely about their tasks, portraying in an American idiom the lot of the contented peasant that Richards' contemporary, the French artist Jean Francois Millet, was pictorializing in his canvases.

It was also in 1859 that John Antrobus placed his easel painting *Song of the Cotton Plantation* on public view in New Orleans. The review in the *New Orleans Daily Crescent* closely describes the content of the painting.

The picture, which is of large size, was painted from a real life scene on the plantation of Col. Watts, on Bayou Macon, in this State, and represents the negroes engaged in picking and carrying cotton to the gin-house. The perspective coloring and drawing is very fine. Far in the background are seen the banks of the bayou and objects beyond; in the middle ground the gin-house, the overseer upon his horse, and other plantation aspects; while in the foreground is the grouping of the negroes at their work in various attitudes, carrying the baskets high-piled with the fleecy staple, which seems to lay so lightly that a breath of wind would waft it from the canvas. . . .The blue haze of the autumn atmosphere seems to veil without dimming the rich and mellow coloring in which the objects are drest [*sic*], and the clouds are piled in the further background of the sky, as seemingly natural as though by nature's hand itself. So beautiful is the painting as a work of art, so truthful is it as a representation of peculiar and locally characteristic life and nature that we do not wonder that all who see it are filled with admiration, as were we.[16]

In terms of content alone, the review could just as easily have been describing a painting by William Aiken Walker.

Articles about the South's agrarian economy written after the war appealed to national curiosity about the region's recuperation. These articles were often accompanied by illustrations in which the black figured prominently. In the immediate post-war period Edwin Forbes (1839-1895) drew *Gathering Corn* for *Harper's Weekly* which appeared as a wood engraving in the issue dated October 14, 1865. In it a black and a white man work side by side in binding corn stalks together, a reflection of Northern editorial optimism that working relations between the races were becoming equitable following emancipation.

Far removed from Forbes' depiction in both spirit and scene is *Cotton Culture-Covering in the Seed*, a drawing by Edwin Austin Abbey (1852-1911). Featured in the April 24, 1875 issue of *Harper's Weekly*, this sketch portrays a gang of blacks working in the field, watchfully supervised by a white overseer mounted on horseback. In its juxtaposition of a non-laboring white to blacks engaged in the physical drudgery of sowing, it has less in common, as regards race relations, with the Forbes image than it has with the ante-bellum painting by Antrobus.

FIGURE 40. After **MATT MORGAN** (1839–1890). *A Day's Work Ended,* circa 1887, wood engraving, 8 13/16 x 13 11/16 inches. Reproduced in *Frank Leslie's Illustrated Newspaper,* volume 64, December 31, 1887, p. 333. General Research Division; The New York Public Library; Astor, Lenox, and Tilden Foundations.

Contemporary to Walker's plantation scenes, *A Day's Work Ended* shows tired, bent, black field workers walking in regimental fashion out of the cotton field at the end of the day, their care-worn facial expressions and slumped postures proof positive of their lives of toil. Morgan's view seems to be starkly realistic in depicting the hard life of rural black workers, their sad, exhausted faces eliciting the viewer's sympathy for their plight. But this is not how the *Leslie's* reader was supposed to respond to the scene. The article's author dispelled all ambiguities of the intent of the picture when he wrote:

It reminds one of Jules Breton's or Millet's studies of the toil, the 'homely joys and destiny obscure,' of the French peasants. Even more picturesque, and perhaps happier in their way, are these Alabama negroes, with their shining ebon faces, broad smiles, and woolly heads. They have been gathering the fleecy store of the luxuriant cotton-field all day beneath the brilliant sun. Now, when the twilight sky is rosy behind the pines and magnolias that fringe the horizon, they wend their way cheerily homewards, in single file, by the narrow, poppy-bordered path that winds to their clustered cabins.[17]

As the images cited make clear, arduous field labor as performed by blacks had been positively portrayed in the visual arts in the ante-bellum and post-bellum periods. Whether in the romantic, painterly style of Antrobus or Richards, or the more straightforward manner of the illustrator Forbes, the message clearly was that the blacks—handsome, healthy, and content—were cheerful, willing participants in the Southern agricultural system. Thus, the spirit of happy productivity conveyed by Walker's plantation scenes is not without precedent.

When in New Orleans, Walker often wandered along the levee observing the mighty Mississippi River steamboats, their towering twin smokestacks the skyscrapers of his day. He also saw ocean-going brigs and packets flying the colors of foreign nations, and he heard the whistles, songs, and bawdy shouts of the stevedores and roustabouts as they trundled their massive loads.

By 1883 Walker concluded that scenes of commerce on the levee were subjects suitable for his brush, having enough color, figures, and activity—criteria which he had already found to be fulfilled by cotton plantations at harvest time—to inspire lively compositions. (See figure 41.) The levee scenes that he began to paint by no means represent a departure from his Cotton Kingdom theme, for they are invariably crowded with cotton bales and black laborers who perform the menial tasks of carting and loading. These works simply represent the commercial, rather than the agricultural, side of the Cotton Kingdom.

Though he was inspired to paint these dockside scenes at New Orleans, they were scenes familiar to him from his hometown. English artist Eyre Crowe

FIGURE 41. ***Where Canal Meets the Levee***, oil on academy board, 12 x 10 1/4 inches, signed lower right: *WAWalker.* Collection of Mr. and Mrs. Robert J. Hussey, Jr.

FIGURE 42. EYRE CROWE (1824-1910). *Cotton is King*, 1853, illustration appearing in Crowe's book, *With Thackeray in America* (London: Cassell and Company, Ltd., 1893). Photograph Collection; Miriam and Ira D. Wallach Division of Art, Prints and Photographs; The New York Public Library; Astor, Lenox, and Tilden Foundations.

(1824-1910) on a visit to the United States with William Makepeace Thackeray in 1852-1853 had been fascinated with the plight of blacks. Of their stay in Charleston, Thackeray noted that in the evenings, "Mr. Crowe and I sit in my room and draw pictures of niggers."[18] Crowe sketched a black man resting atop a bale of cotton on one of Charleston's wharves. Entitled *Cotton is King*, the sketch became an illustration to his book *With Thackeray in America* (1893). Similarly posed figures appear in levee scenes that Walker painted in the 1880s.

In 1883 Walker painted *The Levee*, an action-packed scene that thrust him into national prominence when a lithograph was made after it by the country's most

THE LEVEE - NEW ORLEANS.

FIGURE 43. Currier & Ives, lithographers. After WILLIAM AIKEN WALKER. *The Levee—New Orleans,* 1884, lithograph printed in colors, 21 x 29 1/2 inches, signed and dated on the stone, lower center: *WAWalker./1883.* The Library of Congress, Washington, D.C.

Walker's painting entitled *The Levee* (1883) that served as the model for this lithograph is in the collection of J. Cornelius Rathborne, New Orleans, Louisiana. It measures 19 1/2 x 29 1/2 inches and was purchased by Mr. Rathborne's grandmother in New Orleans in 1945.

FIGURE 44. *The Quai at New Orleans*, oil on academy board, 4 x 8 inches, signed center left: *WAWalker*. The Warner Collection of Gulf States Paper Corporation, Tuscaloosa, Alabama.

successful lithography firm, Currier and Ives of New York City. Both painting and print are crowded with people, boats, and goods, and give a lively indication of what New Orleans' shipping traffic was like at the time. At least seven steamboats are docked at the levee, including the famous *Natchez*. Countless others lie at anchor in midstream awaiting their turn to dock, while many more dot the far shore at Gretna, Louisiana. Spread out before the boats is an array of produce—cotton bales weighing in excess of five hundred pounds, great hogsheads filled with cane syrup, sacks of rice, raw timber, and lumber—waiting to be loaded. The black workers who have brought the produce to the levee either converse in small groups or lounge about, waiting their turn to bring forward the goods for which they are responsible. In 1884 Currier and Ives published *The Levee—New Orleans* (figure 43) as well as *A Cotton Plantation on the Mississippi* (figure 36), also after a painting by Walker. Each image was printed in a large folio format. Because of the manner in which Currier and Ives mass-marketed the lithographs they published, these images found their way into many homes and probably did more than the most glowing of newspaper reviews to broaden Walker's fame.

FIGURE 45. *Newsboy* or *Post No Bills*, 1883, oil on academy board, 11 x 6 inches, signed and dated lower left: *WAWalker./1883.* Inscribed upper left on wall: *POST NO/BILLS.* The Warner Collection of Gulf States Paper Corporation, Tuscaloosa, Alabama.

The subject who posed for *Newsboy* is another example of the many unskilled blacks that Walker found in Southern cities. Here Walker merged his interest in the juvenile street vendor that he had encountered on the streets of Baltimore with the poor, raggedly-clad black of the Deep South of the post-Reconstruction era. The young man carries copies of the *Florida Times Union*, which was published in Jacksonville, Florida. The youth has a somewhat comical appearance as he stands with one shoe off and wears on the other foot a cast-off brogan that is far too large for him. Walker painted the enlarged lips red to further emphasize a feature long associated with satirical renderings of blacks.

Typical of Walker's cotton plantation scenes described earlier, the lithograph *A Cotton Plantation on the Mississippi* (figure 36) features mule-drawn carts, black field hands standing waist-deep in cotton plants, the gin house, and other essential buildings. In the background a paddle wheel steamer belching thick, gray smoke into the air identifies the setting as the Mississippi River delta.

Another lithographed cotton plantation scene by Walker was issued for advertising purposes by the Kitson Machine Company of Charleston. It shows a wagon loaded with cotton bales and drawn by a pair of oxen and a pair of mules. A field of cotton in full bloom stretches across the middle ground of the composition. In the background may be seen the gin house and several rickety cabins constructed of rough-hewn boards, and at far left, the planter's house with a roof typical of domestic architecture in southern Louisiana. In fact, Walker's view actually represents a

FIGURE 46. *Cotton Pickers*, oil on board, 6 1/8 x 12 1/4 inches, signed lower left: *WAWalker*. Private Collection, Huntsville, Alabama.

Louisiana cotton plantation. Nonetheless, the adaptation of the image by a South Carolina manufacturer attests to the widespread popularity of the artist and his theme in his native state.

In the fall of 1884, Walker found New Orleans business and civic leaders in a whirl of activity as they prepared for the opening of the city's first industrial exposition, the World's Industrial and Cotton Centennial Exposition. Manufactured goods, handwork, new strains of produce, and works of art from the United States as well as abroad were to be laid out in multitude in the pavilion under construction in Exposition Park (now Audubon Park). The Exposition was expected to draw tens of thousands of sightseers to New Orleans, and more importantly, investors. It was hoped that traders from Latin American countries would see how easily goods manufactured anywhere in the United States could be obtained in New Orleans and thereby enhance the Crescent City's position as a center of international trade. New Orleans had taken on a gala appearance by the time the Exposition officially opened on December 16, 1884.

The Exposition site included an art gallery, but Walker did not exhibit paintings

FIGURE 47A. *Louisiana*, circa 1885, oil on brass plate, 12 inches in diameter, titled lower center and signed lower left: *WAWalker*. The Roger Houston Ogden Collection, New Orleans, Louisiana.

FIGURE 47B. *New Orleans*, circa 1885, oil on brass plate, 12 inches in diameter, titled lower center and signed lower right: *WAWalker*. The Roger Houston Ogden Collection, New Orleans, Louisiana.

FIGURE 48. **Cabin Scene**, oil on board, 6 1/8 x 12 1/4 inches, signed lower left: *WAWalker*. Private Collection, Huntsville, Alabama.

in it.[19] Instead, revealing himself to be an astute businessman, he turned to producing souvenir paintings which he sold to tourists. On brass plates measuring ten or twelve inches in diameter and academy board pieces cut no larger than 12 x 6 inches, he painted levee scenes, cotton field scenes, and full-figure portraits of blacks dressed in tattered finery, often bearing a battered valise. He would inscribe these works with his interpretation of black dialect. Walker is said to have made his studio on the street corners of New Orleans, and it is likely that during the course of the Exposition he stationed himself somewhere in Exposition Park or on one of the steamboats that took visitors from the foot of Canal Street on the one hour ride to the Park.

It may have been at this time that a Walker legend was born. According to New Orleans hearsay, Walker painted quite literally for the man on the street. He would dress himself in a crisply-pressed suit and perfectly knotted silk cravat, and donning a beret (he was sensitive about his bald head, and all portraits of him after the age of forty show him wearing a hat) and colorful smock, would take himself, his easel, and his palette outside to spend the day painting. He is said to have stood at the corner of Royal and Dumaine streets in the heart of the *Vieux Carre*.

Walker used an assembly line method of execution. On his easel he would place a large academy board which he would score into rectangles measuring 12 x 6 inches or 8 x 4 inches. He would then commence to paint a series of portraits of field hands, beginning with alternating strips of sky, cotton bushes, and dirt horizontally across his board, then superimposing raggedly-clad black figures at intervals of a few inches. He would dash them off quickly, and when he had completed the board of figures, he would take his knife and divide them from one another to sell for six, seven, or eight dollars each. A pair of such paintings would sell for eleven, thirteen, or fifteen dollars. His mechanical approach is borne out by these small works themselves, where often a rounded bulge in the jacket or skirt of a figure upon close examination turns out to be the impasto of a painted-over cotton blossom.

Walker was a clever retailer who employed shrewd sales strategies. One finds on the backs of his academy board pictures a figure of "$6.00," for instance, written in pencil, crossed out, and replaced with a figure of "$4.00," all in Walker's hand. This suggests that Walker wished to travel unencumbered; when he was ready to leave New Orleans in late spring, he would slash his prices in order to rid himself of unsold pictures and gain cash. Although few of Walker's small academy board paintings are dated, it is to be assumed that he continued to paint on New Orleans' street corners for many years after the Exposition. The broad public exposure attracted many customers, both tourists and local residents.

While Walker stood at the corner of Royal and Dumaine making small compositions for the common man, other of his paintings were on view in Seebold's annual exhibition of works by New Orleans artists in November 1884. A critic for the *Daily Picayune* observed, "Resident artists are represented by some charming pictures, and persons—particularly strangers—who are unfamiliar with the works of such men as Chapin, Buck, Molinary, Walker and Perelli will find good examples of these. . . ." Of Walker's work in particular, the writer went on to note:

During the past summer Walker, who has been in Florida and South Carolina, has made a whole easeful of intensely Southern scenes. His drawings of the Negro in his native cotton and cane field is immutably given with all the half pathetic ruggedness of costume and love of gay colors that render the darkey such good artistic material for one who has the skill. 'The Ripe Rice Field,' 'Gwine ter der Expersition,' and a third picture showing a cotton field with a distant fringe of cypress swamp, are all worthy of special note.[20]

At the conclusion of the show the paintings were sold at auction, but the prices were pronounced by a reviewer as being "absurdly low." *The Ripe Rice Field* brought only forty-five dollars.[21]

In July 1885, Walker lent several of his paintings of black cotton pickers to an exhibition at Blessing's gallery. Walker's treatment of the subject earned a glowing review. The critic, however, had some difficulty in reconciling the depravity of the subject with Walker's glorification of it.

Walker, that dashing and audacious artist, is at his summer studio at Arden, N.C. A few of his last season's pictures may yet be seen at Blessing's—scenes taken from that often scorned, yet difficult line of portrayal, plantation life and negro character sketches. Mr. Walker's compositions are homely, every day scenes, seemingly uninteresting and often repulsive. They are vigorous, however, beautiful and full of interest to the stranger. The works of this artist are fine exemplifications of the art of treating homely subjects artistically. Here the painter has so modified or idealized his work so as to give chaste and strongly picturesque effect, and yet retain all its forcible naturalness. This is art! This is genius! It raises the artist above the level of a mere copyist. He selects his themes from the lowly walks and elevates them, portraying only the better side, without losing the realistic effect. Some of Mr. Walker's works are now on their way to France to be placed in the gallery of the coming Paris Exposition.[22]

By 1884 Walker had begun to paint wagon scenes. (See figures 52 and 53.) Derived from his larger plantation pictures, these wagon groups included an open, wooden, two or four-wheel farm wagon, black driver and riders, one or more pairs

FIGURE 49. *Portrait of Napoleon Johnsing*, circa 1880, oil on canvas, 18 1/4 x 10 1/8 inches, signed lower left: *WAWalker. 188[?]*. Inscribed on valise: *Napoleon Johnsing./City Hotel. N. O.* Inscribed on cotton bales: *NO* and *570*. Collection of Mr. and Mrs. George Brandt III.

In inscribing the names and destinations of his subjects on their baggage, Walker made use of the cartoonist's device that had first appeared in American periodicals in the ante-bellum period. Johnsing is probably an adaptation made by freedmen of the English surname *Johnson*. The name was not Walker's invention, for it appears in connection with several black figures in the series of satirical lithographs entitled "The Bric-A-Brac Mania," published by Currier and Ives in the 1880s.

FIGURE 50. ***The Cotton Pickers***, oil on wooden palette, 7 1/4 x 5 inches, signed lower right: *WAWalker*. The Morris Museum of Art, Augusta, Georgia.

FIGURE 51. ***The Rice Harvest***, 1885, oil on canvas, 10 x 20 inches, signed and dated lower right: *WAWalker. 1885.* The Roger Houston Ogden Collection, New Orleans, Louisiana.

of mules or oxen, and a canine escort—a sign of the times, for dog ownership had been forbidden to slaves.[23] Often the dog is portrayed as it defecates. Whether the inclusion of this act is Walker's commentary on the subject matter or a humorous attempt at verisimilitude is left to the viewer's imagination. He depicted the workers either as they went to market, their wagon piled high with cotton bales, or returning to the plantation, the load gone, singing and drinking from a communal jug of moonshine, their reward for a hard day's work. Occasionally one finds in Walker's oeuvre a wagon loaded not with cotton but with moss. The gathering and selling of moss had been one of the few means of earning money allowed blacks under slavery. Walker must have found the continued practice a pleasant reminder of the earlier days of plantation life.

When exhibited in New Orleans, Walker's wagon scenes met with critical approval. In the fall of 1885, he and Charles Giroux together exhibited paintings of black subjects at Blessing's. Among the works discussed at length by the newspaper reviewer was *A Wagon Scene* by Walker.

Among the many New Southern scenes reflected on canvas are several spirited compositions—life-like pictures, painted from nature, and taken from homely subjects. Plantation scenes, with just enough ideality to make interesting and at the same time not destroy their truthfulness. One of the above compositions, by Mr. W. A. Walker, is now exposed at Blessing's, 'A Wagon Scene.' Two genuine piny woods mules, in a make-up harness that is characteristic of the backwoods, are hitched to a rickety wagon that is loaded with bales of cotton, on top of which are perched several ragged negroes, form the chief objectives, mid a barren, dreary, landscape. The whole composition possesses a strange realism that at a glance inspires the spectator with its truthfulness. In the above style of graphic art Mr. Walker is peculiarly at home. He was the first to enter the field of Southern character sketches, and in his chosen field is without a rival. A work of the same order by Mr. Giroux is on exhibit at the same place. The composition portrays the cotton picking season. Six darky figures, plantation hands, with baskets of cotton

FIGURE 52. ***Taking Cotton to Market***, oil on canvas, 10 x 17 7/8 inches, signed lower right: *WAWalker*. The Sewell Family Collection, Vidalia, Louisiana.

Figure 53. **Hauling Moss**, 1884, oil on canvas, 6 x 10 inches, signed and dated lower right: *WAWalker. 1884.* Inscribed on verso: *Hauling Moss / $15.00.* The Warner Collection of Gulf States Paper Corporation, Tuscaloosa, Alabama.

on their heads, are the central objects of attraction. Behind them is a broad field of the fleecy staple with here and there hands in the distant perspective gathering the white 'fleecy gold that grows on bushes.' In the far distance are several cabins well defined against an autumnal forest. This work is remarkably well finished. The same careful study and painstaking care that characterize all Mr. Giroux's works is apparent in every line and shadow.[24]

Giroux's painting described above is lost; however, we may look to his *Cotton Plantation* (figure 56) for a comparison of his style to Walker's. *Cotton Plantation* shows black hands at rest, their attention focused on a distant, undisclosed event. A placid bayou and sandy road, rendered in warm golden tones, bisect the canvas. A neat, white-washed cabin is set off to the left. A cotton field is relegated to the far right of the composition. Figures, trees, house, and fields are bathed in a shimmering, silvery

FIGURE 54. JEROME NELSON WILSON, photographer (1827-1897). *Fifteenth Amendment: Bringing His Crop to Town*, 1871, stereograph, 3 3/8 x 6 7/8 inches. Photograph Collection; Miriam and Ira D. Wallach Division of Art, Prints and Photographs; The New York Public Library; Astor, Lenox, and Tilden Foundations.

light. Though the artists occasionally exhibited together, Giroux's and Walker's paintings are in marked contrast to each other. In the hands of Giroux, the unity and sublimity of the landscape was of prime importance; figures of field workers, their labor, and their cabins were incidental anecdotes which serve to anchor his paintings in time and place. Conversely, from the brush of Walker, who was a literalist in recording appearances, the figures, the cotton they pick, and the efficient plantation system are his subjects; the landscape background is incidental. Walker used flat-topped cypress trees to distinguish Louisiana cotton fields from palmetto-bordered Carolina fields; a lemon or orange tree set next to a cabin served to identify a Florida locale. Giroux, as a landscapist, was primarily interested in broad, atmospheric effects. Walker instead placed emphasis on human activity, revealing himself to be a committed genre painter.

The fact that Giroux and Walker painted identical subject matter in the 1880s and that they more than once exhibited their work together suggests that they were quite close. Giroux was working in New Orleans by 1868. It seems that off and on he lived in the home of Mr. and Mrs. Dawson Blanchard at 744 Magazine Street and instructed their daughter Blanche in painting. There are canvases that show evidence of both Giroux and Miss Blanchard having worked on them, but that are

FIGURE 55. ***Wagon Scene with Barrels***, 1884, oil on canvas, 18 x 30 inches, signed and dated lower left: *WAWalker.1884*. The Warner Collection of Gulf States Paper Corporation, Tuscaloosa, Alabama.

FIGURE 56. **CHARLES GIROUX** (born circa 1828). ***Cotton Plantation***, oil on canvas, 22 x 36 inches, signed lower left: *C. Giroux*. The Museum of Fine Arts, Boston, Massachusetts; Gift of Maxim Karolik for the Karolik Collection of American Paintings, 1815-1865.

signed "Blanchard."[25] Significantly, Walker too gave Miss Blanchard art lessons with the same result. A portrait of an elderly black field hand in Walker's distinctive style, though at variance with his technique, bears the signature "Blanche Blanchard."[26] Walker and Giroux had ample opportunities to know each other well, and it is extremely likely that they enjoyed each other's company in the relaxed environment of the Blanchard home. Thus, it is no mere coincidence that their paintings were exhibited together at Blessing's in the summers of 1883 and 1885. The pictures they showed, all plantation scenes, would have made a unified exhibition as satisfying as any present-day curator could hope to arrange.

In the spring of 1886 Walker went to Charleston. There he painted *Bombardment of Fort Sumter* (figure 57), modeled upon a sketch (now lost) and the miniature painting he had made on a playing card in 1864. Until recently the painting hung in the Edmonston-Allston House in Charleston, a building that offers approximately the same view across Charleston Harbor as is represented on Walker's canvas, which recreates the Union monitor assault on Fort Sumter of April 7, 1863.

Time may have dimmed Walker's memory of that historic day. In other images of the event, we see the Battery crowded with people, all craning to get a glimpse of the monitors and the damage they might be doing, but in Walker's view the scene is nearly devoid of animation. With the exception of two men in Confederate grays—one of whom points out something to his companion, who crouches to get a better look—everyone is at best only mildly attentive to the naval engagement. Those most obviously disinterested are the pair of black women conversing at lower left and their counterparts at lower right, two black men who actually have their backs turned to the scene of action.

Walker has taken deliberate pains here to show blacks as decidedly indifferent to the white man's war, the purpose of which was, among other things, to decide their fate. He portrays them as physically detached—removed from the possibility of any contact with whites and the white world. These small figures in *Bombardment of Fort Sumter*, seemingly insignificant in the total scheme of the picture, are Walker's most telling statement of just how outside the mainstream of life he considered the black race.

Walker was back in New Orleans in the fall of 1886. There he exhibited paintings in the first annual exhibition of the Artists' Association of New Orleans. This organization had been formed the preceding year in an effort by the artists of New Orleans to mutually promote the sale of their work. The Southern Art Union had not proved to be effective at realizing its stated goals, and in the spring of 1886 it had released its rented rooms and turned its collection over to Tulane University.

The Artists' Association, on the other hand, was extremely successful. It operated an art school and mounted an annual exhibition of its members' works. Although the association held a formal exhibition and reception only in the late fall, its doors

FIGURE 57. **Bombardment of Fort Sumter**, 1886, oil on canvas, 20 x 36 1/4 inches, signed and dated lower left: *WAWalker. 1886.* Collection of the Historic Charleston Foundation, Charleston, South Carolina. On loan to the Gibbes Museum of Art, Charleston, South Carolina.

remained open year-round, and visitors were welcome to browse and buy pictures directly off the walls. The galleries of the Artists' Association soon became the prime showcase in New Orleans for viewing the works of local artists. In fact, so successful was the Association in its mission that by 1887 Blessing's, Wagener's, and Lilienthal's galleries had ceased holding exhibitions of the work of local artists.

Walker was one of twenty professional members of the Artists' Association when it opened the doors of its headquarters at 31-33 Camp Street to the public for the first time on November 6, 1886. The rooms were festively decorated with evergreens, palmettos, and moss, and all the member artists were on hand to welcome visitors to the gala affair and to discuss their work.[27] Walker exhibited three paintings entitled *Cotton Picker*, one called *Wagon Team*, and five watercolor sketches of unspecified subjects.[28] Walker also participated in exhibitions of the Artists' Association held in 1887, 1889-1892, and 1894. His work in these showcases was often cited by the press, as will be noted.

Exhibitions, classes, and other art activities in American cities generally ceased with the advent of summer. New Orleans artists typically left their city studios for resorts on the Gulf of Mexico or the mountains of Georgia or the Carolinas, where they would spend the summer filling sketchbooks with material that would become the subject of future easel paintings. By 1881 Walker had discovered the Asheville, North Carolina area of the Blue Ridge Mountains, and from that time until the last summer of his life, a period of nearly forty years, he worked there each June through September.[29] The Blue Ridge had long attracted affluent Southerners in the summer months. Many stayed in the various inns, boarding houses, and resort hotels that abounded in the area, while others built summer cottages of their own. Walker lodged at the Bonnycrest Inn at Skyland throughout the eighties, and after the turn of the century, was an annual guest of Arden Park Lodge in neighboring Arden. As in New Orleans, Walker here found a ready market among fellow summer visitors for small, souvenir paintings. His income from the sale of these works would cover his expenses of room and board.

These small mountain communities offered Walker a quiet change of pace from his life in New Orleans. At Skyland and Arden he could paint with less distraction and accumulate a body of paintings to submit to the fall exhibitions in New Orleans. Only one large-scale painting of a North Carolina scene is known, Walker's *View from the Reverend D. C. Howell's Farm, N. C.* (figure 58). So specifically is the canvas inscribed as to the identity and date of the scene that we may assume it was commissioned from Walker and not painted for speculative purposes. The scene on the Howell farm is set in late summer; the corn that grows behind the house is mature, but the trees are not yet wearing their autumnal foliage. Fields have been cleared for crops or pasture by the controlled burning of forest, as evidenced by the patchwork pattern of denuded trunks along the mountainsides. Rails are piled by the house in preparation for the coming winter's work of fence repair. It is a panoramic view that assigns equal value to things both near and distant, and it is highly descriptive and brightly colored in the manner of the folk artist. This is a departure from Walker's style as seen in the cotton plantation scenes, where he gives his composition depth by confining brighter colors and crisper delineation to foreground elements, while depicting distant trees with a hazy blend of gray and green. Such inconsistency should be seen as suggestive not of artistic immaturity, but rather of flexibility. Walker's business-like attitude and savvy enabled him to adapt his choice of color and handling of form to meet the varied demands of his clientele.

On several occasions Walker painted the creeks and brooks in the vicinity of Arden. *Richland Creek*, dated July 18, 1887, and *Waterfall*, painted two years later, are among his earliest efforts in the watercolor medium. Both are worked on a paper measuring 13 x 9 inches and depict rock-strewn waters framed and backed by masses of dark green foliage. Walker's most sophisticated North Carolina landscape is the undated *Mountain Creek* (figure 59). The waters of the creek, clear and green, flow in a zigzag pattern from upper right to gather in a pool at lower center. Despite the painting's diminutive size, Walker's successful handling of the principle of vanishing point perspective and the clarity with which he rendered the sparkling mountain water serve to draw the viewer into the composition. Furthermore, *Mountain Creek* is a significant piece, for it shows Walker's blossoming interest in pure landscape devoid

Figure 58. ***View from the Reverend D. C. Howell's Farm, N. C.***, 1881, oil on canvas, 22 x 36 inches, signed and dated lower left: *WAWalker. 1881.* Inscribed lower right: *View from Revd. D. C. Howell's Farm. N. C.* Robert M. Hicklin Jr., Inc., Spartanburg, South Carolina.

FIGURE 59. ***Mountain Creek***, oil on academy board, 12 x 9 1/2 inches, signed lower left: *WAWalker*. Collection of Mr. and Mrs. Francis M. Pinckney.

Walker used dark shadows to lend high relief to this painting, thereby achieving an unusual degree of depth.

FIGURE 60. ***North Carolina Mountain Landscape****,* oil on paper mounted on panel, 8 x 10 1/2 inches, signed lower right: *WAWalker.* Private Collection.

of human activity. Landscape painting was a genre in which he would work more and more as the years went by, painting not only mountain streams, but also Florida beaches and the sandy terrain of the sea islands near Charleston. Walker exhibited "four views of North Carolina scenery" at the fourth annual exhibition of the Artists' Association of New Orleans in 1889.[30] The following year he submitted five sketches made at Edisto Island, South Carolina and seven sketches of the environs of Arden.[31]

FIGURE 61. **Old Bald, Western North Carolina**, 1887, watercolor on pa-
per, 10 x 6 7/8 inches, signed and dated lower left: *WAWalker. July 11./87.*
Inscribed lower right: *Old Bald. Wn N. C.* The Sewell Family Collection,
Vidalia, Louisiana.

In the late 1880s Walker turned to painting the homes of poor black plantation workers. In December 1887, he publicly exhibited for the first time a painting titled *Cabin* at the second annual exhibition of the Artists' Association of New Orleans.[32] The cabin scene would remain a mainstay of Walker's oeuvre for years to come. In these works, appealing in their realism, Walker focused on one cabin, usually seen from the front. Family members who dwell in it are gathered on the porch, or lacking a porch, are shown standing about the yard or engaged in domestic chores. The solitary cabin was a reflection of a new social order in the Southern black community. During Reconstruction blacks had eschewed the communal slave quarters, seen as "a relic of their former subjection," for individual tenancies scattered across the plantation.[33] This pattern of settlement remained the norm in the 1880s when Walker turned to painting the homes of rural blacks.

Walker painted these dwellings everywhere his annual peregrinations took him—Louisiana, the sea islands, Florida, and the Blue Ridge Mountains. The cabins reveal regional characteristics in building materials and style of construction. Those of western North Carolina are constructed of logs and have sturdy stone or brick chimneys, while the typical Louisiana cabin is built of boards and often has a raised front porch. Yet another regional variant is the "rude, pine-log cabins" of the sea islands, their yards dotted with palmetto trees and rows of cotton planted right up to the door. From whatever region, the vast majority of cabins painted by Walker lack windows, although a few have openings in their walls that are covered by wooden shutters. Locally available materials were generally used in cabin construction, and in rural areas glass was scarce and costly.

Walker's cabin scenes follow a formula that he found successful. The foreground yard is given to bare dirt, which to poor whites and blacks in the South was considered fashionable. The woman of the house would rake her yard as carefully as she would sweep her house. Grass, on the other hand, was for the pasture, and it was viewed as poor housekeeping to have grass growing near the house. In Walker's views, chickens scratch around in the dirt and children play with sticks and mud pies, the only toys available. Dominating the middle ground is the cabin itself with a chimney of wood, mud, stone, brick, or a combination of materials. Those of wood

FIGURE 62. ***Cabin by the Cornfield***, oil on canvas, 10 1/4 x 16 inches, signed lower left: *WAWalker.* The Greenville County Museum of Art, Greenville, South Carolina.

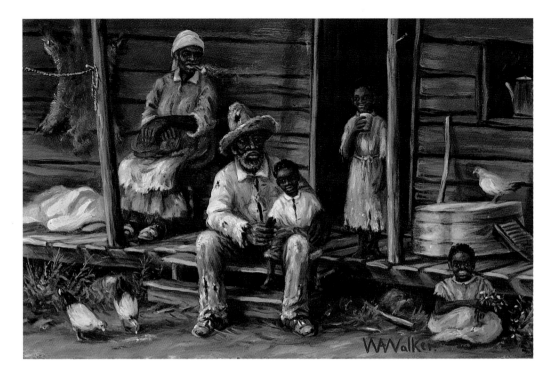

Figure 63. ***Family on Porch***, oil on academy board, 5 3/8 x 8 3/8 inches, signed lower right: *WAWalker*. The Warner Collection of Gulf States Paper Corporation, Tuscaloosa, Alabama.

and mud often have one or two wooden poles buttressed against them. If the chimney caught fire, the poles would be removed, allowing the chimney to collapse and the cabin to be saved. The front wall of the cabin may have hanging on it a bunch of red peppers or a possum skin stretched and tacked up to dry. Hollowed gourds hang from poles as tall as palmettos. The gourds were placed there to attract martins, which would keep the yard free of mosquitoes. A pig's trough may be artlessly set directly in front of the cabin door. Orange and lemon trees sometimes add a spot of color, as do the costumes of the women, each clad in an eclectic array of fabrics from turban to kerchief to homespun dress and long work apron. The yard is littered with the props of living: chairs and barrels, baskets and pots, wooden buckets, tables, and abandoned cartons. The cabin was so small (usually one room) and the limited number of openings in its walls admitted so little light that it was

FIGURE 64. ***Sharecroppers in the Deep South***, oil on canvas, 12 x 19 inches, signed lower right: *WAWalker*. The Sewell Family Collection, Vidalia, Louisiana.

Figure 65. ***Charleston County Cabin***, oil on canvas, 8 1/4 x 16 1/4 inches, signed lower left: *WAWalker*. Robert M. Hicklin Jr., Inc., Spartanburg, South Carolina.

Figure 66. ***North Carolina Cabin***, 1887, watercolor on paper, 10 x 13 inches, signed and dated lower right: *WAWalker./Aug 29. 1887.* The Sewell Family Collection, Vidalia, Louisiana.

common for black women to perform the chores of cooking and washing clothes in the yard and for the family to spend their time outside as well.

By and large, Walker painted his cabin scenes on academy boards, though some have been found whose support is canvas. Walker's boards generally came from one of two manufacturers, the F. W. Devoe Company of New York (and its successor Devoe & Raynolds of New York and Chicago) and Frost & Adams of Boston. He purchased them in stores that stocked art supplies in New Orleans, Charleston, Jacksonville, and other Southern cities. Labels on the backs of at least three boards reveal that Walker acquired them from J. Gumbinger, jeweler and optician of Jacksonville, Florida. He bought many from the Standard Photo Company in New Orleans, with which he had a business relationship.[34]

Figure 67. **O. Pierre Havens**, photographer (1838-1912). ***Folks All Home****,* stereograph, 3 7/8 x 7 inches. Printed on cardboard mount: *Havens. (Successor to Wilson & Havens) Photographer, 141 & 143 Broughton Street, Savannah, Ga. Publisher of the Largest Collection of Southern Views in The United States.* Photograph Collection; Miriam and Ira D. Wallach Division of Art, Prints and Photographs; The New York Public Library; Astor, Lenox, and Tilden Foundations.

Walker cut his boards himself. The vast majority of the cabin scenes measure approximately 6 x 12 inches, while a lesser number he cut to a 9 x 12-inch format. The twelve-inch side was usually the horizontal measurement; in only a handful of known examples did he turn his board in order to paint a vertical composition. The firm, smooth surface of the academy board allowed Walker to inscribe the back in pencil. His cabin scenes he titled simply *Cabin,* in a big, flowing, penciled script. He sometimes noted prices on the back, also in pencil. The cabin paintings ranged from five to twenty-seven dollars. One of what was once a pair is now in the collection of the Gibbes Museum of Art in Charleston, South Carolina. Measuring the smaller size of 6 1/4 x 12 1/4 inches and showing evidence of having been painted in a free and quick manner, Walker's inscription on the back of this painting indicates that he asked eighteen dollars for it and its companion (presently unlocated).

From 1860 until the end of his life, Walker's signature on his paintings showed no major variation. In that year he began, consistently, to sign his works with his three initials conjoined and followed by his last name written in full, like this: *WAWalker*. Usually he placed a period after his surname, but he rarely placed a period after the first or second initial. On those paintings that he dated, the year is inscribed following the period at the end of his name, either on a line with it or immediately below it. He usually placed a period following the year also. Infrequently he would include the month (always abbreviated) and day preceding the year. (See figure 80.) His signature is found on the painted surfaces of his boards, canvases, papers, and brass plates in red, brown, or less frequently, black paint, in either the lower left or lower right corner. Occasionally he placed the signature obliquely on a cotton bale or rock if such were conveniently located near a lower corner of the composition. Most commonly, he adopted a straight up and down style for his signature, though a few slant to the left in backhand fashion.

The cabin scenes were tremendously popular with a public eager to have pictures to hang on its walls. Walker painted and sold hundreds of them from the late 1880s until the end of his career. However, the subject did not win critical approval. The newsletter of the Artists' Association offered the following observation when Walker showed his first one there in December 1887: "'Cabin,' by Walker, has a good deal of detail work in it, but it lacks effect and depth. The watercolors are better."[35] Walker was undeterred. He pursued the theme with a vengeance, and to the sixth annual exhibition of the Artists' Association of New Orleans in 1891 he submitted *Simon's Cabin* and *Davis' Cabin*.[36] And his new theme was adopted by other artists. In 1888 Mrs. Walter Saxon (circa 1855-1927), a student of the Artists' Association, exhibited a picture called *Shanties* that won her a gold medal.[37]

By 1885 Walker had developed yet another vehicle for painting blacks. Inscribed no earlier than that year are many full-length pictures of standing black men and women. These paintings range from pocket-sized 8 x 4-inch academy boards to canvases measuring fifty inches in height and represent some of Walker's most ambitious work. He painted the figures singly or in pairs, and with few exceptions, he painted them in the context of the Cotton Kingdom. Field hands are posed before

FIGURE 68A & 68B. ***Charleston Market Vendors***, oil on academy board, 8 x 3 13/16 inches each, female figure signed lower left: *WAWalker*. Male figure signed lower right: *WAWalker*. The Morris Museum of Art, Augusta, Georgia.

cotton plants in full bloom, while dock workers are painted standing in front of cotton bales. One such dock worker, in a painting in the collection of Jay P. Altmayer, holds in his right hand a stevedore's hook, a tool that was used for grabbing hold of a bale in order to hoist it onto a wagon or boat. Another variation featured vendors, usually women, who bear baskets of produce on their arms or who stand in a stall at a city market. (See figures 68A and 68B.)

Six large-scale canvases of cotton pickers are known. They are: *Old Cotton Picker* (frontispiece, p. ii); *"I'll Stick to Cotton as Long as it Sticks to Me"* (figure 69); *Old Jeb* (figure 70); *The Old Cotton Picker* (figure 71); *Chums Befo' Duh War* (figure 72); and *Uncle Sam* (Collection of Jay P. Altmayer). The subjects of all the paintings are men; all have full, gray beards and stooped, bow-legged postures; all smoke corncob pipes; and all are posed amidst cotton plants, four with baskets of cotton at their sides. There is no evidence for any of the six having descended through a black family. It is probable that, like the large paintings of cotton plantations, these figure paintings were commissioned by whites with an interest in the cotton business. In fact, one of them, *The Old Cotton Picker*, has a history of ownership in England, the biggest buyer of Southern cotton after the war. Despite the care that Walker took to render the features of their weathered faces, the subjects were painted not so much to immortalize individuals, as portraits would, but rather to capture the humble poverty and benign demeanor of anonymous, black field workers, qualities that were acceptable to a white, art-buying public. Two of them traditionally have been titled *Uncle Sam* and *Old Jeb*. It is not known if these titles were assigned by Walker, but whether given by him or subsequent owners of the paintings, they provide further evidence that the subjects were to be remembered as stereotypes rather than as individuals.

The most complex of Walker's large figure paintings is the double portrait of 1893 titled *Chums Befo' Duh War* (figure 72). The subjects pose casually, with hands thrust in their pockets, though one has removed his hat for the sake of having his picture made. They are clothed in the patchwork costumes that all Walker's black characters wear. The prices that plantation stores charged to sharecroppers were exorbitant, making new garments an impossible luxury. It seems that the man on the left has been compelled by necessity to wear two right shoes. The presence of flat-

FIGURE 69. *"I'll Stick to Cotton as Long as it Sticks to Me,"* 1886, oil on canvas, 42 1/8 x 24 1/4 inches, signed lower left: *WAWalker. 1886.* Collection of Judith S. Vane.

FIGURE 70. ***Old Jeb***, 1889, oil on canvas, 42 x 24 inches, signed lower left: *WAWalker. 1889.* Lagakos-Turak Gallery, Philadelphia, Pennsylvania and Robert M. Hicklin Jr., Inc., Spartanburg, South Carolina.

topped cypress trees in the far background of the painting suggests a Louisiana setting, and it is likely that Walker found the pair on a plantation in the Mississippi Delta, although the painting has a Charleston provenance.

In 1888 Walker painted a picture of two elderly black field hands that has long been known as *Calhoun's Slaves* (Collection of Jay P. Altmayer). Recently this pair has come to light in another painting with the same date, titled *"What Do You Think?"* (figure 74), and in a third version, with the descriptive title *Two Men with Canes* (The Warner Collection of Gulf States Paper Corporation, Tuscaloosa, Alabama). The overwhelming trait that links the three paintings—and one that they share with the six large canvases previously discussed—is the positioning of the subjects in the extreme forefront of the picture plane. It is as if Walker saw the men as players on a stage and the cotton field, which he painted behind them, as a backdrop to their scene. This positioning, as well as the still, posed quality of the subjects, recalls Walker's painted photograph, *Portrait of A. A. Trescott* (figure 28), and it is likely that one or more photographs served as the models from which Walker painted his pictures of the two elderly men. At the fourth annual exhibition of the Artists' Association of New Orleans in December 1889, a painting like these, if not one of these, was singled out for praise: "Some much admired plantation and darky painting is exhibited by Mr. W. A. Walker. One is in [*sic*] his favorite, showing two ragged old negroes in the cotton field, which is in full bloom."[38]

Walker carried this theme into a painting that represents a woman and child in a cotton field (figure 75). The woman, whose grizzled hair and walking stick suggest an advanced age, is attired in frayed skirt, patched shirt, and colorful, plaid tignon or head kerchief. Her costume and the clay pipe she holds in her mouth are typical features of Walker's paintings of black women. Her broad nose, thick lips, furrowed brow, and heavy-lidded eyes combine to create a weathered, careworn visage. The well-formed head of the child, whose gaze is directed away from the viewer, is one of Walker's most sensitive portraits. The youngster, who wears a faraway, dreamy look, smiles shyly, exposing two small white teeth.

The fact that Walker places both the youngest and the eldest blacks in the field underscores the spread of sharecropping in the post-war South. Immediately follow-

FIGURE 71. ***The Old Cotton Picker***, oil on canvas, 42 x 24 inches, signed lower left: *WAWalker*. The Warner Collection of Gulf States Paper Corporation, Tuscaloosa, Alabama.

This painting was discovered in England in 1988. It is quite likely that it was commissioned from Walker by an English mill owner or shipper involved in the cotton trade.

ing the war black women had been housekeepers in their own homes, while black children attended school, much to the disdain of some members of the white population, who accused blacks of mimicking the family patterns of middle-class whites.[39] The Depression of 1872, coupled with the end of the Republican mandates of Reconstruction that had made land available to all races, meant that blacks could no longer afford to own land and in some areas were denied the right to purchase it by white consensus. As a result, sharecropping became the predominant system of labor for rural blacks. Under the system, the more cotton a family could raise, the greater its share of the crop at harvest time. It behooved families to return their women and children to the fields to work alongside the men. By the mid-1880s when Walker painted *In the Cottonfields*, this practice had become the norm.

Walker found a ready market for plantation scenes among wealthy cotton brokers and mill owners, as well as less affluent collectors who wanted to spend only five to twenty-five dollars for a painting. The image of the poorly dressed black, his small, crude cabin, his mule, the cotton field in which he worked, and the wagon that he drove to market were familiar, comforting images for most white Southerners. Moreover, these subjects were recognized around the world as icons of the American South, the "Land of Cotton." Such images were mass produced, primarily in the form of paired, mounted photographs for viewing through a stereoptican, from the 1870s through the turn of the century.

Photographer J. A. Palmer (op. 1870s) of Aiken, South Carolina offered a series of stereo views entitled *Characteristic Southern Scenes*. His label on the back of each stereo card bore the advertisement, "A large Stock of Views of Negro Groups, Cabins, Teams, Cotton Fields and Plants, etc., kept constantly on hand." Photographers in North and South Carolina, Virginia, Georgia, Florida, and Louisiana, as well as a few very large firms in the Northeast, maintained a stock of such subjects that they sold much like modern postcards in hotels, bookstores, and newsstands, thus making them readily accessible to the tourist market. One photographer printed titles on the backs of his stereo cards in seven languages, while another advertised that his stereo views could be purchased through the mail. A comparison of several of Walker's types of black paintings to contemporary stereo views exemplifies the extent to which

FIGURE 72. ***Chums Befo' Duh War***, 1893, oil on canvas, 50 x 35 inches, signed and dated lower left: *WAWalker. 1893.* Private Collection. On loan to the Greenville County Museum of Art, Greenville, South Carolina.

FIGURE 73. JEROME NELSON WILSON (1827–1897) and O. PIERRE HAVENS (1838–1912), photographers. *Jack and Abby Landlord, Aged 100 and 110 Years*, stereograph, 3 7/8 x 7 inches. Printed on cardboard mount: *Photographed by Wilson & Havens, Savannah, Ga.* Photograph Collection; Miriam and Ira D. Wallach Division of Art, Prints and Photographs; The New York Public Library; Astor, Lenox, and Tilden Foundations.

he was producing with similar commercial objectives in mind. For nearly every black subject in his repertory—the cotton field scene, cabin scene, wagon scene, levee scene, and portraits of field hands—a corollary may be found in commercial photography of the period. (Compare figure 34 to 38; 55 to 54; 62 and 63 to 67; and 72 to 73.)

Did Walker himself work from photographs? Perhaps. Several Walker family members mentioned having seen or owned photographs taken by Walker. Whether Walker worked from photographs or from life certainly is a question of interest to the art historian, but from both the sociological and the commercial perspectives, Walker's choice of subjects and those subjects' pervasiveness in contemporary photography, which by definition was mass-produced, reflect a consensus of what was widely accepted as "typically Southern subjects" in the post-Reconstruction era.

FIGURE 74. *"What Do You Think?"*, 1888, oil on canvas, 20 1/8 x 16 1/8 inches, signed and dated lower left: *WAWalker. 1888.* Private Collection.

Walker's plantation scenes, levee scenes, cabin scenes, and portraits of blacks in the cotton fields were popular wherever he went throughout the South. They earned a broader, national reputation for him as well when they were purchased by visitors to the South, and especially when two of his most monumental paintings were selected for publication by Currier and Ives. At least one Northerner, Stephen Weld, commissioned a large cotton plantation scene from Walker because of the wondrous way in which it portrayed the Cotton Kingdom. Complementary works by his predecessors Eyre Crowe and John Antrobus, as well as contemporary artists like Charles Giroux, may have contributed to his inspiration. These scenes were quite successful with the public and earned glowing reviews in the press. Sheer numbers indicate the vast extent of these subjects' appeal. But what explains these paintings' commercial popularity and critical acclaim? Why were these scenes that seem to portray the black man as slave popular with Walker's public, and why, in that constant nonverbal dialogue that goes on between artist and public, producer and consumer, did Walker respond to public demand by the production of what in the late twentieth century are viewed as biased works?

Historian Thomas B. Alexander, in a paper delivered at a symposium at the University of Mississippi in 1983, raises a provocative question, which provides a glimmer of insight into the motivation of William Aiken Walker and his audience. Professor Alexander proposes that ante-bellum attitudes died hardest among those who were children during the War Between the States. He maintains that despite what he calls the "planter's wartime disenchantment with the attitudes and behavior of the black," the Sambo myth survived and that it was the *children* of the Confederacy who later revived the myth and, more importantly, who *believed* in it.[40]

In the 1880s, Walker's contemporaries held the positions of civic authority; they were the generation responsible for erecting statues to Robert E. Lee and other Confederate heroes. It is no coincidence that as Walker's peers were building memorials in every courthouse square across the South and otherwise celebrating the glorious days of the Confederacy, Walker himself began to concentrate his work on the depiction of blacks in extremely servile attitudes.

FIGURE 75. *In the Cottonfields*, oil on canvas, 20 x 12 inches, signed lower right: *WAWalker*. The Morris Museum of Art, Augusta, Georgia.

FIGURE 76. *Happy Charley*, 1890, oil on academy board, 12 1/4 x 9 1/4 inches, signed and dated lower left: *WAWalker./Nov. 8th. 1890*. Inscribed lower center: *Happy Charley*. Inscribed in pencil on verso: *Not for sale Copy $25.00, 9 x 12 size*. Collection of Mr. and Mrs. G. Thomas Ludwig, Williamsburg, Virginia.

Happy Charley captures in oil the stereotype of the eternally happy black youth. We learn from Walker's inscription on the verso that he expected this subject to be in great demand, for though he would not sell this particular board, he would make a copy of it for twenty-five dollars.

FIGURE 77. *Three Children Eating Sugarcane*, watercolor on paper laid down on board, 3 1/2 x 3 1/2 inches, initialed lower left: *WAW*. Imprinted on verso: *Harris/Photo/Daytona, Fla*. The Warner Collection of Gulf States Paper Corporation, Tuscaloosa, Alabama.

For the cotton plantations of the Mississippi Delta to flourish again on Northern capital during Reconstruction was to revive the appearance of the Carolina cotton economy from which Walker's father had earned his living. The cotton trade was a major proponent of Walker's early reality, and he embraced its reincarnation joyfully. His joy is attested to by the intricate manner in which he painted and the contented demeanor he assigned to his human subjects. A love for the minutiae of the scene infuses each painting. Each cotton boll, each cabin board, each frayed shirt is painstakingly rendered. In a field full of black pickers each woman and man is uniquely dressed. All smile, happy to be working, as they bend to pick the fleecy white staple. It is an idyllic view.

It is astonishing that many people believe Walker to have been a black man, for his vision is profoundly white. He painted blacks solely in roles of servitude to whites, whether as cotton pickers to plantation owners or as stevedores to supercargoes. In no instance did he portray the rich culture developed by Southern blacks that we now know gave peace and meaning to lives of debilitating physical labor, pain, and penury. It is significant that in his portrayals of blacks Walker almost exclusively painted older subjects—those who had been born and raised as slaves and had spent a good part of their working lives under slavery. They were the men and women who chose to stay on the plantations of their birth rather than flee across the Mississippi, as did some of their bolder, emancipated children. Was there something in the faces of this older generation to which Walker could relate—a benignity, a resignation to their lot in life? And conversely, did he see a restlessness in the faces of younger black adults that unnerved him? A frustration that he could not understand? A longing that was not appropriate in a race that was supposed to know its place in Walker's world?

In the 1880s and for most of the nineties, Walker wintered in a city that historically had one of the largest populations of free blacks in the South. New Orleans had black doctors, lawyers, merchants, preachers, and even a black newspaper. Here was a viable community of black citizens, yet in Walker's oeuvre there is not to be found a single portrait of an educated, professional black. No such work exists because, for William Aiken Walker, no such person existed. Walker's views reflect the bias of his race, his class, and his era. He painted what he saw, and what he saw was filtered through a Southern, white, ante-bellum consciousness. Walker's vision is but another window on the selective nature of human perception and values.

CHAPTER FIVE

A More Tranquil Life

FIGURE 78. ***Boat on Ocklawaha River***, oil on board, 10 x 6 inches, signed lower left: *WAWalker.*
Inscribed on verso: *#17 Ocklawaha Riv. $12.00.* The Vickers Florida Collection, Jacksonville, Florida.

As Walker approached his sixties his sojourns in New Orleans became less regular. He wintered there in 1897 and did not return again until 1905, his final visit to the city. Behind him were the days of intense involvement in the Artists' Association of New Orleans, where he exhibited for the last time in 1894.[1] Ahead lay easy, glorious days of fishing, reading, and recording in sketch books languorous yachting trips made with friends down the Florida coast, or when in Arden, North Carolina, solitary woodland rambles to paint the mushrooms, ferns, and other flora of the forest. Between seasons he enjoyed lengthy stays in Charleston where he always maintained close ties. Financially secure and personally satisfied with the artistic stature he had attained, he was his own master.

In these later years Walker's rate of artistic production slowed, and he worked exclusively on surfaces of a small, easily managed format. Cotton picker and cabin scenes, painted on academy board generally measuring 8 x 4, 6 x 12, or 9 x 12 inches, remained his major source of income, but after 1893 he painted no full-length figure paintings measuring upwards of three feet in height or any large plantation scenes with their multiple layers of activity.[2] He painted numerous, small-scale beach scenes in oil—showing a white strip of sand, a sliver of ocean often accented by a ship on the horizon, the scene framed by palmetto trees and yucca plants. As money was not a pressing concern, Walker generously made many pictures to present as gifts. He would send his friends homemade Christmas cards, each a little coastal view painted in oil or watercolor, measuring no more than 2 x 3 inches with a greeting penciled on the reverse. (See figures 79A and 79B.) He would also give these miniatures to the children of his nieces and nephews as birthday remembrances.

In addition to beach scenes, Walker displayed a renewed interest in still life painting, a subject he had abandoned in the late 1870s. Instead of the game pictures that had occupied his youth and the tabletop still lifes of his early forties, however, Walker took on the role of naturalist. He painted the variety of flowers, leaves, berries, and birds' nests discovered on forest explorations, simply arranged on a plain, dark background, imitating with his brush their intricate variations of form, texture, and color. Similarly, on fishing trips he would paint his catch and that of his friends', taking care to inscribe each rendering with the fish's proper scientific name.

Figure 79A. **Miniature Beach Scene**, 1906, oil on paper, 2 3/16 x 3 5/16 inches, initialed lower left: *WAW.* Inscribed on paper backing: *Christmas Greeting with best wishes to Lottie, from your old friend Wm. A. Walker. 1906.* The Historic New Orleans Collection, New Orleans, Louisiana (1953.136).

This Christmas gift to Lottie Mitchell is representative of the sketches that Walker sent to friends and relatives, either bearing Christmas greetings or birthday wishes. Sometimes he would make his oil sketch on a very small piece of paper suitable for framing. At other times, he would embellish the top of his writing paper with a small pen and ink sketch, which would be followed by a brief message.

Figure 79B. **Compliments of the Season**, 1905, pen and ink on paper, 6 3/4 x 5 inches (sight). The inscription reads as follows: *Compliments of the Season./from Wm. A. Walker./Christmas. 1905./To Mr & Mrs C. Lewis Diehl.* Location unknown; photograph courtesy of the author.

The nature studies, beach scenes, and other landscapes that crept into Walker's oeuvre in his later years share one important characteristic: they are devoid of the human figure. This turning away from the depiction of human life and activity may be reflective of the increasing isolation that Walker felt as he grew older. After he turned seventy, his correspondence reveals that he was often lonely as he waited out rainy January days in his room at Ponce Park, Florida, anticipating the arrival of old friends and a return to the beach to draw and paint. During Walker's summer stays at Arden, he often eschewed company for long, solitary hours of sketching. A fellow guest of Arden Park Lodge wrote years later, "He, his easel and paint brushes were inseparable. Each day he set forth to capture the beauties of the mountain country."[3]

FIGURE 80. ***First Snow, Pisgah***, 1890, oil on paper, 13 3/16 x 9 7/8 inches, signed and dated lower left: *WAWalker./Oct. 28. 1890.* Inscribed on verso: *No 19. Pisgah. from Arden Park Hotel. N. C. first snow $15.00.* The South Carolina State Museum, Columbia, South Carolina; Gift of Henry M. G. Walker, Jr.,

As the 1890s began Walker was in St. Augustine, Florida. His stay there is documented by two pictures, one an oil painting dated March 8, 1890, that shows the old gates to the city flanked by a pair of stone piers and another titled *The Plaza and Hotel Ponce de Leon, St. Augustine,* which he exhibited later that year in New Orleans.[4] The Ponce de Leon was one of a group of luxury hotels built throughout Florida by Henry Morrison Flagler, partner to John D. Rockefeller in the oil business. Designed by Carriere and Hastings of New York in the Moorish style, it was by far the largest and most opulent of the hotel chain. A series of interconnected artists' studios was incorporated into the Ponce de Leon complex. Martin Johnson Heade, Frank H. Shapleigh, George W. Seavey, W. Staples Drown, Robert S. German, Charlotte Buell Corman, Marian Foster, Felix de Crano, Laura Woodward, and Otto Bacher all had studios there at one time or another.

Heade (1819-1904) occupied studio number seven beginning in January 1888 when the Ponce de Leon officially opened. Having taken up permanent residence in St. Augustine four years earlier, Heade painted the marshes just a mile outside the city in luminous glazes of green and gray punctuated by fiery sunsets. Still life paintings of magnolias, orange blossoms, and Cherokee roses were also part of his Florida oeuvre. Shapleigh (1842-1906), a Bostonian, visited St. Augustine seasonally. While displaying his New England landscapes and interiors in his Ponce de Leon studio, he would paint St. Augustine's picturesque landmarks, including the cathedral, the sea wall, and her narrow streets with overhanging balconies. De Crano (died 1908) painted floral still lifes and coastal views. Bacher (1856-1909), who had made a name for himself with his etchings of Venice, portrayed the people of St. Augustine as they went about their day-to-day tasks in the city's dark, winding streets.

The Ponce de Leon artists held a weekly reception at which time their studios were thrown open to the public. Whether or not Walker personally knew these artists is unknown, but working winter after winter as he did in St. Augustine, he had to have been aware of their work. His paintings of the Florida coast, still life arrangements, and sites of local interest such as the Plaza and Hotel Ponce de Leon place his subjects in the mainstream with that of contemporary Florida artists.

While in St. Augustine the Magnolia Hotel was Walker's home, and he made his

FIGURE 81. ***Bringin' in the Dory***, 1895, oil on academy board, 6 1/8 x 12 1/4 inches, signed and dated lower left: *WAWalker. 1895.* Inscribed on verso: *6 x 12 price $5.00.* The Warner Collection of Gulf States Paper Corporation, Tuscaloosa, Alabama.

The fisherman stands on the bank of the Halifax River. In the background is the roof of Pacetti House and the adjacent cottage that also housed guests. Pricing the painting at $5.00, Walker hoped that it would be purchased by a guest of the hotel. This is less than the average price he asked for paintings of blacks' cabins and black field hands, perhaps suggesting that he undervalued this type of work.

studio in Thomas Tugby's curiosity shop at the corner of St. George Street and Hypolita. The gossipy local newspaper reported his arrival for the winter of 1895:

> Mr. Walker, who has for a number of years spent his winters here, a guest of the Magnolia, does [now] have a studio exhibiting his pictures characteristic of Southern plantation life at Tugby's. He especially affects the negro as he was thirty-five years ago—cotton fields, 'The Quarters,' all strong and typical.[5]

The Magnolia, though not nearly as grand as the Ponce de Leon, was a handsome Victorian structure, three stories tall, wood-framed and turreted. It was located on St. George Street, the city's main thoroughfare. The Magnolia's rate was between three and four dollars per day (as compared to the Ponce de Leon's five-dollar daily rate), with special weekly rates available, allowing Walker to live quite comfortably for relatively little money.[6]

Tugby's, where Walker painted, was only a few blocks away. We might well picture him there, working away at his easel in the same assembly line method of production that he had adopted in New Orleans, all the while benefitting from a steady stream of passersby and potential buyers who visited the shop. Once dry, his small, sturdy paintings could easily be packed in valise or steamer trunk and taken home as fitting souvenirs of a Florida vacation.

Later each winter Walker went further south on Florida's Atlantic coast to Ponce Park (now Ponce Inlet), a fisherman's paradise approximately twelve miles south of Daytona. There the pace of life slowed. It was a quiet resort, where, if the weather was warm and sunny, Walker loved nothing better than to spend his day on the beach sketching or to meander in his boat or that of a friend through lagoons in search of bass or bluefish.

Ponce Park was a place to which Walker developed a deep, personal attachment. He spent many weeks each year at Pacetti House, a modest boarding house run by the Pacetti family, and he came, over time, to be treated like a member of that clan. Bartola C. Pacetti (1821-circa 1898) came to Ponce Park in 1843 to work as a pilot of ships, settling and building his home on property that he would eventually inherit. After the War Between the States, when tourism began to develop in Florida, Bartola also guided fishing parties in the waters he knew so well. To cater to the needs of sportsmen who were flocking to the area in ever increasing numbers, he and his wife Martha eventually decided to open a boarding house. In 1886 construction of Pacetti House was completed, and it began to attract a circle of well-heeled, avid sportsmen and their families from the East Coast and the Midwest. (See figure 81.) After Bartola's death, Martha and her children continued to run the establishment until it was sold out of the family in the 1920s.[7]

While in residence, Walker acted as receptionist for Pacetti House. He converted the office into a studio and so was never far from his paints and brushes. His part in

running the establishment partially compensated for his room and board. He also was generous in making gifts of his paintings to the Pacetti family.[8] Some of his paintings belong to Pacetti descendants, while two remain in the house that Bartola and Martha built.

Walker made many close and lasting friendships at Pacetti House. W. H. ("Colonel") Piper from Pennsylvania was a fishing and drinking companion. Piper's absence from Ponce Park in 1909 elicited a friendly, humorous poem from Walker's pen, which he copied into the back of his manuscript book, "Mes Pensées."[9]

Dr. C. Lewis Diehl (1840-1917), a pharmacist and the first president of the Louisville College of Pharmacy, vacationed at Ponce Park usually in the late winter or early spring. He and Walker shared a passion for the game of whist, as well as for fishing and sailing. A group of letters written by Walker to Diehl over a fifteen-year period attests to their friendship. Additionally, six paintings by Walker were part of Diehl's granddaughter's estate. Included among them were five views of the beach at Ponce Park, three of which date to 1895, and one small painting of a black man standing in a cotton field.

Another Ponce Park friend was the wealthy St. Louis industrialist William Henry Gregg (1831-1916). His career culminated in the presidency of the Southern White Lead Company from which he retired in 1889 to devote himself to travel and the pursuit of a social life. Each year Gregg fished for weeks at a time in Florida and thereby became an expert on the bounty the state's waters had to offer. He sailed his own yacht, the *Orian,* named after his wife, the former Orian Thompson. Walker was his companion on well-documented voyages made in 1899, 1900, and 1908.

From his experience Gregg wrote a book titled *Where When and How to Catch Fish on the East Coast of Florida* (1902), in which he proffered practical advice to the sports fisherman in an anecdotal and entertaining manner. The book is illustrated with one hundred engravings in black and white plus a dozen chromolithographs. Three of the latter are after original oils by Walker, though he is not credited as the artist. However, Gregg mentions Walker in several places in his text—referring to him as "Professor Walker" of Charleston—when he describes for his readers certain fish that he and Walker caught together.

Gregg, like Diehl, was the recipient of paintings by Walker. *The Cove at Ponce Park* (1895), *Bluefish,* and *Sheepshead,* both of which were painted in 1900 and served as models for chromolithographs in Gregg's book, were originally owned by the industrialist and today remain in his family. *Blackberry Winter* (figure 39) was also part of Gregg's collection.

In the spring of 1899, Walker accepted Gregg's invitation to make a fishing trip from Daytona to the Florida Keys on the *Orian.* Walker meticulously recorded their journey in a series of pencil sketches—his earliest surviving drawings, many of which were preserved by the Walker family. He recorded them in sketchbooks which he was careful to fill chronologically from the front of each book to the back, each sketch a clear rendering of a particular spot and carefully inscribed as to location, date of execution, and sometimes even the hour of the day. Often he squeezed two to four sketches made on the same day onto one page so that he could begin the next day with a fresh sheet, so methodical was he in his work habits. He signed each sketch with his initials in monogram, (*WAW*), rather than with his surname written in full, as was his custom on oil paintings.

The first sketches in the group are a pair dated April 11, 1899, three days into the voyage. They depict the St. Lucie River and Sewells Point at the mouth of the river (figure 83). Drawn a couple of hundred yards from land, they are panoramic in scope, offering a sweeping view of the shore. A bank of dense tree growth is broken here and there by towering palm trees, whose shaggy tops Walker depicted by masses of quick, short lines, made by not lifting his pencil from the paper. Denser and more distant growth seems enveloped in haze, an effect that Walker created by using the side of his pencil.

In a letter to Diehl, Walker vividly described what he and Gregg had seen, experienced, and, most importantly, caught on the voyage:

> Since our start 8th Apl. the cruise has been delightful, and the weather superb, barring some rain lately, which did not hurt. . . . It would take a volume to describe the beautiful scenery that I have seen, far more lovely than I dreamed of, and every day is one of joy. At Gilbert's Bar we caught Blue fish trolling,

FIGURE 82A. Photograph of William Aiken Walker on porch of Pacetti House, Ponce Park, Florida. Private Collection.

FIGURE 82B. Photograph of William Aiken Walker and Dr. C. Lewis Diehl at Ponce Park, Florida. Private Collection.

FIGURE 82C. Photograph of Dr. C. Lewis Diehl, William Aiken Walker, and Gomecinda Pacetti at Ponce Park, Florida. Private Collection.

FIGURE 83. *St. Lucie Riv[er], Fla.* and *Sewells Pt., Mouth of St. Lucie Riv[er]*, 1899, pencil on paper, 8 x 12 inches (sheet); each sketch is inscribed with title lower left; initialed and dated lower right: *WAW. 11th Apl. 1899.* Collection of Mrs. Lucia Cogswell Heins.

& still fishing, some fine 10 lb. groupers and snappers. . . . .We are living well, and our cook edits the culinary menu in good style. We arrived at Palm Beach 18th and it is the loveliest spot I have ever seen. The Royal Poinciana is a dream of beauty, but you have seen it. . . . [10]

The Royal Poinciana on Lake Worth was another in the chain of Flagler hotels. Walker was so impressed by the Royal Poinciana that he made three sketches of it from various vantage points across the water. (See figure 84.) He precisely delineated its long, mansard roof studded with dormer windows and crowned by a square cupola. The lush vegetation that rises around the structure he suggested by quick diagonal rubs with the side of his pencil, while simultaneously maintaining the flatness of the

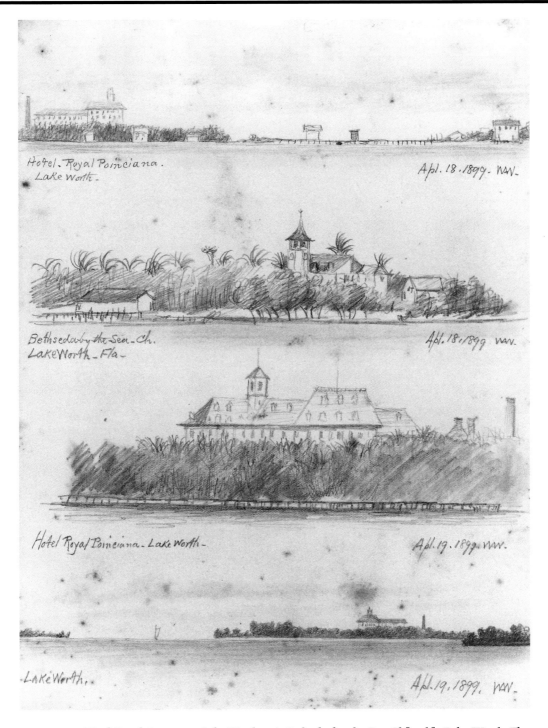

FIGURE 84. *Hotel Royal Poinciana, Lake Worth* and *Bethseda-by-the-Sea-Ch[urch], Lake Worth, Fla.*,
1899. Each sketch inscribed with title lower left; dated and initialed lower right: *Apl. 18. 1899.
WAW. Hotel Royal Poinciana, Lake Worth* and *Lake Worth*, 1899. Each sketch inscribed with title
lower left; dated and initialed lower right: *Apl. 19. 1899. WAW.* Pencil on paper, 12 x 8 inches
(sheet size). Collection of Mr. and Mrs. Stephen Cogswell, Atlantic Beach, Florida.

FIGURE 85. *Saunders House, Indian Key, Florida,* 1899, pencil on paper, approximately 4 x 8 inches. This sketch shares a 8 1/4 x 10 1/2 inch page with three other sketches. Inscribed and dated top of sketch: *Saunder's house. Indian Key. Fla—May 4, 1899. (13 Acres).* Collection of Constance Cogswell Miller.

sea level terrain. These sketches convey an accurate description of place, as well as the tranquil mood of the tropical environment. A contemporary guidebook described Lake Worth as a place inhabited by Northerners in the winter, having three miles of "tasteful cottages and costly mansions." Twenty-two miles in length, it abounded with many varieties of ocean fish including pompano, tarpon, millet, and sea trout.[11]

Another sketch Walker made on the trip represents, according to his own inscription, "Saunders house, Indian Key, Fla. May 4, 1899". The one-story wooden cottage with porch across the front is flanked by two smaller structures and set in a yard liberally dotted with young palms. A year or more later Walker made an oil painting (figure 86) after the sketch.[12] Though he initially intended to sell the painting, he wound up presenting it as a gift to Gomecinda and Flora Pacetti, son and daughter-in-law of Bartola and Martha Pacetti. Besides having once borne the price Walker sought for it (and subsequently crossed out with pencil), the back of the academy board is inscribed in Walker's hand: "To Mr & Mrs G A Pacetti/. . . best wishes for health and happiness in their/new home from Wm A. Walker/Indian Key Fla. Oct 190[?]."

FIGURE 86. ***Saunders House, Indian Key, Florida***, circa 1900, oil on academy board, 6 3/8 x 12 inches, signed lower left: *WAWalker*. Inscribed on verso: *To Mr & Mrs G A Pacetti/. . . best wishes for health and happiness in their/new home from Wm. A. Walker/Indian Key Fla. Oct 190 [?]*. The Sewell Family Collection, Vidalia, Louisiana.

Walker intended to copy more oil paintings from the sketches he made on the trip with Gregg. Three other sketches are inscribed, "This has been used," meaning that he had used them as the basis for oil paintings. For Walker one very important purpose of the trip was to garner new material for his brush. Southern Florida was increasingly being developed as a tourist haven at this time, as indicated by the opening of the Royal Poinciana and Flagler's Royal Palm at Miami, another subject sketched by Walker, as well as the number of elegant homes that were under construction in the Lake Worth and Miami areas. Walker was wise to expect ready purchasers for landscapes and views of the attractions in south Florida.

After more than five weeks on the water Walker sketched the familiar facade of Pacetti House at Ponce Park on May 17, 1899. Perhaps the lengthy trip tired him a great deal, for he extended that summer's visit to Arden far into the fall, perhaps to the brink of the Christmas holidays. Walker did manage to travel to Charleston to visit with his nephew Henry Mazyck Walker before heading south again for St. Augustine. 1899 was a hard year, and at its end Walker was plagued with rheumatism and other unnamed ailments.

In the autumn of 1902 Walker again cruised south, revisiting many of the best fishing spots that he and Gregg had discovered three years earlier. As before, Walker sketched appealing scenery that he passed along the way. Though his preferred vantage point remained a boat on the open water, the 1902 sketches reveal him to have moved considerably closer to the shore. From this new perspective, creeks and inlets, previously seen as mere breaks in the vegetation, appear as watery recesses that draw the viewer into the depths of the composition. The 1902 sketches (all in the collection of the Carolina Art Association, Gibbes Museum of Art) abound with small details, while at the same time retaining the broad, atmospheric effects of the earlier drawings. A house, dock, boat, and the individual rocks forming an embankment are drawn with care in *Fish House, New Smyrna* (October 16), while in *Newfound Harbor Key* (December 17) and *Knights Key* (December 19), Walker took great care to delineate several varieties of beach grasses, conveying their differences by varying the pressure and angle of his pencilled marks. Conversely, some of the sketches display an elegantly sparing use of the pencil. In *Canal, Hillsboro River* (figure 87) the white of the paper lends a luminous effect to the water's quiet surface and gives vegetation the appearance of being touched by sunlight.

Walker continued to visually document not only the places he visited, but also the very fish that he caught. He eschewed the wood panel background of the fish still lifes of his youth, adopting at this time, for paintings on canvas, a solid background of deep sea green or light brown; for those on paper, he allowed the creamy color of the paper itself to provide the background. Walker exercised a literal and precise application of pencil and brush, and applied a wide range of colors in subtle, transparent glazes that capture the luminosity of the fishes' scales. The resulting renderings are anatomically correct and beautifully colored in the superb tradition of eighteenth century botanical illustration.

Walker would either position his fish horizontally on the picture surface (figure

FIGURE 87. ***Canal, Hillsboro River***, 1902, pencil on paper, 7 x 10 inches, dated lower right: *Nov. 20. 1902.* Inscribed lower center: *Canal. Hillsboro Rivr.* The Carolina Art Association/Gibbes Museum of Art, Charleston, South Carolina.

89), or, as was the custom of his contemporaries, New Orleans artists George D. Coulon (1822-1904) and Achille Perelli (figure 88), turn the picture surface on the vertical axis and render the fish suspended from a nail by a string through its mouth. (See figure 90.) He would first draw the fish in pencil upon his paper or the prepared ground of an unstretched canvas tacked to a board. Then he would fill in his drawing either with watercolors or oil paints. These paintings show Walker to have been an accurate student of animal classification, for many are inscribed with the fishes' precise scientific and common names. Additionally, a large number of the paintings are dated. Walker's purpose in dating these works was probably so that he or the friends for whom he painted could remember not so much the circumstances of the painting, but rather the memorable catch that the painting celebrated.

In *Yellowtail* (figure 90), Walker excelled, capturing the glowing quality of the scales while subtly blending areas of color, from silver to peach to gold. In other

FIGURE 88. ACHILLE PERELLI (1822-1891). *Bass*, watercolor and gouache on paper, 28 x 22 inches, signed lower right: *A. Perelli N. O.* Collection of Mr. and Mrs. Guy B. Scoggin.

pictures, perhaps ones which he had to complete rapidly, he sacrificed his technique. They appear to be thick and dull in color, showing that he overpainted them instead of allowing the spontaneity of his original pencil drawing to guide his hand. In the fish pictures of this period, we see the widest range of quality of which Walker was capable, from his most sophisticated use of color and control of line to his most primitive.

FIGURE 89. *Sea Trout*, 1903, oil on canvas, 15 7/8 x 30 1/8 inches, signed and dated lower left: *WAWalker. 1903.* The Morris Museum of Art, Augusta, Georgia.

FIGURE 90. *Yellowtail,* 1902, oil on canvas, 17 3/8 x 11 3/8 inches (sight), signed and dated lower left: *WAWalker. 1902.* Inscribed on canvas at stretcher: *Ocyurus Chrysunis. Rabirabia./Yellowtail.* The Parrish Art Museum, Littlejohn Collection, Southampton, New York.

It will be recalled that during the War Between the States Walker had lived in the home of his brother Joseph and was an involved and loving uncle to Joseph's children. At the turn of the century, those children were grown and had families of their own. It was in the homes of two of them that Walker stayed on his semi-annual visits to Charleston. Henry Mazyck Walker (Harry) lived on St. Michael's Place, and his younger brother George lived at various times in Charleston and the nearby village of Summerville, South Carolina. George was married to Claudia Louise Chapman of Charleston, whose gracious and loving nature always made Walker feel welcome; Walker became as fond of her as he was of any of his blood relatives. In addition to their eight children, George's mother Emma Mazyck Walker lived with the family. (Emma was the widow of Walker's brother Joseph.) William Aiken Walker and his sister-in-law, seated opposite each other at the dinner table, would enliven family discussions with stories of their youthful days in Charleston.

In June 1904 the George Walkers lived in Summerville, South Carolina, and it is there that Uncle Willie (as Walker was called by the family) visited them before he journeyed to the mountains at Arden. As usual he enjoyed himself immensely. He wrote to Diehl a few days after his arrival at Arden:

> I came here on 16th much improved in health for the dry pine laden air of Summerville, much sleep, and good late dinners, plenty of fresh milk from fine Jersey (not tin) cow, and good rest and fresh vegitables [*sic*], recuperated my old anatomy very much, and the pleasure of being with my folks counted for much. It was a great pleasure to go to Charleston often and meet my old friends, and be among refined, polite people. Charleston is looking very pretty, for there are many beautiful homes of varied architecture with lovely flower gardens and shade trees, all at their best at this season. I made 3 trips to Isle of Palms, the seashore resort just beyond Sullivan's Island, via ferryboat & electric railway, and made a lot of sketches of scenery very similar to that of Ponce Park that I painted last season, only a far greater number of Palmetto trees on the hills, and the beach and surf is fine. I can sell them next season,

thereby inflating my purse. We had a pic-nic [*sic*] there one day, a fine dinner, and staid [*sic*] until 10 P.M. at the Friday night Hop.

This letter reveals a great deal about Walker's modus operandi. He continually sought opportunities to sketch, and the specificity of locations sketched was of little concern. As Walker himself relates, he visited the Isle of Palms to make sketches for paintings he would execute at Arden and then sell the following winter at Ponce Park as souvenirs of the latter place. This insight is a relief to someone trying to pinpoint the location of Walker's beach views, for the terrain and vegetation on the Atlantic coast of South Carolina and Florida are practically indistinguishable, the only difference between the two states being, as Walker points out, their relative number of palmetto trees. This interchangeability offers a plausible explanation of why Walker, with the exception of paintings made either to fulfill commissions or as gifts to friends or family, dated few of his paintings and inscribed even fewer with their place of execution. Such non-specificity gave Walker flexibility in marketing his wares. Whether landscapes, cabin scenes, or paintings of cotton pickers, Walker was satisfied that he was providing the tourist segment of his clientele with Southern scenes. Beyond being distinctly Southern, it mattered not that the scenes were site-specific.

Walker continued his June 1904 letter to Diehl by describing how he found things at Arden Park Lodge:

> Everything is lovely here, and I am delightfully installed in my former room which is large and pretty, and quiet. The table is exceedingly good, good cooking and variety, and plenty of fresh vegitables [*sic*], which I enjoy hugely after so much tin goods. It is quite cool, too cool night and morning for me, and we sat by fire last night. Two of my friends are building pretty cottages very near the hotel, and another is going to build, all Charlestonians, so I will have more pleasant houses to visit at. Society is fine here, as many nice people have permanent homes nearby, all of whom I visit.[13]

FIGURE 91. *Isle of Palms, South Carolina*, 1904, pencil on paper, 9 x 13 inches, inscribed and dated lower left: *Isle of Palms. S.C./10th June. 1904*. Collection of Mrs. Lucia Cogswell Heins.

Colonel and Mrs. Charles Cotesworth Pinckney may have been two of the Charleston friends that Walker had in mind as he wrote to Diehl. The Pinckneys had a lovely plantation home, Runnymede, on the banks of the Ashley River not far from Charleston, where Walker was often a guest. He made a small oil sketch of Runnymede, as well as of the woods at Arden that surrounded their summer dwelling (figure 59). These pictures are still in the Pinckney family.

Walker had a miserable summer in 1904. He was growing deaf and suffered the entire season with influenza compounded by erysipelas, a bacterial infection causing inflammation of the skin and mucous membranes, which he contracted in August.[14] Perhaps because of his ailments he wanted to flee the mountains before the weather turned terribly cold. He spent part of October in Charleston and was in residence at

Figure 92. ***Orange Grove***, oil on canvas, 12 x 20 inches, signed lower right: *WAWalker*. Collection of Judith S. Vane.

FIGURE 93. *Lighthouse at Ponce Park*, 1904, oil on canvas, 7 3/4 x 17 1/4, signed lower left: *WAWalker*. Dated on canvas at stretcher: *March 22, 1904*. The Sewell Family Collection, Vidalia, Louisiana.

Bartola and Martha Pacetti sold the land on which Ponce de Leon Lighthouse was built to the United States government. Construction was begun in 1883 and completed in 1886, the lighthouse commencing operation in 1887.

Ponce Park by November 18, on which date he again wrote to Diehl, "here I am very much engaged making sketches on the beach and sand hills every day, which I want to finish before it gets too cold. It is pleasant work."[15]

The weather that season remained good, for Walker reported to Diehl just after Christmas, "I have made lots of new sketches and enjoyed the work very much for the scenes are lovely and the sunshine and air health giving."[16] Although no sketches made by Walker at Ponce Park at the end of 1904 have been located, we may look to those done the preceding summer and autumn at the Isle of Palms for an idea of their appearance. (See figure 91.) Executed with a free, spontaneous touch, the Isle of Palms sketches represent small sand hills dotted with palm trees, palmettos, yuccas, and beach grasses. Two of them dated October 6 depict the wispy quality of sea oats, their heavy heads bowed by the breeze. One of these is inscribed with Walker's color notation to himself, "Oct. flowers under Pal[metto]."

Walker's beach scenes in oil and watercolor are truthful to the spirit of his drawings. He made them in small to medium sizes—from miniatures measuring less than two inches square to one canvas that is seventeen inches across. In the paintings, as in the drawings, emphasis is placed upon the scene's natural elements. Clouds, trees, the ocean surface, sand, and grass were the components with which Walker worked. Only occasionally did he admit a structure to the space as he did in *Lighthouse at Ponce Park* (figure 93), a painting that shows the brick lighthouse near the Pacetti establishment. Though set in the distance and nearly blocked from view by plant life, it is nonetheless the focal point of the composition. Another beach view entitled *Edisto Island, South Carolina* (figure 94), painted on academy board, was originally one of a pair. Walker priced it alone at $20.00. The pair could be bought for $35.00, prices comparable to what he charged for cabin scenes.

In the spring of 1905 Walker visited St. Augustine, Biloxi, Mississippi, and, for the first time in eight years, New Orleans. He left Ponce Park earlier than usual, due to the fact that his relationship with the Pacetti family had grown strained. Bartola had died, and while Martha Pacetti still ran the kitchen, their son Gomecinda had taken over the financial management of Pacetti House. "Gome," as he is referred to in Walker's letters, increased Walker's board from $10 to $12 per week, an action that offended the artist deeply, since he had worked for the family for so many years. There may also have been another unpleasant incident, for Walker wrote to Diehl from Biloxi in June, "Our exodus from P. [Ponce] Park seems like a miserable nightmare to look back upon? Beastly. I wrote Gome a few lines, business letter to ship my box of tackle to me here & received a very friendly letter, begging me to write . . . but I have not forgotten my 'send off.'"[17]

Perhaps Walker's visit to the Crescent City was encouraged by his cousin George Langtry, who had invited him to come in 1900, an invitation that Walker apparently declined.[18] Walker did not stay with the Langtrys in 1905, but rather with his "old

FIGURE 94. ***Edisto Island, South Carolina***, oil on academy board, 12 x 9 1/8 inches, signed lower right: *WAWalker*. Inscribed on verso: *9 x 12 $20.00 pair $35.00 Edisto Island, S.C.* Robert M. Hicklin Jr., Inc., Spartanburg, South Carolina.

FIGURE 95. *House at Edisto*, 1889, oil on paper mounted on masonite, 9 7/8 x 14 inches, signed and dated lower left: *WAWalker. Mar. 1889.* Private Collection.

FIGURE 96. ***Biloxi Lighthouse, Biloxi, Mississippi***, 1888, watercolor on paper, 12 x 9 3/4 inches, signed and dated lower left: *WAWalker. April. 28./88.* Inscribed lower center: *Biloxi, Miss.* Courtesy of the Mariners' Museum, Newport News, Virginia.

FIGURE 97. **Lower Matecumbe Key**, 1908, oil on canvas laid down on board, 6 1/4 x 20 3/8 inches, signed and dated lower left: *WAWalker. 16 Dec. 1908.* The Vickers Florida Collection, Jacksonville, Florida.

Lower Matecumbe Key was painted from the deck of William Henry Gregg's yacht, the *Orian.* Walker never mounted the canvas to a stretcher. Rather, the canvas was laid down on board after the paint had dried. Six paintings of fish—three dating to 1902, two to 1908, and one undated—similarly were never stretched. This suggests that on fishing trips Walker would paint *en plein aire,* tacking his canvas to a firm surface in order to work on it, and after it had dried, rolling it up to take back to his base at Ponce Park.

Lower Matecumbe Key was discovered in St. Louis in 1992. Thus, it is likely that it was originally owned by Gregg, a St. Louis resident, who acquired it either by gift or purchase from Walker.

---

landlady" in the French Quarter. His visit seems to have been a social whirl as he caught up with long-time friends:

> At last I am 'highly civilized' having dined elegantly at 6 P.M., with old friends in their beautiful home on Esplanade Ave. last Saturday, day of my arrival, attending the theatre, and Club after the play, and I have had fine dinners ever since, 2 invites for last Sunday—query, why can't I eat 2 dinners on same day? My friend's home contains many of my best paintings, old friends to look on again. . . . He is the one I told you has his lovely summer home at Biloxi, where I may possibly pass the summer.[19]

In a later letter to Dr. Diehl, Walker further described his stay:

> An old friend, leading Portrait Painter in N. O. took me to a fine table

FIGURE 98. **Winter Nest**, 1905, oil on academy board mounted on wood panel, 18 1/2 x 12 1/4, signed and dated lower left: *WAWalker. 1905*. The Warner Collection of Gulf States Paper Corporation, Tuscaloosa, Alabama.

d'hote dinner near Poydras Market, a fine place; dinner begins at 6 P.M. served in 6 or 7 courses, fine soup & salads, chicken every day I was there, everything finely cooked, all the wine you chose to drink, ending with dessert and roquefort cheese & coffee. All this for 75c!! Think of it! The dining room is pretty, the company good, and the kitchen a marvel of cleanliness; it is French, and I told the Madame who presides over the kitchen (in French) that her kitchen was a picture.

As much as he enjoyed renewing old acquaintances, Walker felt a stranger in the city that had once been his home. This was to be his last visit. Continuing his letter to Diehl, he wrote:

I spent one month in N. O. Never have I seen such a great change in a city in 8 years! Improvements everywhere, Canal St. crowded all the time, people walk fast now. . . . It is no longer the quiet, easy going city of a few years ago, but one of progress, and is destined to be a great city, it is now a big one. It is all fine and progressive, but alas, it was pleasanter to me in the olden time.[20]

From New Orleans, Walker went to Biloxi on the balmy Gulf Coast. He was no newcomer to the resort community, for he had sketched Biloxi's lighthouse in watercolors on a visit in 1888. (See figure 96.) He found a few changes from the old days, but they left a more favorable impression upon him compared to the changes he had in found New Orleans. He wrote to Diehl:

This place is very pretty and much improved also, has trolly [*sic*] cars, Yacht Club, Theater and many lovely homes with the grand old oaks on the lawns, quite a little city. I have a fine cool room on the beach, fine view of the Gulf & Ship Island (13 miles away) only rooms rented, & I take my meals 2 doors away, fine table and pleasant company, so I am quiet in my room, which means much, no children to bother me. I have not been fishing yet, but am now rigged up and expect an old friend soon who will keep house here, to fish with, fine old sport from Charleston who has spent much time here. . . .[21]

He got to Arden later that summer and stayed quite late into the fall before going to Florida. He spent most of the month of December 1905 in St. Augustine from where he again wrote to Diehl:

Hier bin ich endlich aus dem 'Cold Storage,' Gott sei dank. I was about to write today when your letter reached me forwarded from Skyland, which place I left on afternoon of 1st arriving here a little afer [*sic*] 11 A.M. 2d Saturday. The mercury stood 15° above zero early the morning of the day I left (horribly cold) and I landed here amid flowers, & lovely green lawns & trees, in a warm atmosphere, about 70°, and never have trees & grass looked of such welcome green to me before! Sunday was warm also, but Monday cold, 33° I heard, high winds, cloudy at times, but warmer now, & I can keep warm as a toast in my snug den (the old one) at Tugby's where I am very comfortable.

This little city is more beautiful than ever, many new cottages built in past 3 years, & many large palmetto trees set out, adding much to the picture. I have had a warm welcome from many old friends, which is pleasant. Hotel Magnolia opens on 11th & I will then take my meals there as usual & play whist. The hotel is being put in fine shape.

I am still suffering from a severe cold caught during a freeze three weeks ago, much pain in my back, head out of fix & c., [get] about but poorly, and sleep but little, but this climate will right the latter after awhile. How glorious the white breakers and green sea look after the bare cold brown mountains. Ah![22]

He was quite happy at St. Augustine; in fact, he was having such a good time that he questioned whether he would return to Ponce Park that season in light of how he had felt towards the Pacettis when he had last left.[23] Not until March 1908 is there evidence of his having gone again to Pacetti House.

Walker's hearing, which for unknown causes he had partially lost in 1904, was suddenly and just as mysteriously restored to him in 1908. He wrote a poem in celebration of his cure. Entitled "Ode to a Mosquito," he penned it at Arden on August 5, 1908:

Oh you dear little musical skeeter!
How dear were the notes of your sweet little song.
You charming, delectable pestiferous creeter
That gladened [sic] my ears that were deaf for so long!

Enjoy thy bright life of biting and stinging,
I'll not begin this new life by a killing;
There's room in this world for you and me singing.
Pursue thy gay life, I am perfectly willing.

To be in this world and yet not be of it,
Has been for long years my lot in this life;
The sounds that I missed how much did I covet
Why should I rejoyce [sic] now in murder and strife.[24]

At Arden the summer of 1910 Walker added colorful studies of forest vegetation to his oeuvre. In some paintings, he depicted mushrooms, lichen, and fungi *in situ*, that is, actually growing from the woodland floor and backed by a dark, impenetrable mass of tree trunks and leaves (figure 99). The dark, moist undergrowth of a wood as a subject in painting was the invention of seventeenth century Dutch artist Otto Marseus van Schrieck (1619?-1678). In van Schrieck's work flowers, mushrooms, and creeping vines form the setting for the playing out of the *vanitas* theme: hidden amongst the plant life snakes lie in wait for toads and, in turn, toads for butterflies. While Walker's paintings lack this ghastly drama, the manner in which he portrayed forest vegetation is ultimately rooted in the work of the Dutch artist. Van Schrieck had many followers in the Netherlands and Italy in the 1600s. In the nineteenth century, the painting of plants and insects as they existed in nature was revived by the Pre-Raphaelites, most notably in the writings of British critic John Ruskin and in paintings and watercolors by the American John William Hill.

As an alternative to the forest floor still life, Walker would cut his flora and carry it back to the studio, either to paint it as a spray floating against a solid brown background or as a tabletop arrangement. In either case, he employed a shallow

FIGURE 99. *Forest Floor at Arden*, 1910, oil on canvas, 7 1/4 x 11 3/4 inches (sight), signed and dated lower left: *WAWalker./Sep. 17. 1910.* Collection of Mrs. Edward Hall Walker, Charleston, South Carolina.

---

picture space, placing emphasis upon the natural objects and their varied colors, forms, and textures.

After the autumn of 1910, Walker's painting and sketching activity decreased drastically. He wrote to Diehl the following February from Ponce Park:

> There have been plenty of vacant rooms so far and I have my easel still in your room adjoining mine although I have done very little painting since the Col. arrived and will vacate it as soon as Mrs. Gome tells me to do so.[25]

Walker was left to his own resources. It was a time of introspection. The only self-portraits he ever painted date to 1913 and 1914, when he was seventy-five years old. (See figure 101.) Both show his full, white beard, well-combed, its ends twisted and neatly arranged atop his collar, and the waxed ends of his handlebar moustache

FIGURE 100. *Still Life with Watermelons, Peppers, and Corn*, oil on paper, 6 1/4 x 5 3/4 inches. The Sewell Family Collection, Vidalia, Louisiana.

groomed with equal precision. They reveal Walker's concern for persona. His shoes were always polished to a mirror finish, and his colorful cravats were a matter of great pride to him. When complimented on one, he would hold his head high, lift his shoulders, and say slowly, obviously happy to be asked, "My dear, that is pure silk and it comes from France."[26]

His grandniece Josephine Walker Martin, daughter of George and Claudia Walker, was a child and teenager when she knew him. She recalled, "Uncle Willie was a charming gentleman. As I remember he very often wore a dinner jacket that went halfway down his thigh. He was a very dapper, very particular gentleman of the old school."[27]

Notwithstanding his fastidious ways, he knew how to have fun. Mrs. Martin's

sister Julia Walker Bradley remembers the circus coming to Charleston when she was a teenager and that Uncle Willie went along with the family. "His eyes just twinkled, he was so delighted and amused by everything. He had never been to the circus before."[28]

Mrs. Martin and Mrs. Bradley said that it was their mother, Claudia Chapman Walker, who was responsible for Walker landing more often at their house than at the home of one of his other nephews or nieces. When he would visit them at 134 Cannon Street in Charleston, their brothers moved out of their bedroom so Walker could have a room to himself. The room was located on the second floor right over the front door. It had a window facing the street through which the breezes would blow from the Ashley River, only one-and-a-half blocks away.

There was a piano in the parlor of the Cannon Street house, and knowing how Walker loved to sing and play, Claudia would encourage him to do so for the family. Mrs. Bradley recalled, "He had a lovely baritone voice, and he would play the piano without reading any music. Mother would say, 'you children come listen to your Uncle Willie,' and we'd go into the front parlor and have to be as quiet as mice. We sat there and he'd sing. We had a lot of fun with him."[29]

The pleasure that his grandnieces found in Walker's visits seems to have been mutual. On his first visit to the family after they had moved from Summerville into the house on Cannon Street, Walker, with childlike enthusiasm, wrote to his friend Diehl about the modern conveniences of the new house, as well as the pleasure he took in doing things with the family.

> Charleston, SC
> 134 Cannon Street
> 26 May 1912
>
> My dear doctor,
>
> I received a kind letter from Miss [Katie] Diehl a few days ago which I will answer soon, but owing you a letter I will cancel that debt today. . . . My time has been most pleasantly passed here as I am living in a beautiful house with large rooms, electric lights throughout and gas for cooking, and my

nephew & his wife are devoted to me and so are his nice children, all vie to make it pleasant. We go to bed at 12 o'clock or after, quite a change from Pacetti house, breakfast at 8:30 (Sundays at 10) and dine after 3, suits me fine. The lot is over 100 ft wide & 270 feet deep, flower & vegitable [*sic*] gardens and fruit & shade trees, one of the largest lots in the city, one block & a half from the Ashley river so get all the breezes. I gave my three pretty young nieces & the father and mother of two of them a Theatre party one night and felt pleased to escort such a pretty, beautifully dressed party. I have two good games of whist a week which I enjoy heap much. My nephew's eldest boy [William Walker] is a cadet at the S. C. Military Academy—the 'Citadel'—a fine institution and the Col. Commandant is a friend of the family so we have him in our whist games, a very agreeable gentleman. My niece and I went to view the dress parade of the cadets Friday afternoon and saw it from the window of Col. Bond's office in the Citadel who entertained us; I was much interested as they are a fine body of young men, over 200, and stand very high in their drill.

Their band is composed of cadets, 25 in number, and the boys get a splendid education at the Academy. My nephew's wife is a bright well educated woman and good looking, and her children have inherited brightness and good looks *and politeness* for all say 'yes' or 'no thank you, sir' in place of 'yes' or 'no' of twentieth century rudeness! So was I and their father and mother educated, and it is delightful to me to be among my compatriots here for politeness is the rule and Charlestonians are noted for their politeness.

We have had a delightful month of May, and the flowers and shade trees make the old city look lovely and the many magnolias perfume the air. We have the latter in our garden, but yesterday was hot 95° fahr I heard, but was pleasant up here; it is 86° in my room, noon, but nice breeze and I am comfortable. Been cold at Asheville, NC 54°-56° so presume I will need fire in my room at Arden next week as I expect to go thither and my old comfortable den is prepared for me. I have had a good rest and want to get to work again. I have done some sketching on the little cabin pictures. I will

FIGURE 101. *Self-portrait of William Aiken Walker*, 1913, oil on panel, 12 1/4 x 9 1/2 inches, signed and dated lower left: *WAWalker./1913.* The Carolina Art Association/Gibbes Museum of Art, Charleston, South Carolina.

paint in the mountains, in my room here, but want to settle down to real work. . . . A splendid breeze is blowing through my window now. I will close with kindest regards to all at your home.

Yours sincerely,
Wm. A. Walker[30]

Walker passed the remainder of the summer of 1912 quietly at Arden, as he would do for the next eight summers. Over the years he had become a close friend to the Beale family, owners of Arden Park Lodge. At Beale Manor, their nearby home, they hosted colorful dances for which the musical accompaniment was the fiddle, dulcimer, and harmonica of the local mountain folk.

As a young girl, Evelyn Saffold Taber was a guest at Arden Park Lodge during the summer of 1916. From that one visit, she was left with vivid memories of the Beale family and the colorful Mr. Walker. Writing years later, she recalled that by day Walker was off into the woods with his art supplies, but by evening he was quite sociable. Seated on the wide porch of the lodge, he would attract a large circle of persons around him, old and young alike, and entertain them into the night with tales of his adventures in Cuba, New Orleans, and Baltimore, as well as his camping trips in Florida. "I recall one story he told us of a solitary fishing trip, camping in the woods under most primitive conditions. He said 'And on this particular expedition, I dined entirely from tins.' The incongruity of *dining* under such bucolic circumstances struck our sense of humor and all of us laughed heartily. But that was William Aiken Walker: he *dined* whether from tins or at The Ritz."[31]

Walker suffered the inevitable losses of someone who lives a long life. Dr. Diehl, who seems to have been an intimate, and Martha Pacetti, his landlady and friend of thirty years, both died in 1917. Arden Park Lodge burned to the ground shortly thereafter; the exact date is uncertain. Walker resided at Pacetti House—his last documentable stay there—in 1919 and spent the summer of that year at Arden. There he painted the ruins of the inn where he had enjoyed so many happy days. *Ruins, Arden Park Lodge* (1919; The Warner Collection of Gulf States Paper Corporation, Tuscaloosa, Alabama) and *Chimney, North Carolina* (1918; Collection of

FIGURE 102. **Cabin**, circa 1905-1920, watercolor on paper, 7 1/4 x 10 1/8 inches (sight), signed lower left: *WAWalker*. Collection of Mrs. Edward Hall Walker, Charleston, South Carolina.

Mrs. George Walker Cogswell, Atlantic Beach, Florida) each show a lone chimney surrounded by trees and rubble.[32] He returned to Arden the following summer for what would be his last visit. Nearing eighty-two years of age, Walker had outlived most of his contemporaries, yet he remained vigorous to the very end. That final summer he tromped around outside with pencils in hand. He set down on paper, in a firm hand, a sketch of two black children standing beside a shack. It is inscribed, "Arden Oct. 15, 1920." Drawn eleven weeks before he died, it is Walker's last documentable work of art.[33]

From Arden, Walker went to Charleston to spend Christmas with George and Claudia Walker. At their home he took ill. He died on January 3, 1921, of acute cardiac dilatation, or enlargement of the heart.[34] His funeral was held two days later in the parlor of the house in which he died, the house that had for nine years felt so much like home. Afterwards, his body was buried in Charleston's Magnolia Cemetery. His obituary read:

> Mr. William A. Walker died yesterday at the residence of his nephew, Mr. George William Walker, of Charleston. For some years Mr. Walker had made his home in Arden, N.C., in the summer and in Ponce Park, Fla., in the winter, dividing his time between these places, usually stopping in Charleston, his native town, for several weeks in going from one to the other.
>
> A few days ago he contracted a severe cold and failed to rally from its effects. He was in his eighty-second year. He was recognized as an artist in representing the scenes of the Old South, his paintings attracting much attention. He was also gifted as a musician. In spite of his advanced age Mr. Walker's faculties were almost unimpaired. The funeral will be held tomorrow afternoon at Mr. George W. Walker's residence, 134 Cannon Street. The J. M. Connelley Company has charge of the funeral arrangements.[35]

Walker died intestate, although, as his heirs were surprised to discover, he died a prosperous man. His total estate was valued at $13,441.28, which included deposits at banks in Charleston and Augusta, Georgia, $105 in cash found in his trunk, and 110 "Water and Oil Sketches" left at Ponce Park, at Charleston, and with the Standard Photo Company of New Orleans.[36]

In the 1890s Walker had discovered new and appealing Southern scenes that distracted him from his trademark cotton fields and laborers. He turned to subjects that were personally significant and pleasing: Mount Pisgah from his window at Arden Park Lodge; the Ponce de Leon Hotel at St. Augustine; the lighthouse at Ponce Park; and fine fishing spots that lured him and his companions further down the Florida coast. He found that other people appreciated these views and would

FIGURE 103. ***Bird in Flight, Ocklawaha River***, oil on board, 10 x 6 inches, signed lower right: *WAWalker*. Inscribed on verso: *#18 Ocklawaha Riv. $12.00*. The Vickers Florida Collection, Jacksonville, Florida.

buy them as souvenirs, just as they had purchased scenes celebrating the Cotton Kingdom. Still life painting, a genre which he had largely abandoned after 1879, captured his interest again. He painted fish caught in Florida waters and the berries, leaves, and mushrooms that grew abundantly in the forest at Arden.

These later years, which found Walker as artistically active as ever, also offer a close look at Walker the man. From his letters we know that he enjoyed fishing, fine dining, and fine wines. He formed enduring friendships and was a steadfast correspondent. He cherished family ties and made a point to spend time with his relatives in Charleston on a regular basis.

Walker's personal drive and professional commitment were such that he remained a practicing artist to the end. Though plagued with various illnesses and the handicap of deafness in later years, he never completely lost his will to paint and draw.

Epilogue

After Walker's death, the popularity of his paintings hardly suffered. In 1939 one of his cotton picker portraits entitled *Calhoun's Slaves* was included in the first exhibition of American genre painting ever to be held at the Metropolitan Museum of Art in New York City. This landmark exhibition, *Life in America*, coincided with the New York World's Fair of that same year.

A mere four months later Harry MacNeill Bland of the Bland Gallery in New York assembled a one-man show of the work of William Aiken Walker. The exhibition showcased thirty-one paintings and two lithographs by Currier and Ives after paintings by Walker. Thirteen of the paintings were on loan from private collections, two of those in the Northeast. The remaining eighteen were apparently purchased by Bland and offered for resale in his gallery. Drawing upon the knowledge of museum professionals in New Orleans and Charleston, as well as recollections from Walker family members, Bland was able to compile a brief, fairly accurate biography of the artist, which was printed in the flyer accompanying the show.

The magazine, *Art News*, in reviewing the Bland Gallery show was impressed by the intense realism of the scenes, one of the qualities New Orleans critics had responded to thirty and forty years earlier. The anonymous reviewer wrote, "[The pictures] make an uncommonly good display. For instance, in *Negro Cabin Showing Outdoor Fireplace*, note the gourds for purple martins hanging on the queer-looking bare tree to the left of the cottage. In *Negro Home and Family* note the care lavished upon expressing the quality of Spanish moss. Note the accuracy of the scenes of the cotton plantations." This was Walker's first notice in a national arts publication. The reviewer was obviously ignorant of the widespread reputation Walker and his paintings commanded in the South, citing the lithographs made by Currier and Ives as saving the artist from obscurity. He wrote, "These pictures, though by a man born in Charleston, are not only of South Carolina but of Florida and Louisiana.

Most of them date from the eighties. Currier & Ives lithographed two of the Louisiana views and it was from their lithographs that one of the definite clues to the painter was found."[1]

Scattered attention continued to be paid to Walker's paintings in museum publications dating to the late 1940s through the fifties. One of Walker's fish still lifes painted in 1860 was illustrated in the catalogue of the M. and M. Karolik Collection of American paintings published by the Museum of Fine Arts of Boston in 1949.

Mississippi Panorama, a book published by the City Art Museum of St. Louis in 1950, offered no new biographical information on Walker and no critical commentary on his paintings. What it did do, however, was illustrate three of Walker's paintings and one lithograph, all set on the levee of the Mississippi River at New Orleans.

A breakthrough in Walker scholarship was made by art critic and author Marie Louise D'Otrange Mastai in her article, "The World of William Aiken Walker," published in *Apollo* magazine in June 1961. A footnote to the article stated that the author was preparing a book on Walker. It is a loss that Mastai's book was never published, for she was one of the first scholars to recognize Walker as a quintessential American artist. Mastai's only fault was that she, like Harry Bland before her, wrote under the false assumption that "cotton fields . . . rude but picturesque cabins . . . and last, the busy quays of the far-off port" were the subjects of Walker's paintings for the entirety of his career.[2]

Lastly, and until now the chief resource on William Aiken Walker, is the book *William Aiken Walker, Southern Genre Painter*, by Roulhac Toledano and the late August Trovaioli, published by Louisiana State University Press in 1972. It is a commendable achievement. Trovaioli, a junior high school principal, completed all the research and prepared the book in his spare time. The book's strengths are numerous. Beginning his research in the 1960s, Trovaioli interviewed many people who had personally known William Aiken Walker, including the artist's grandnieces and -nephews, Gomecinda Pacetti, proprietor of Pacetti House, and the Misses Beale, whose parents owned Arden Park Lodge at Arden, North Carolina.

The book also succeeds in representing through illustrations nearly every type of subject matter that Walker painted, including, for the first time, selected portraits of white subjects and two hand-colored photographs of the artist himself. Also presented are some of the numerous pencil sketches, made late in Walker's career, that depict the beaches of South Carolina and Florida. The book provides a unique visual record of many paintings and drawings that have subsequently changed hands and in many cases are "lost" today.

Where Trovaioli and Toledano's book falls short is in documentation. Letters written by Walker are frequently misdated; in some cases, two or more letters written as much as a year apart are strung together to read as one, making for chronological confusion. Certain broad assumptions are made without any verification, such as the assertion that Walker's mother, as a young widow, took her boys from Charleston to live in Baltimore. Additionally, it misidentifies William Aiken Walker as the Captain W. A. Walker who was a Confederate cavalry officer. Yet, so comprehensive a treatment of the life and works of William Aiken Walker is the Trovaioli/Toledano book that it has ever since been recognized as the ultimate authority on the artist and has been quoted or otherwise cited in all subsequent material until the present, including articles in newspapers and journals, entries under Walker's name in artists' dictionaries, and catalogue entries prepared by galleries and museums.

It is hoped that *The Sunny South: The Life and Art of William Aiken Walker* not only corrects misinformation presented in the Trovaioli/Toledano book, but also offers scholars a clear, chronological arrangement of material about William Aiken Walker upon which future discoveries may be hung. Historical background, where provided, is intended to help the reader understand Walker's personal and professional choices—choices steeped in the history and heritage of the Old South.

To survey Walker's entire career is to look first to the live animals and dead game still lifes of his youth, painted to grace the dining rooms and parlors of ante-bellum Charleston. There followed the hand-colored photographic portraits, all the rage in the South on the eve of the War Between the States, to which every artist rushed to claim proficiency. The war itself called for the skills of painters who were trained observers, and here Walker's detail-oriented hand and eye won him a job with the Engineers Corps and resulted in a map of Charleston drawn under his supervision. The age of sentimentality that swept the country in the aftermath of the war found Walker in Baltimore painting genre scenes of the city's street urchins, idealized and industrious.

The failure of Reconstruction brought with it the death of any real hope for meaningful opportunity on the part of Southern blacks. It was at this time that Walker, living in the Deep South, discovered a subject with universal appeal, a signature subject that would forever be identifiable as his own. The rural black field hand, toiling under a merciless sun, and the urban black laborer, who could at best find a day's work at arduous tasks, became Walker's—and his audience's—enduring symbols of the South. These he painted in a range of prices to satisfy any pocketbook, from large canvases painted on commission to postcard-size souvenirs. Finally there were the small, quiet landscapes and still lifes of Walker's advanced years, to which he brought techniques perfected over a lifetime.

What all this adds up to is a life's work full of variety, always adaptable to changing circumstances and changing tastes. Walker's paintings and drawings mirror his surroundings, showing, for instance, the appearance of Lake Worth when it was a tropical retreat, Charleston's Circular Church before its post-war reconstruction, and the costume of black sharecroppers in the 1880s. They also tell the story of changing social attitudes, of how Walker as a white Southerner viewed blacks and how, in turn, his patrons viewed them as well. This is Walker's legacy. As a chronicler of bygone times and people and places that today retain only a shadow of their former appearance and meaning, Walker's creations will be valued as long as there are those who seek to know the past and who value pictorial expression.

Chronology

Under each year, works of art are listed first. The title of each work is given in italics, followed by the month and day on which it was done (if known), medium, dimensions, its present or last known location, and for works of art illustrated in this book, their figure number. Unless otherwise specified, medium is oil on canvas or academy board, and dimensions are given in inches. Only works of art which are dated in the artist's hand have been given a place in the chronology; works with circa dates—no matter how sound they may be—have not been entered. Not all works of art listed herein have been examined by the author; therefore the chronology is not to be interpreted as a definitive listing of authentic works. For those works whose present location is unknown, a source is cited where an illustration of the work may be found. Complete reference information on these sources can be found in the bibliography.

Following the works of art under each year are listed other accomplishments, activities, and facts pertinent to that year.

1839	William Aiken Walker born in Charleston, South Carolina, March 11.
1841	Father, John Falls Walker, dies, June or July.
1849	First home on East Bay Street, Charleston, South Carolina sold by older brother George William Walker in accordance with terms of their father's will.
1850	Exhibits oil painting(s) at the South Carolina Institute Fair, Charleston, South Carolina, November.

1858   *Still Life with Virginia Partridges.* December 21. 18 1/2 x 14 1/4. Robert M. Hicklin Jr., Inc., Spartanburg, South Carolina. (figure 5)

Exhibits "a copy of one of Herring's farmyard scenes" at Messrs. Courtenay and Co.'s store, Charleston, South Carolina, June.

1859   *Dog 'Wasp'.* 14 5/8 x 12. The Carolina Art Association/Gibbes Museum of Art, Charleston, South Carolina. (figure 6)

Bulls Defending a Cow. 18 x 26. The Sewell Family Collection, Vidalia, Louisiana. (figure 7)

Exhibits "a game study showing a few ducks suspended against a wall" at Messrs. Courtenay's and Co.'s book store, Charleston, South Carolina, February.

One Oil Painting, Bulls Defending a Cow and *One Oil Painting, Copy of an Old Picture* (a pair, no. 57) exhibited in the ninth annual fair of the South Carolina Institute, Charleston, South Carolina, November 15.

1860   *Blue-winged Teal Drakes.* 19 3/4 x 16. The Warner Collection of Gulf States Paper Corporation, Tuscaloosa, Alabama.

Duck, Bob-whites and Rails. 24 x 20. Collection of J. H. Woodward, 1964. Illustrated in Mastai, *Connoisseur*, p. 79.

Dollarfish and Sheepshead. 24 x 20. The Museum of Fine Arts, Boston, Massachusetts.

Still Life with a Bottle of Cognac, Crabs, and Prawns. 32 x 16. Location unknown. Illustrated in Mastai, *Connoisseur*, p. 78.

Address as it appeared in Charleston, South Carolina city directory: "Walker, W. A. artist home Rutledge corner Doughty." Brother, Joseph Flint Walker, also at this address.

1861   Enlisted in Second Palmetto Regiment, South Carolina Volunteers, at Charleston, May 9.

Discharge from Confederate States Army signed at Richmond, Virginia, August 31.

1862   *Confederate Encampment at Seven Pines (Fair Oaks), Virginia.* 7 x 10. Collection of Jay P. Altmayer.

1863   Records Union ironclad attack on Charleston Harbor in original sketch, April 7.

Mother, Mary Elizabeth Flint Walker, dies, July 19.

In his capacity of draughtsman, Confederate Engineer Corps, produces *Map of Charleston and its Defences,* [*sic*] November 28.

1864   *Sheepshead.* 20 x 14 1/8. The Warner Collection of Gulf States Paper Corporation, Tuscaloosa, Alabama.

Set of playing cards, sixteen of which are hand decorated by Walker in oil, ink, and watercolor. Painted at Charleston, South Carolina, September. 3 1/4 x 2 inches, each. Collection of Jay P. Altmayer. (figure 12)

Composes music and lyrics to "My Love is Far Away," July 4.

Composes "La Manola (Polka Redowa)," July 21.

Writes poem, "Belle ange que j'aime," at Charleston, South Carolina, October.

Exhibits *Ruins of Ft. Sumter as Seen from Ft. Johnson* at Dr. Aimar's drug store, Charleston, South Carolina, October.

1866   *Ducks and Woodcocks.* 24 x 18. Collection of Jay P. Altmayer. (figure 2)

Dollarfish and Sheepshead. 21 x 17. Collection of Jay P. Altmayer. (figure 8)

Completes "Mes Pensées," a manuscript book of poems, at Charleston, South Carolina. "Mes Pensées" is owned by the Carolina Art Association/Gibbes Museum of Art, Charleston, South Carolina. (figure 14)

1868   *St. Finbar's Roman Catholic Cathedral.* 11 3/4 x 18 3/4. The Carolina Art Association/Gibbes Museum of Art, Charleston, South Carolina. (figure 11)

Circular Church in Ruins. 19 1/2 x 15 1/2. Private Collection. (figure 10)

Address as it appeared in Baltimore, Maryland city directory: "Walker Wm. A. artist and teach. of languages 16 1/2 N. Charles."

1869 *Trophies of the Hunt.* A pair of paintings, each 27 x 20. Location unknown. Illustrated in sale catalogue, Parke-Bernet, New York, New York, January 27, 1965, lot no. 32. One of the pair, *Hanging Rabbit, Duck and Quail* is illustrated in Trovaioli and Toledano, p. 103, fig. 9.

Self-portrait of William Aiken Walker. Photograph colored with oil paints. 6 1/2 x 4. The Sewell Family Collection, Vidalia, Louisiana. (figure 1)

Negro Youth with Basket on Head or *Flower Boy.* 10 x 6. Collection of Jay P. Altmayer.

Leaves New York on steamship *Eagle* for Havana, Cuba, Thursday, December 9.

Arrives in Havana, Cuba and starts to work in the gallery of C. D. Fredricks y Davis, Calle de la Habana 108, December 15.

1870 Completes forty-seven pictures in his Havana, Cuba studio by January 1.

Sees performance of comic opera "El Campanorel" at Grand Teatro Tacon, Havana, Cuba, Saturday, January 8.

Visits Guanabacoa, Cuba, Sunday, January 16.

Visits Marianao, Cuba, Sunday, January 23.

Makes a sketch in oil of "Habana St." from his studio window, Saturday, January 29.

Makes a sketch of "Relea de Gallos," Monday, January 31. Writes in his journal that he has completed eighty-seven pictures for a total compensation of $221.60.

Writes in Cuban diary for the last time; contemplates returning home, February 13.

1871   *Newsboy Selling the Baltimore Sun.* 11 1/4 x 7 1/2. The High Museum of Art, Atlanta, Georgia; Gift of Mr. and Mrs. George E. Missbach (74.7). (figure 18)

Gathering Herbs. 12 1/4 x 9 1/8. Collection of Mr. and Mrs. Quincy Scarborough, Fayetteville, North Carolina. (figure 15)

The Surprize. [*sic*] June. 12 x 16. Collection of August P. Trovaioli, Grand Bay, Alabama, 1972. Illustrated in Trovaioli and Toledano, p. 103, fig. 8.

One of the Attractions of the Seashore and *A Native of South Carolina* included in an exhibition of the work of Baltimore, Maryland artists at Perrigo & Kohl's gallery, Fayette and Charles Streets, Baltimore, Maryland, April.

A Native of South Carolina purchased by Mr. Orndorff for $16 and *One of the Attractions of the Seashore* purchased by W. W. Remington for $18 at auction in Baltimore, Maryland, April 25 and 26.

Paintings by Walker included in second annual exhibition of the Maryland Academy of Art, Baltimore, Maryland, December.

On the Lawn purchased by Mr. Wilson for $25 at auction, Myers and Hedian's Store, Baltimore, Maryland, December 17.

1872   *Boy with Goat.* 11 x 8. The Morris Museum of Art, Augusta, Georgia. (figure 20)

A Few Bars' Rest. 27 x 22. Location unknown.

Exhibits *The Homeless Boy, Home Again,* and *On the Lookout* in Louisville Industrial Exposition, Louisville, Kentucky, September - October.

Currier & Ives publishes lithograph entitled *A Free Lunch.* 11 1/4 x 14. The Library of Congress, Washington, D.C. (figure 23)

Address as it appeared in Baltimore, Maryland city directory: "Walker Wm. A., artist, 20 North Charles; dwelling 109 North Charles."

1873   *A Young Girl.* Photograph colored with oil paints. 13 1/4 x 10 1/2 (oval). Location unknown. Illustrated in sale catalogue, Sotheby's, New York, New York, January 31 - February 3, 1979, lot no. 498.

Self-portrait. Photograph colored with oil paints. 5 1/2 x 5 1/2. Collection of Felix H. Kuntz, New Orleans, Louisiana, 1972. Illustrated in Trovaioli and Toledano, p. 67, fig. 16.

Address as it appeared in Louisville, Kentucky city directory: "4th, southwest corner Green; residence 212 5th, near Walnut."

1874   *View of Galveston Harbor.* 29 x 63. The Rosenberg Library, Galveston, Texas. (figure 21)

1875   Address as it appeared in Galveston, Texas city directory: "Walker, William A., artist, cor. Market and 21st, r[esidence]. same."

1876   *Still Life with Cheese, Bottle and Mouse.* 20 x 16. Collection of Malcolm W. Monroe, New Orleans, Louisiana.

San Jose Mission. 23 1/4 x 35. The Witte Museum and the San Antonio Museum Association, San Antonio, Texas. (figure 22)

Portrait of Kate Wilson Smith. 17 1/4 x 14 1/4. Private Collection. (figure 29)

Several paintings by Walker sold at auction in New Orleans, Louisiana, February 23.

1878   Composes "O, Salutaris Hostia" at Sullivan's Island, South Caro-
            lina, August.

1879   *Old Shoe with Mice.* Oil on wood. 9 x 12. The Louisiana State
            Museum Collection, New Orleans, Louisiana.

            Oysters at the Charleston Hotel. 17 7/8 x 21 3/4. The Warner Collec-
            tion of Gulf States Paper Corporation, Tuscaloosa, Alabama.
            (figure 30)

            Address as it appeared in Augusta, Georgia city directory:
            "Walker, William A., artist, 206 Broad, r[esidence] 113 Greene."

1880   *Portrait of Lottie Mitchell.* 7 7/16 x 6 3/4. The Historic New
            Orleans Collection, New Orleans, Louisiana. (figure 27)

            Poker Game. 7 x 10. Collection of Jay P. Altmayer. (figure 24)

            Ruins of the Church at Old Dorchester. 12 x 7 1/2. Robert M. Hicklin
            Jr., Inc., Spartanburg, South Carolina. (figure 31)

            Address as it appeared in Augusta, Georgia city directory:
            "Walker, William A., painter, 702 Broad."

1881   *The Cotton Plantation.* 21 1/2 x 35. Private Collection. (figure 37)

            Cotton Wagon. 20 x 24. Collection of F. Walton Bailey, Spring-
            field, Ohio, 1961.

Big B Cotton Plantation. 25 x 40. Collection of Jay P. Altmayer. (figure 34)

Mica-Dale. Watercolor and ink on paperboard. 11 x 8. Collection of Mrs. Lisa Cogswell Kirk, Springfield, Massachusetts.

Ruffles and Rags. 16 x 12. Collection of Jay P. Altmayer.

The Sunny South. 22 1/8 x 36 1/8. Collection of Dr. and Mrs. Ron Lawson, Memphis, Tennessee. (figure 35)

View from the Reverend D. C. Howell's Farm, N. C. 22 x 36. Robert M. Hicklin Jr., Inc., Spartanburg, South Carolina. (figure 58)

1882   *Portrait of Miss Percy Ferguson, Greenville, Mississippi.* 50 x 30. Collection of Helen S. Martin. (figure 25)

1883   *Newsboy* or *Post No Bills.* 11 x 6. The Warner Collection of Gulf States Paper Corporation, Tuscaloosa, Alabama. (figure 45)

             Going to Market. 22 x 14. The Warner Collection of Gulf States Paper Corporation, Tuscaloosa, Alabama.

             The Levee. 19 1/2 x 29 1/2. Collection of J. Cornelius Rathborne, New Orleans, Louisiana. (See figure 43.)

             A Cotton Plantation on the Mississippi. 20 x 30. Gilcrease Museum, Tulsa, Oklahoma. (See figure 36.)

Cotton Plantation on the Mississippi. 13 x 26. Collection of Jay P. Altmayer.

Plantation Scene, Sharecroppers. 14 1/4 x 23 3/4. The Warner Collection of Gulf States Paper Corporation, Tuscaloosa, Alabama.

Cotton Gin, Adams County, Mississippi. 14 x 22. Didier's Inc., New Orleans, Louisiana, 1973. Illustrated in *The Magazine Antiques*, April 1973, p. 706.

Policeman Spies Darkies Pilfering Cotton from Bales, New Orleans Levee. 6 7/8 x 12 3/4. Collection of Malcolm W. Monroe, New Orleans, Louisiana.

Exhibits *Rattlesnake Bayou, Mississippi* at Blessing's, New Orleans, Louisiana, July.

Exhibits four paintings at Lilienthal's Art Gallery, 121 Canal Street, New Orleans, Louisiana.

1884   *Negroes Returning from Market*. 18 x 30. The Warner Collection of Gulf States Paper Corporation, Tuscaloosa, Alabama.

Hauling Moss. 6 x 10. The Warner Collection of Gulf States Paper Corporation, Tuscaloosa, Alabama. (figure 53)

Negro Cotton Hands with Wagon. 14 x 24. With Kennedy Galleries, Inc., New York, New York, 1972. Illustrated in Trovaioli and Toledano, p. 114, fig. 15.

Gwine ter Der Expersishun. 16 1/2 x 11. Collection of Jay P. Altmayer.

Wagon Scene with Barrels. 18 x 30. The Warner Collection of Gulf States Paper Corporation, Tuscaloosa, Alabama. (figure 55)

Currier & Ives publishes lithographs of *The Levee, New Orleans* (figure 43) and *A Cotton Plantation on the Mississippi* (figure 36), both painted in 1883.

Spends summer in Florida and South Carolina.

Exhibits *The Ripe Rice Field, Gwine ter Der Expersishun,* and a picture "showing a cotton field with a distant fringe of cypress swamp" in fall exhibition, Seebold's Art Gallery, New Orleans, Louisiana, November.

The Ripe Rice Field sells for $45 at Seebold's, New Orleans, Louisiana, December 2.

1885   *The Levee at New Orleans.* 11 1/2 x 17 1/2. With Hirschl & Adler Galleries, Inc., New York, New York, 1969.

Auntie in Wagon with Oxen. 10 x 18. Formerly with Kennedy Galleries, Inc., New York, New York. Illustrated in Trovaioli and Toledano, p. 119, fig. 25.

Portrait of Cuffy. 18 x 10 1/8. Collection of Mr. and Mrs. Quincy Scarborough, Fayetteville, North Carolina.

The Levee at New Orleans or *New Orleans Docks.* 12 3/8 x 18 3/8. The Warner Collection of Gulf States Paper Corporation, Tuscaloosa, Alabama.

Negro Family on Cabin Steps. Dimensions unknown. Location unknown. Illustrated in Trovaioli and Toledano, p. 89, fig. 5.

The Rice Harvest. 10 x 20. The Roger Houston Ogden Collection, New Orleans, Louisiana. (figure 51)

Plantation Portrait. 14 x 24. The Morris Museum of Art, Augusta, Georgia.

Figure in a Field. 13 x 6. The Roger Houston Ogden Collection, New Orleans, Louisiana.

Boy. 11 3/4 x 5 3/4 (sight). Collection of J. Cornelius Rathborne, New Orleans, Louisiana.

Exhibits scenes of plantation life and negro character sketches at Blessing's, New Orleans, Lousiana, July.

At Arden, North Carolina, by July 26.

Exhibits *A Wagon Scene* at Blessing's, New Orleans, Louisiana, October.

Exhibits *Cotton Plantation* (Collection of W. J. Warrington) in the Creole Exhibition, North Central and South American Exposition, New Orleans, Louisiana, November 1885 - April 1886.

1886   *"I'll Stick to Cotton as Long as it Sticks to Me."* 42 1/8 x 24 1/4. Collection of Judith S. Vane. (figure 69)

Negro Couple on Cotton Wharf. 6 1/2 x 12 1/4. Collection of Jay P. Altmayer.

Negro Woman with Pipe. 18 x 10. Collection of Judith S. Vane.

Bombardment of Fort Sumter. 20 x 36 1/4. The Historic Charleston Foundation, Charleston, South Carolina. On loan to the Gibbes Museum of Art, Charleston, South Carolina. (figure 57)

Smoked Hams. 28 3/16 x 22 3/16. Private Collection.

In the Cottonfield. 6 1/8 x 12 1/8. The Warner Collection of Gulf States Paper Corporation, Tuscaloosa, Alabama.

Single Figure. 12 1/4 x 6 1/4. Formerly with Robert M. Hicklin Jr., Inc., Spartanburg, South Carolina.

At Charleston, South Carolina, May.

Exhibits three pictures titled *Cotton Picker*, one titled *Wagon Team*, and four untitled watercolors in first annual exhibition of the Artists' Association of New Orleans, Louisiana, November.

1887   *Old Bald, Western North Carolina.* July 11. Watercolor. 10 x 6 7/8. The Sewell Family Collection, Vidalia, Louisiana. (figure 61)

Richland Creek, North Carolina. July 18. Watercolor. 13 x 19. Location unknown. Illustrated in sale catalogue, "W. A. Walker Painting Collection," Morton's, New Orleans, Louisiana, August 28, 1973.

North Carolina Cabin. August 29. Watercolor. 10 x 13. The Sewell Family Collection, Vidalia, Louisiana. (figure 66)

Exhibits three watercolors and a landscape in oil in second annual exhibition of the Artists' Association of New Orleans, Louisiana, December.

1888   *Calhoun's Slaves.* 20 x 16. Collection of Jay P. Altmayer.

The Cotton Wagon. 14 x 21. Collection of Jay P. Altmayer.

On the Road to Natchez. 12 x 20. Private Collection.

"What Do You Think?" 20 1/8 x 16 1/8. Private Collection. (figure 74)

Biloxi Lighthouse, Biloxi, Mississippi. April 28. Watercolor. 12 x 9 3/4. The Mariners' Museum, Newport News, Virginia. (figure 96)

Cabin in the Cornfield. October. 12 1/4 x 20. Private Collection, Georgia.

1889   *Old Jeb.* 42 x 24. Lagakos-Turak Gallery, Philadelphia, Pennsylvania and Robert M. Hicklin Jr., Inc., Spartanburg, South Carolina. (figure 70)

House at Edisto. March. Oil on paper mounted on masonite. 9 7/8 x 14. Private Collection. (figure 95)

Brook in North Carolina. August 17. Watercolor. 12 1/2 x 9 1/2. Location unknown. Illustrated in sale catalogue, "W. A. Walker Painting Collection," Morton's, New Orleans, Lousiana, August 28, 1973.

Exhibits four views of North Carolina scenery, a picture of "two ragged old negroes in the cotton field, which is in full bloom," and other plantation scenes in fourth annual exhibition of the Artists' Association of New Orleans, Louisiana, December.

1890   *Trompe L'oeil: Mallard, Pocket Knife, Scissors and Buckshot.* 24 1/2 x 18 1/2. The Warner Collection of Gulf States Paper Corporation, Tuscaloosa, Alabama.

South Battery, Charleston. 6 1/4 x 12 1/4. Collection of Miss Louise Crane, New York, New York.

The Gates of St. Augustine. 9 x 12. Location unknown. Illustrated in sale catalogue, "W. A. Walker Painting Collection," Morton's, New Orleans, Louisiana, August 28, 1973.

On the Way to Knowledge. October 15. 14 x 8. The Roger Houston Ogden Collection, New Orleans, Louisiana.

First Snow, Pisgah. October 28. 13 3/16 x 9 7/8. The South Carolina State Museum, Columbia, South Carolina; Gift of Henry M. G. Walker, Jr. (figure 80)

Happy Charley. November 8. 12 1/4 x 9 1/4. Collection of Mr. and Mrs. G. Thomas Ludwig, Williamsburg, Virginia. (figure 76)

Exhibits fourteen pictures including *The Plaza and Hotel Ponce de Leon, On the Way to Knowledge,* and several mountain views in the fifth annual exhibition of the Artists' Association of New Orleans, Louisiana, December.

1891   *Mountain View.* October 17. 8 x 13. Location unknown. With Chapellier Gallery, New York, New York, circa 1964-1966.

Exhibits *Simon's Cabin, Davis' Cabin, Palmettoes, S. C.,* and *Pond, Edisto* in sixth annual exhibition of the Artists' Association of New Orleans, Louisiana, December.

1892   *Cotton Picker.* 7 1/2 x 4 1/2. Estate of W. E. Groves, New Orleans, Louisiana.

Florida Gulf Coast near Fort Walton. 5 1/2 x 7. Collection of Jay P. Altmayer.

North Carolina Landscape. October 21. 9 3/4 x 14. Collection of Philip Walker, Columbia, South Carolina.

Participates in the annual exhibition of the work of the industrial drawing and manual training classes of Tulane University and High School and art work of students of H. Sophie Newcomb Memorial College, New Orleans, Louisiana, February.

Exhibits *Way Down South in the Land of Cotton* in seventh annual exhibition of the Artists' Association of New Orleans, Louisiana, December.

Congratulated on his "selection for the world's fair," referring to the World's Columbian Exposition to be held the following year in Chicago. *New Orleans Daily Picayune*, 13 December 1892.

1893   *Chums Befo' Duh War*. 50 x 35. Private Collection. On loan to the Greenville County Museum of Art, Greenville, South Carolina. (figure 72)

1894   Exhibits "one of his familiar negro studies" in the ninth annual exhibition of the Artists' Association of New Orleans, Louisiana, December.

1895   *Lighthouse at Walker's Florida Residence*. 6 x 12. Private Collection.

The Cove at Ponce Park. 6 1/2 x 12 1/2. Collection of August P. Trovaioli, 1973. Illustrated in Trovaioli and Toledano, pl. 3.

Lighthouse. 6 1/2 x 13. Collection of Jay P. Altmayer.

Bringin' in the Dory. 6 1/8 x 12 1/4. The Warner Collection of Gulf States Paper Corporation, Tuscaloosa, Alabama. (figure 81)

The Cove at Ponce Park, Florida. November 14. 6 1/2 x 12 1/2. Private Collection.

Exhibits "pictures characteristic of Southern plantation life at Tugby's," St. Augustine, Florida, January.

1896   Resides at the Magnolia Hotel and has a studio at Tugby's, St. Augustine, Florida, January.

1898   *Ponce Lighthouse, Ponce Park, Florida.* 6 1/2 x 12. Collection of August P. Trovaioli, 1973. Illustrated in Trovaioli and Toledano, p. 45, fig. 10.

1899   The following works, all pencil sketches, document a trip that Walker made with Mr. William Henry Gregg in the spring down the east coast of Florida. The voyage on the yacht *Orian* began in Daytona on April 8 and ended at Ponce Park on May 17. Unless otherwise noted, all are from a sketchbook, the leaves of which measure 8 1/4 x 10 1/2 inches. Where two or more titles are listed together as one entry, it indicates that they occupy one page in the sketchbook. The sketchbook descended to Walker's grandniece Lucia Walker Cogswell. In 1992 it was divided in order that individual leaves could be distributed to her children and grandchildren.

          St. Lucie Riv[er], Fla. and *Sewells Pt., Mouth of St. Lucie Riv[er].* April 11. Collection of Mrs. Lucia Cogswell Heins. (figure 83)

          Fish Camp, Gilbert's Bar, Indian River Florida; Gilbert's Bar, East; and a smaller, unidentified sketch. April 12.

          Jupiter Narrows, Florida-Mouth; Jupiter Narrows; and *Hobe Sound.* April 13.

          Hobe Sound, Florida. April 13. *Jupiter Light, Florida.* April 14. Illustrated in Trovaioli and Toledano, p. 49, fig. 14.

Jupiter Inlet, Florida-South. April 14. *Mr. C. Carlins, Jupiter, Florida.* April 15.

Mouth of Indian River, Florida. April 15. *Fishing Boats, Jupiter Inlet-Catching Pompano.* April 16.

Lake Worth Inlet, Florida and *Lake Worth, Florida, Pitts Island Looking North from Inlet.* April 16.

Lake Worth Inlet, Florida-South. April 16. *The* Orian *Aground Lake Worth, Florida, Near Inlet* and *Lake Worth, Florida.* April 17.

Hotel Royal Poinciana, Lake Worth and *Bethseda-by-the-Sea Ch[urch], Lake Worth, Fla.* April 18. *Hotel Royal Poinciana, Lake Worth* and *Lake Worth.* April 19. Collection of Mr. and Mrs. Stephen Cogswell, Atlantic Beach, Florida. (figure 84)

Lantona, Lake Worth; Lake Worth opposite Hypoluxo; Canal Lake Worth; and *Everglades, Florida.* April 19.

Lake Wyman, Everglades; Hillsboro River, Florida; and *Hillsboro Inlet.* April 20. *Crooked River.* Undated.

Bay Biscayne, Miami. April 22. *Miami;* and *Brickells, Miami, Mouth of Miami River.* April 24. Illustrated in Trovaioli and Toledano, p. 45, fig. 12.

First Presbyterian Church, Miami, Florida; Miami; Royal Palm, Miami; and *Narres Cut, Bay Biscayne, Miami, Florida, Virginia Key.* April 25. Illustrated in Trovaioli and Toledano, p. 49, fig. 13.

Hotel Royal Palm, Miami, Florida; Royal Palm from Bears Cut; and *Bears*

Cut Six Miles from Miami. April 26. *Cape Florida, Key Biscayne* and *Soldier Key, Florida.* April 27.

Ragged Key, Florida. April 27. *Sponge Kraal, Elliott Key, Florida; Caesars Creek;* and *Elliott Key, Florida, Sea Face from Caesars Creek.* April 28. *Angelfish Creek, Old Rhodes Key, Florida.* April 29.

Bonefish, Key Largo, Florida. May 1.

Entrance to Blackwater Bay, Florida; Bay of Florida; and *Bay of Florida: Formation of Keys by Mangrove Tree Seeds.* May 2. *Indian Key, Florida, Southern End of Cruise.* May 3. *Saunders House, Indian Key, Florida* . May 4. Collection of Constance Cogswell Miller. (figure 85)

Indian Key, Florida (three drawings with this title) and *Alligator Reef Light, Florida.* May 4.

The Orian *Filling Her Tanks at Indian Key, Florida.* May 5. *Indian Key Florida from the Atlantic* and *The Hole, Upper Matecumbe Key, from the Atlantic Ocean.* May 6.

Long Island or Plantation Key, Florida (two drawings with this title) and *Planter, Key Largo, Florida.* May 6. *Angelfish Creek between Key Largo and Angelfish Key.* May 9.

Bay, Cards Sound, Florida, Fishing for Barracuda. May 9. Illustrated in Trovaioli and Toledano, p. 95, fig. 1.

Arsenicker Key, Florida, Cards Sound. May 11. *Steamboat Creek, Key Largo, Florida* and *Sponging in Cards Sound, Florida.* May 12.

Key West Sponger, Miami, Florida. May 13. Dimensions unknown. Location unknown. Illustrated in Trovaioli and Toledano, p. 50, fig. 15.

Earthworks, Spanish War, Miami, Florida. May 13. 5 1/4 x 7 3/4. From another sketchbook in the Walker Family Collection.

Bears Cut, Six Miles from Miami, Fla. May 13. 5 1/4 x 7 3/4. From another sketchbook in the Walker Family Collection.

Off the Florida Coast. May 13. 5 1/4 x 7 3/4. Collection of Mrs. Lisa Cogswell Kirk, Springfield, Massachusetts.

Gilbert's Bar, Florida. May 14. 5 1/4 x 7 3/4. Collection of Mrs. Claudia Cogswell Bolduc.

Fish Camp, Gilbert's Bar, Florida. May 15. Dimensions unknown. Location unknown. Illustrated in Trovaioli and Toledano, p. 121, fig. 27.

Pacetti House, Ponce Park, Florida, End of the Cruise of the Orian. May 17. Collection of Mrs. Claudia Cogswell Bolduc.

Lodges at Magnolia Hotel, St. Augustine, Florida, by February 4; returns later in year, by December 30.

1900 *Bluefish.* December. 18 x 12. Private Collection.

Sheepshead. December. 18 x 12. Private Collection.

Lodges at Pacetti House, Ponce Park, Florida, April.

1901   *Fort Pierce Hotel, Florida.* November 6. Pencil on paper. 4 3/4 x 7 3/4. Collection of Mrs. Claudia Cogswell Bolduc.

Menhadin. Fort Pierce, Florida. November 8. 11 7/16 x 15 11/16 (sight). The Parrish Art Museum, Littlejohn Collection, Southampton, New York.

St. Lucie, Florida. November 16. Pencil on paper. 4 3/4 x 7 3/4. Collection of Mrs. Claudia Cogswell Bolduc.

Trachinotus Carolinus, Common Pompano. Jupiter, Florida. November 19. Oil on paper. 11 1/2 x 15 5/8 (sight). The Parrish Art Museum, Littlejohn Collection, Southampton, New York.

South End of Lake Worth. November 23. Pencil on paper. 4 3/8 x 7 5/16 (sight). Collection of A. McLeish Martin, M.D., Charleston, South Carolina.

Indian Key, Florida. December 6. 8 x 10. The High Museum of Art, Atlanta, Georgia; Gift of Mr. and Mrs. George Missbach (74.6).

Fish Seller, Key West and *Key West, Unloading Sponges.* December 23. Pencil on paper. 4 1/4 x 7 3/4 (sight). Collection of Josephine Walker Martin, Ph.D., Columbia, South Carolina.

1902   *Florida Pompano.* 16 x 12. Collection of Dr. Ted Wingard, Jacksonville, Florida.

Striped Mullet. 17 7/16 x 11 7/16 (sight). The Parrish Art Museum, Littlejohn Collection, Southampton, New York.

Yellowtail. 17 3/8 x 11 3/8 (sight). The Parrish Art Museum, Littlejohn Collection, Southampton, New York. (figure 90)

Red Grouper. 19 7/16 x 11 7/16 (sight). The Parrish Art Museum, Littlejohn Collection, Southampton, New York.

Head of Dog. April. 17 3/4 x 11 3/4. Dr. and Mrs. John Ward, Columbia, South Carolina.

Ponce Park, Florida. April. 8 1/4 x 11 3/4. Location unknown. Number 28 in Walker exhibition, Bland Gallery, New York, New York, 1940.

Sand Smelt or *Silversides.* Ponce Park, Florida. May. Oil on paper. 15 9/16 x 11 5/16 (sight). The Parrish Art Museum, Littlejohn Collection, Southampton, New York.

Isle of Palms, S. C. June 14. Pencil on paper. 4 3/4 x 7 3/4. Estate of Lucia Walker Cogswell, Charleston, South Carolina.

The pictures made in the remainder of 1902, except where otherwise noted, are pencil sketches, made by Walker in a single sketchbook, the pages of which measure 7 x 10 inches. The sketchbook descended to Walker's grandniece Lucia Walker Cogswell. In 1992 it was given to the Carolina Art Association/Gibbes Museum of Art in Charleston, South Carolina.

Fish House, New Smyrna, Florida. October 16.

San Sebastian Hotel. October 26.

Wrasse Fishes, Pudding Wife. Angelfish Creek, Florida. November. 11 1/2 x 15 5/8 (sight). The Parrish Art Museum, Littlejohn Collection, Southampton, New York.

Jensen, Indian River (two drawings with this title on one page). November 7.

Sergeant Fish, Robalo. Fort Pierce, Florida. November 7. 17 9/16 x 11 5/8 (sight). The Parrish Art Museum, Littlejohn Collection, Southampton, New York.

Bessey's. Indian River, Florida. November 8.

Florida Coastal Scene. November 8. Oil, support unknown. 11 x 17. Location unknown. Illustrated in sale catalogue, Sotheby Parke Bernet, Los Angeles, sale no. 139, October 29, 1974, lot no. 206.

Gilbert's Bar, Entrance to Jupiter Narrows and *Jupiter Narrows*. November 11.

Canal, North Entrance to Lake Worth. November 14.

Canal, North End Lake Worth. November 14. *Munyons Island, Lake Worth*. November 17.

Lake Worth Inlet and *Oak Lawn, Lake Worth*. November 17. Pencil on paper. 4 1/2 x 7 1/8 (sight). Collection of A. McLeish Martin, M.D., Charleston, South Carolina.

Canal, Hillsboro River. November 20. (figure 87)

Hillsboro River Inlet. November 20. *New River Inlet.* November 21.

New River Inlet. November 21. *Miami.* November 22.

Cocoanut Grove. November 24.

Spanish Mackerel Trolling, Bay Biscayne. November 25.

Cape Florida, Old Light. November 28.

Cape Florida. November 28. Pencil on paper. 4 3/4 x 7 3/4.

Near Bonefish Grounds, Barnes Sound. December 2. *Bonefish Banks.* December 3.

Newfound Harbor Key and *Key West, Florida.* December 7.

Black Turbot. Key West, Florida. December 17. 11 7/16 x 15 5/8 (sight). The Parrish Art Museum, Littlejohn Collection, Southampton, New York.

Newfound Harbor Key. December 17. *Bahia Honda Key.* December 18.

Knights Key. December 19.

Knights Key. December 19. *Ragged Keys.* December 23.

Writes a poem entitled "The Cruise."

1903   *Crab.* 16 x 12. Collection of George Deneger, New Orleans, Louisiana, 1972. Illustrated in Trovaioli and Toledano, pl. 25.

Sea Trout. 15 7/8 x 30 1/8. The Morris Museum of Art, Augusta, Georgia. (figure 89)

Allamanda and Pyrostegia. 13 x 9 1/2. With Herman Schindler, Charleston, South Carolina, 1972. Illustrated in Trovaioli and Toledano, p. 102, fig. 7.

1904   *Lighthouse at Ponce Park.* March 22. 7 3/4 x 17 1/4. The Sewell Family Collection, Vidalia, Louisiana. (figure 93)

Ponce Park, Florida. May 20. Four views with this title and date in a 1902 - 1904 sketchbook. Each pencil on paper. 7 x 10. The Carolina Art Association/Gibbes Museum of Art, Charleston, South Carolina.

Lighthouse at Ponce Park. May 26. In a 1902 - 1904 sketchbook. Pencil on paper. 7 x 10. The Carolina Art Association/Gibbes Museum of Art, Charleston, South Carolina.

Isle of Palms, South Carolina. June 10. Four views with this title and date in a 1904 - 1905 sketchbook. Each pencil on paper. 9 x 13. Estate of Lucia Walker Cogswell, Charleston, South Carolina.

Isle of Palms, South Carolina. June 10. Pencil on paper. Dimensions unknown. Collection of Josephine Walker Martin, Ph.D., Columbia, South Carolina.

Isle of Palms. June 14. Pencil on paper. 4 7/16 x 7 3/16 (sight). Collection of A. McLeish Martin, M.D., Charleston, South Carolina.

Isle of Palms, South Carolina. October 6. In a 1904 - 1905 sketchbook. Pencil on paper. 9 x 13. Estate of Lucia Walker Cogswell, Charleston, South Carolina.

Isle of Palms. October 6. Two views with this title and date in a 1904 - 1905 sketchbook. Pencil on paper. 9 x 13. Estate of Lucia Walker Cogswell, Charleston, South Carolina.

Spends winter at Ponce Park, Florida.

Visits nephew George Walker and his family at Summerville, South Carolina, early June.

Arrives Arden Park Lodge, Arden, North Carolina, June 16.

Suffers from influenza all summer; confined to bed in August.

Visits Charleston, South Carolina in October.

Lodges at Pacetti House, Ponce Park, Florida, by November 18; spends Christmas there.

1905   *Winter Nest.* 18 1/2 x 12 1/4. The Warner Collection of Gulf States Paper Corporation, Tuscaloosa, Alabama. (figure 98)

Acorns and Oak Leaves. Biloxi, Mississippi. 12 x 9. The Warner Collection of Gulf States Paper Corporation, Tuscaloosa, Alabama.

Automobile Road, Ponce Park, Florida. April 1. In a 1904 - 1905 sketchbook. Pencil on paper. 9 x 13. Estate of Lucia Walker Cogswell, Charleston, South Carolina.

Visits St. Augustine, Florida and New Orleans, Louisiana in the spring.

Visits Biloxi, Mississippi in June.

Spends part of summer and all of autumn in Blue Ridge Mountains, North Carolina; leaves Skyland, North Carolina, December 1.

Arrives St. Augustine, Florida, December 2.

1906   *Red Drum Caught and Painted by William Aiken Walker.* 12 1/4 x 32 1/4. Robert M. Hicklin Jr., Inc., Spartanburg, South Carolina.

Autumn Foliage, North Carolina. October 25. 9 x 9. The Carolina Art Association/Gibbes Museum of Art, Charleston, South Carolina.

Small Cabin. 9 3/16 x 9 7/8. The Carolina Art Association/ Gibbes Museum of Art, Charleston, South Carolina.

Miniature Beach Scene. 2 3/16 x 3 5/16. The Historic New Orleans Collection, New Orleans, Louisiana (1953.136). (figure 79A)

1907   *Runnymede on the Ashley.* 3 3/8 x 4 1/2. Private Collection.

1908   *Cabin.* 10 x 12 1/4. Collection of Josephine Walker Martin, Ph.D., Columbia, South Carolina.

             Wash Day, Arden. September 21. 9 1/2 x 12. Private Collection.

             Woodland Scene at Arden. September 21. 10 1/2 x 7 1/2. Collection of Mrs. George Walker Cogswell, Atlantic Beach, Florida.

             Barrel and Bucket Mountain Scene, North Carolina. September 25. 10 x 12 1/4. Collection of A. McLeish Martin, M.D., Charleston, South Carolina.

             My Cabin. October 2. 9 x 13 5/8. Location unknown. Number 29 in Walker exhibition, Bland Gallery, New York, New York, 1940.

             Cornstalks. October 3. Dimensions unknown. Collection of Floyd A. Walker, 1940. Number 30 in Walker exhibition, Bland Gallery, New York, New York, 1940.

             Mountain Scene, Arden, North Carolina. October 5. Collection of Josephine Walker Martin, Ph.D., Columbia, South Carolina.

             Cottage and Corn. October 6. Dimensions unknown. Location unknown. Number 31 in Walker exhibition, Bland Gallery, New York, New York, 1940.

             Amber Jack. December 9. 19 x 13 1/4 (sight). The Parrish Art Museum, Littlejohn Collection, Southampton, New York.

Planter P. O. Key Largo, Florida and *Torpedo Boat Fleet off Alligator Reef Light.* December 15. Pencil on paper. 4 5/16 x 7 3/8 (sight). Collection of A. McLeish Martin, M.D., Charleston, South Carolina.

Red Grouper. Lower Matecumbe Key, Florida. December 16. 19 3/16 x 13 1/4 (sight). The Parrish Art Museum, Littlejohn Collection, Southampton, New York.

Lower Matecumbe Key. December 16. 6 1/4 x 20 3/8. The Vickers Florida Collection., Jacksonville, Florida. (figure 97)

Knight's Key Sea End of R. R. and *Shore End of R. R.* December 18. Pencil on paper. 4 5/16 x 7 1/8 (sight). Collection of A. McLeish Martin, M.D., Charleston, South Carolina.

F. E. C. R. R., Duck Key (Below Long Key) and *Viaduct, F. E. C. R. R., Long Key.* December 18. *Cut between Black Water Bay and Bay of Florida.* December 19. Pencil on paper. 4 3/4 x 7 3/4, sheet size. The Carolina Art Association/Gibbes Museum of Art, Charleston, South Carolina.

Crayfish. December 19. 19 1/2 x 14. With The Sporting Gallery, Middleburg, Virginia, 1972. Illustrated in Trovaioli and Toledano, p. 11, fig. 11.

Boggy and *Cabin, Broad Creek.* December 20. *Fowey Rock Light.* December 21. Pencil on paper. 4 3/4 x 7 3/4, sheet size. The Carolina Art Association/Gibbes Museum of Art, Charleston, South Carolina.

Lodges at Pacetti House, Ponce Park, Florida, March and April.

Writes poem, untitled, for "S. S. S." at Ponce Park, Florida, May 8.

Writes poem, "Ode to a Mosquito," at Arden, North Carolina, August 5.

Writes poem, untitled, for "Colonel W. H. H. P." at Ponce Park, Florida, December 21 .

1909   *Florida Beach Scene: Palms and Water.* May 26. 12 x 21. Robert M. Hicklin Jr., Inc., Spartanburg, South Carolina.

1910   *Carolina Toadstools.* 9 1/2 x 16 1/2. Location unknown. Number 32 in Walker exhibition, Bland Gallery, New York, New York, 1940. Illustrated in Mastai, *Connoisseur,* p. 77.

Arden, North Carolina. September 16. 8 1/8 x 12. Collection of Dr. and Mrs. John Ward, Columbia, South Carolina.

Forest Floor at Arden. September 17. 7 1/4 x 11 3/4 (sight). Collection of Mrs. Edward Hall Walker, Charleston, South Carolina. (figure 99)

Mushrooms. September. 15 1/2 x 11. Private Collection.

Stays at Pacetti House, Ponce Park, Florida, January.

1911   *Barracuda.* 12 15/16 x 22 1/2. The Warner Collection of Gulf States Paper Corporation, Tuscaloosa, Alabama.

Takes sick while at Ponce Park, Florida, February.

1912   *Ocean Waves Breaking on Beach.* 7 1/2 x 14 3/8. The Carolina Art Association/Gibbes Museum of Art, Charleston, South Carolina.

Visits nephew and his family at their new home, 134 Cannon Street, Charleston, South Carolina, May.

Goes to Arden, North Carolina for the summer, early June.

1913   *Self-portrait of William Aiken Walker.* 12 1/4 x 9 1/2. The Carolina Art Association/Gibbes Museum of Art, Charleston, South Carolina. (figure 101)

Beach Scene with Steamer on Horizon. June. Pencil on paper. Dimensions unknown. Collection of Josephine Walker Martin, Ph.D., Columbia, South Carolina.

Lemon Tree. November 8. 4 3/8 x 7 1/2. Collection of Josephine Walker Martin, Ph.D., Columbia, South Carolina.

Arrives at Ponce Park, Florida by Christmas.

1914   *Self-portrait of William Aiken Walker.* February. 8 3/8 x 8 5/8. The Columbia Museum of Art, Columbia, South Carolina.

River, Tree and City on Horizon. April. 8 x 12 1/2. Location unknown. Illustrated in Trovaioli and Toledano, p. 42, fig. 7.

Woods Scene. April. 8 x 12. Collection of Jay P. Altmayer.

Resides at Ponce Park, Florida, February.

1915   *Palmetto and Yucca.* May. 8 1/4 x 14 3/8. The Carolina Art Association/Gibbes Museum of Art, Charleston, South Carolina.

1916   *Floral Still-life.* 10 5/8 x 9 1/2 inches. Estate of Mrs. Julia Walker Bradley.

1918   *Autumn Foliage.* October 3. 12 1/4 x 6. The Carolina Art Association/Gibbes Museum of Art, Charleston, South Carolina.

Brilliant Autumn Foliage. October 21. 6 1/8 x 12 1/4. The Carolina Art Association/Gibbes Museum of Art, Charleston, South Carolina.

Mountain Cabin in Landscape. October. 6 1/4 x 12. Estate of Mrs. Julia Walker Bradley.

Chimney, North Carolina. 6 1/2 x 11 3/4. Collection of Mrs. George Walker Cogswell, Atlantic Beach, Florida.

1919   *Ruins, Arden Park Lodge.* October 1. 12 1/4 x 6 1/8. The Warner Collection of Gulf States Paper Corporation, Tuscaloosa, Alabama.

1920   *Arden.* October 15. Pencil on paper. Dimensions unknown. Location unknown. Illustrated in Trovaioli and Toledano, p. 79, fig. 9.

1921   Dies at the home of his nephew, George William Walker, 134 Cannon Street, Charleston, South Carolina, January 3, 4:30 P.M.

Lithographs

AFTER PAINTINGS BY WILLIAM AIKEN WALKER

A Free Lunch (figure 23), 1872, lithograph, 11 1/4 x 14 inches, signed on the stone, lower left: *WAWalker. 1872.* Printed beneath the image: *PUBLISHED BY CURRIER & IVES/Entered according to act of Congress in the year 1872 by Currier & Ives in the office of the Librarian of Congress at Washington/125 NASSAU ST. NEW YORK*

The location of Walker's original painting for this print is unknown.

Collection: The Library of Congress, Washington, D.C.

Attributed to William Aiken Walker. ***The Sunny South***, 1882, lithograph printed in colors, unsigned. Titled on the stone, lower center: *The Sunny South.* Inscribed on the stone above corresponding vignettes: *Orange Grove/Sugar Plantation/Louisiana/Texas.*

The location of the original paintings(s) after which this lithograph was made is unknown.

Collection: The Historic New Orleans Collection, New Orleans, Louisiana.

A Cotton Plantation on the Mississippi (figure 36), 1884, lithograph printed in colors, 21 x 30 inches, signed on the stone, lower left: *WAWalker. 1883.* Printed beneath the image: *Printed in oil colors by Currier & Ives 115 Nassau St. N.Y./A Cotton Plantation on the Mississippi/Copyright 1884 By Currier & Ives, New York.*

Walker's original painting for this print is in the collection of the Gilcrease Museum, Tulsa, Oklahoma.

Collections: Robert L. Moore, M. D., Philadelphia, Mississippi; The Historic New Orleans Collection, New Orleans, Louisiana; The Library of Congress, Washington, D.C.; Amon Carter Museum of Western Art, Fort Worth, Texas; Chicago Historical Society, Chicago, Illinois; Museum of the City of New York, New York.

One known copy of this lithograph has been tampered with. A paper has been pasted over its original letterpress, changing the title to, "A Cotton Plantation near Charleston, S.C." This altered copy is in the Sewell Family Collection, Vidalia, Louisiana.

The Levee-New Orleans (figure 43), 1884, lithograph printed in colors, 21 x 29 1/2 inches, signed on the stone, lower center: *WAWalker/1883.* Printed beneath the image: *PAINTED BY W. A. WALKER. REPRODUCED IN OIL COLORS BY CURRIER & IVES 115 NASSAU ST. NY COPYRIGHT 1884 BY CURRIER & IVES NEW YORK/THE LEVEE-NEW ORLEANS.*

Walker's original painting for this print is in the collection of J. Cornelius Rathborne, New Orleans, Louisiana.

Collections: Knox College, Galesburg, Illinois; The Historic New Orleans Collection, New Orleans, Louisiana; The Library of Congress, Washington, D.C.; The Sewell Family Collection, Vidalia, Louisiana.

A Cotton Plantation, lithograph printed in colors, 18 1/2 x 27 inches (sight). Made for the Kitson Machine Company, Charleston, South Carolina.

Walker's original painting for this print is in a private collection, Birmingham, Alabama.

Collection: The Sewell Family Collection, Vidalia, Louisiana.

Notes

CHAPTER ONE • *EARLY YEARS*

[1] Walter J. Fraser, Jr., *Charleston! Charleston!* (Columbia: University of South Carolina Press, 1989), xi.

[2] Charles Reagan Wilson and William Ferris, eds., *Encyclopaedia of Southern Culture* (Chapel Hill: University of North Carolina Press, 1989), 589, 861, 1097.

[3] Clement Eaton, *The Mind of the Old South, 1790-1860* (New York: Harper & Row, Publishers, 1961), 201-204.

[4] John Falls Walker's tombstone in the yard of St. Philip's Church in Charleston gives December 4, 1798 as his date of birth. This is supported by naturalization records at the National Archives, which record his age as twenty-three on the date of naturalization, October 14, 1822. (See Record Group number 21, United States District Court, Charleston, South Carolina, List of Aliens Admitted to Citizenship, 1790-1860, 68A915 number 2.) There is some uncertainty about the date of Walker's arrival in the United States. A passenger named John F. Walker, age 20, arrived in Charleston from "Great Britain" in the third quarter of 1820, per *United States Secretary of State*, p. 227. This John F. Walker is probably the same person as John Falls Walker, an error of one year having been made in recording his age.

[5] August P. Trovaioli and Roulhac B. Toledano, *William Aiken Walker: Southern Genre Painter* (Baton Rouge: Louisiana State University Press, 1972), 14. Trovaioli and Toledano state that John Falls Walker's second wife was Mary Elizabeth Aiken implying that the artist's middle name came from his mother. They offer no proof of their assertion.

[6] For a fuller explanation of the Flint family and John Falls Walker's two marriages, see the article by his descendant, Mrs. Lucia Cogswell Heins, "A Note on William Aiken Walker," *South Carolina Historical Magazine* 79 (1978): 322-324.

[7] For a discussion of the sale of the Flint house at 23 State Street to John Falls Walker in 1829, see Heins, 323.

[8] John Walker paid $4,500 for a three-story brick house on East Bay Street, located between Inspection and Boundary streets a few blocks from the Cooper River. The house stood on lot number sixty-one, which he purchased in its entirety with half of the adjoining lot. The lots combined to measure sixty feet in width and 120 feet in depth. See Conveyance Deed between

Mary Cooper and George William Cooper and John Falls Walker, dated February 9, 1832, The South Carolina Historical Society, Charleston, South Carolina.

[9] *Fifth Census (1830), South Carolina*, volume 2, p. 14, Records of the Bureau of the Census, National Archives, Washington, D.C.

[10] Joseph Flint Walker was born August 13, 1833, according to Mrs. Lucia Cogswell Heins' research. See Heins, 323.

[11] William Aiken Walker's date of birth has been given as March 23, 1838 and March 11, 1839. The latter date appears on Walker's passport application. Since that document was signed by Walker, we may assume it to be correct.

[12] Will of John Falls Walker, Will Book I and J, 1839-1845, p. 151, Probate Court, Charleston, South Carolina.

[13] The city in which William was raised has been called into question. His previous biographers have written that Mary Elizabeth Walker took her sons Joseph Flint and William Aiken to Baltimore, Maryland shortly after their father's death. (Trovaioli and Toledano, 14.) I have found no evidence to support a Baltimore residency at that time. It does not make sense that a widow in the nineteenth century would have struck out for an unknown city. Mary Elizabeth Walker had been born and raised in Charleston. Her mother was still alive at the time of her husband's passing and living with the family. Furthermore, she was left with a home in Charleston and with the means to maintain it.

[14] Walker's name does not appear in alumni records of either the College of Charleston or the University of South Carolina, the schools that a Charlestonian of that era would have been most likely to attend. In 1856, at the age of seventeen, Walker's name appears for the first time in the Charleston directory; his occupation is identified as clerk. He was then living in the home of his elder brother Joseph F. Walker at 36 Rutledge Street.

[15] Eaton, 117.

[16] Anna Wells Rutledge, *Artists in the Life of Charleston Through Colony and State from Restoration to Reconstruction* (1949; reprint with new preface by John Morrill Bryan, Columbia: University of South Carolina Press, 1980), 160.

[17] Ibid., 169.

[18] Ibid., 134.

[19] *View along East Battery, Charleston* and two paintings entitled *View of Charleston* are in the Mabel Brady Garvan Collection, Yale University Art Gallery, New Haven, Connecticut.

[20]"T. Addison Richards," *Rambler* I, no. 38 (December 30, 1843): 2, as quoted in Rutledge, 166.

[21]John S. Cogdell to Samuel Finley Breese Morse, 1823, as quoted in Rutledge, 131.

[22] *Catalog of Miniature Portraits, Landscapes, and other pieces executed by Charles Fraser, Esq. and exhibited in The Fraser Gallery, at Charleston, during the months of February and March, 1857* (Charleston: James and Williams, Printers, 1857).

[23] Rutledge, 153.

[24] *Charleston Courier,* 27 November 1850.

[25] Francis James Porcher was born May 8, 1821 at Coosawatchie, son of Dr. Francis Yonge Porcher. He came to Charleston as a child, married Abby Louisa Gilman, and died February 20, 1872. He represented St. Philip and St. Michael's parish of Charleston at the Secession Convention in 1861. At that time, the combined value of his real and personal property was $45,000, and he owned nine slaves. In addition to Walker's painting, Porcher owned at least two paintings by John Beaufain Irving, Jr. of Charleston, one of which he commissioned, the other being a gift from the artist. Biographical information courtesy of Stephen Hoffius of the South Carolina Historical Society. A list of paintings owned by Porcher may be found in a manuscript journal of F. J. Porcher, in the collection of the Carolina Art Association/Gibbes Museum of Art, Charleston, South Carolina.

[26] Walker's other painting submitted to the exhibition is listed as "One Oil Painting, Copy of an old Picture." See *Catalogue of Articles on Exhibition at the Ninth Annual Fair of the South Carolina Institute, Held in Charleston, November 15, 1859* (Charleston: Walker, Evans & Co., Steam Printers, 1859), 10.

[27] *Charleston Courier,* 31 August 1842, as quoted in Rutledge, 155.

[28] *Charleston Mercury,* 12 June 1858.

[29] *Charleston Mercury,* 16 February 1859. Other works exhibited by Walker in the late 1850s are "India Ink Drawing - *Sunshine,* Oil Painting - *Entrance to the Castle of Heidelberg,*" and two works described as "Pencil Drawing - *Oliver Twist,*" all of which are included in "Premium List, S. C. Institute, 1857-1859," p. 46. A copy of this document is in the collection of the South Carolina Historical Society. The present location of these four works is unknown.

[30] Emma Huger to Adele Allston, 18 January 1836, Charleston. Allston Papers, South Carolina Historical Society, as quoted in Rutledge, 135.

[31] *Charleston Courier,* 25 February 1841, as quoted in Rutledge, 163.

[32] *Charleston Courier,* 25 January 1848, as quoted in Rutledge, 164.

CHAPTER TWO • *THE WAR YEARS*

[1] Veterans Records, National Archives Records Center, Atlanta, Georgia.

[2] Certificate of discharge, August 31, 1861. Veterans Records, National Archives Records Center, Atlanta, Georgia.

[3] The 1860 census records Joseph F. Walker, age twenty-six, clerk, as head of his household, with the following members of the household: Emma I. Walker, twenty-five [his wife]; Joseph Walker, age two; Henry M. Walker, age one; Mary E. Walker, age fifty; and William A. Walker, age twenty-one, artist. (The age recorded for Mary E. Walker is in error. Mary Elizabeth Walker would have been sixty-three in 1860.) See *Population Schedules of the Eighth Census of the United States, 1860*, roll 1216, South Carolina, volume 2, p. 451. Charleston's City Directory for the year 1860 lists both Joseph Walker's and William A. Walker's residence as "Rutledge cor. Doughty." Charleston city directories do not exist for the period 1861-1865.

[4] The map is inscribed as follows: "Map of Charleston and its Defences. Compiled from Surveys of Portions of St Andrews and Christ Ch. Parishes by Lieut John Johnson C. S. Engrs/The Harbor, James Id, Folly Id, Morris Id, Sullivans Id, & Long Id, from U. S. Coast Survey, Johns Id from Mills Atlas/Under the direction of Maj. Wm. H. Echols C. S. Engr Corps/By Wm A. Walker Draughtsman C. S. Engr Corps/Drawn by John R. Key 2nd Lieut. C. S. Engrs/Charleston S. C./Nov: 28th 1863." The map was reproduced for and published in *Year Book-1885. City of Charleston, So. Ca.* (Charleston: News and Courier Book Presses, 1885).

[5] James Arthur Fremantle, *The Fremantle Diary Being the Journal of Lieutenant Colonel James Arthur Fremantle, Coldstream Guards, on his Three Months in the Southern States*, ed. Walter Lord (Boston: Little, Brown and Company, 1954), 143.

[6] Manuscript journal of Francis James Porcher. Collection of the Carolina Art Association/Gibbes Museum of Art, Charleston, South Carolina.

[7] Rutledge, 170.

[8] I am grateful to Alfred Harrison, who provided transcripts of Charleston newspaper reviews that discuss paintings by Walker, Key, Lawrence B. Cohen, and others that were painted and exhibited in Charleston during the war.

[9] *Conrad Wise Chapman, 1842-1910, An Exhibition of His Works in the Valentine Museum* (Richmond: The Valentine Museum, 1962).

[10] Fremantle, 148.

[11] See Mark E. Neely, Jr., Harold Holzer and Gabor S. Boritt, *The Confederate Image: Prints of the Lost Cause* (Chapel Hill and London: University of North Carolina Press, 1987).

[12] *Charleston Mercury*, 24 October 1864.

[13] Alfred C. Harrison, Jr., "Bierstadt's *Bombardment of Fort Sumter* Reattributed," *The Magazine Antiques* 129 (February 1986): 415-422.

[14] From the manuscript book of poems "Mes Pensées" by William Aiken Walker. Collection of the Carolina Art Association/Gibbes Museum of Art, Charleston, South Carolina.

[15] Interview by the author with Mrs. Josephine Walker Martin, grandniece of William Aiken Walker, Columbia, South Carolina, July 1988.

Chapter Three • *Reconstruction*

[1] Whitelaw Reid, *After the War: A Southern Tour, May 1, 1865 to May 1, 1866* (Cincinnati: Moore, Wilstach and Baldwin, 1866), 57.

[2] Fitzgerald Ross, *Cities and Camps of the Confederate States*, ed. Richard Barksdale Harwell (Urbana: University of Illinois Press, 1958), 96.

[3] It was in Cheraw, South Carolina that Joseph and Emma Walker's fourth child was born on December 16, 1864. He was christened George William Walker, named for his uncle who had died in battle at Gaines' Mill.

[4] The only documentation that exists for Walker's whereabouts in 1866 is the manuscript book of poems discussed in the previous chapter, the cover of which is inscribed, "Mes Pensées/Charleston 1866." This book is in the collection of the Carolina Art Association/Gibbes Museum of Art, Charleston, South Carolina.

[5] *Woods' Baltimore City Directory, 1868-69* (Baltimore: John W. Woods, 1868). This directory was completed by November 1868 according to the dated preface.

[6] Wednesday Club members adopted and put their signatures to a constitution on October 23, 1869. Walker was not among the signers of that document, which suggests either that he became a member at a later date or that he had by then left Baltimore for New York City, an episode that will be discussed subsequently. The constitution of the Wednesday Club is in the Wednesday Club Papers, Maryland Historical Socity, Baltimore.

[7] The history of the Wednesday Club is summarized in an article by Ottilie Sutro, "The Wednesday Club: A Brief Sketch from Authentic Sources," *Maryland Historical Magazine* 38 (1943): 60-68.

The location of Robertson's drawing is unknown. A photocopy of it is in the collection of the Carolina Art Assocation/Gibbes Museum of Art, Charleston, South Carolina. According to Sutro, Walker also made drawings of Wednesday Club activities, which at the time of her article were in the collection of the Maryland Historical Society, Baltimore, Maryland.

[8] *Woods' Baltimore City Directory*, 1872 (Baltimore: John W. Woods, 1872). Walker is listed as "artist, 20 n[orth] Charles dw[elling] 109 n Charles."

[9] William Aiken Walker's passport application was completed in New York and dated December 6, 1869. C. D. Fredricks, as Walker's witness, signed a statement on the application attesting to the fact that he was acquainted with William Aiken Walker and believed him to be an American citizen. *Trow's New York City Directory for 1869* lists Mr. Fredericks as "Fredricks, Charles D. & Co., photographs, 587 B'way," and cites his residence as New Jersey.

[10] William Aiken Walker, "Cuban Diary 1869-70," unpublished manuscript journal in the collection of the Carolina Art Association/Gibbes Museum of Art, Charleston, South Carolina.

[11] Unidentified clipping from the scrapbook of Andrew John Henry Way. Courtesy of the Maryland Historical Society, Baltimore, Maryland.

[12] *Baltimore Sun*, 26 and 27 April 1871.

[13] My thanks to Paul Worman of New York City who is preparing a book on Andrew John Henry Way for information on Way's Baltimore period.

[14] This painting was offered for sale at Christie's, New York, December 2, 1988, lot number 74. The review quoted was taken from an unidentified clipping found at that time on the back of the canvas.

[15] "Our Native Artists. Their Productions in the Exposition, A Critical Examination of their Works," *Louisville Courier-Journal*, 4 October 1872.

[16] "Baltimore Art and Artists - II," *The Capital*, undated clipping from the scrapbook of Andrew John Henry Way. Courtesy of the Maryland Historical Society, Baltimore, Maryland.

[17] Walker helped his fellow Baltimore artists fill the walls of the Maryland Academy of Art for its second annual exhibition in December 1871. The opening night party of the exhibition was "an artistical and musical soiree." The rooms were brilliantly illuminated, and the address that was delivered by Benjamin Henry Latrobe offered an optimistic prospect for the fledgling institution. Though a catalogue does not exist for this show to detail each artist's contribution, it was noted in the press that "excellent pieces" were contributed by Baltimore artists Sauerwein, Norwood,

Mayer, Hovenden, Way, and Walker. (*Baltimore American*, 15 December 1871, clipping in the scrap-book of Andrew John Henry Way. Courtesy of the Maryland Historical Society, Baltimore, Maryland.)

[18] J. Thomas Scharf, *History of Baltimore City and County from the Earliest Period to the Present Day Including Biographical Sketches of their Representative Men* (Philadelphia: Louis H. Everts, 1881), 675.

[19] *Baltimore Saturday Night*, 26 April 1873.

[20] *Baltimore Sun*, 5 November 1881.

[21] *Daily Louisville Commercial*, 11 October 1872.

[22] *Daily Louisville Commercial*, 23 October 1872.

[23] *Caron's Annual Directory of the City of Louisville, for 1873*, volume 3 (C. K. Caron, Publisher, September, n.d.).

[24] "The Great South: Kentucky and Tennessee," *Scribner's Monthly* 9, no. 2 (December 1874): 137.

[25] Ibid., 138.

[26] "Our Native Artists," *Louisville Courier-Journal*, 4 October 1872.

[27] *Fayman and Reilly's Galveston City Directory for 1875-6* (Galveston: Strickland & Clarke, Stationers, Printers and Lithographers, 1875). The other artists listed in the directory for this year are J. C. Evans, L. Eyth, and C. Hofrichter.

[28] *City of Waco* burned one night in October 1875, as she lay at anchor waiting to enter Galveston Harbor. All passengers and crew members were killed.

[29] For the description of the contents of Walker's picture, I have relied upon an article which discusses the picture and Walker's tenure in Galveston. "Historical Sketch of the Port of Galveston in 1874," *Galveston Daily News*, 13 September 1908, was kindly provided by Lise Darst of the Rosenberg Library, Galveston, Texas.

[30] There was at one time a fire in Rose's and the painting was damaged by water. It was then that Mr. Bowen negotiated with Walker about purchasing *Port of Galveston*; Mr. Bowen sent the painting to New Orleans for restoration, and when it came back, it hung in the office of his Galveston business associate E. J. Hart. In 1907 Bowen gave the painting to the Rosenberg Library in Galveston, and there it has remained. Information courtesy of Lise Darst, Rosenberg Library.

[31] "Art Notes," an undated clipping in the scrapbook of Andrew John Henry Way. Courtesy of

the Maryland Historical Society, Baltimore, Maryland. Walker maintained a relationship with art dealer David Bendann for many years. Affixed to the back of *The Beggar and His Dog* (The Warner Collection of Gulf States Paper Corporation, Tuscaloosa, Alabama) is a label that reads: "David Bendann's/Fine Art Rooms/105 East Baltimore St./Baltimore/Looking/Glass/And Picture Frames." Bendann was located at 105 East Baltimore in 1890.

[32] In the Augusta directory for 1879, Walker is listed as, "Walker William A., artist, 206 Broad, r[esidence] 113 Greene." Under photographers in the business section of the directory is a listing for "Usher, John, 206 Broad." (*Sholes' Directory of the City of Augusta*, January 1, 1879, volume 2, A. E. Sholes, Publisher.) In the directory for the following year, we find, "Walker William A., painter, 702 Broad," and under photographers, "Usher J., 702 Broad." (*Sholes' Directory of the City of Augusta*, January 1, 1880. A. E. Sholes, Publisher.) The fact that the artists were at the same address in the first year and moved to a second shared address one year later may be a coincidence, but it suggests that Walker and Usher shared studio space and may have been in business together.

[33] Letter from Robert A. Rowlinski to William A. Walker, 5 December 1916. Courtesy of Mrs. Lucia Cogswell Heins.

[34] Elizabeth Johns discusses the theme of gambling and the rube in her book *American Genre Painting: The Politics of Everyday life* (New Haven: Yale University Press, 1991).

[35] Alberta Collier, "Two Art Works Prompt Quest: Who Was Miss Lottie Mitchell?" *New Orleans Times-Picayune*, 14 April 1974. Louisiana Art Vertical File, Humanities Division, Tulane University Library.

[36] This portrait remained in a private collection in Vicksburg, Mississippi until it was donated to the Old Court House Museum in Vicksburg, where it is displayed in a case beneath the very flag that Trescott holds. I am grateful to Mr. Joseph Cotton, Director of the Old Courthouse Museum, for allowing me to examine and photograph the Trescott portrait and for furnishing biographical information on Austin A. Trescott.

CHAPTER FOUR • *WALKER AND THE RESURRECTION OF KING COTTON*

[1] "Historical Sketch of the Port of Galveston in 1874," *Galveston Daily News*, 13 September 1908.

[2] John A. Mahe II and Rosanne McCaffrey, eds., *Encyclopaedia of New Orleans Artists 1718-1918* (New Orleans: The Historic New Orleans Collection, 1987), 158.

[3] "A Fine Picture," *New Orleans Daily Crescent*, 26 January 1859. Courtesy of the Historic New Orleans Collection.

[4] "Local News. The Southern Art Union," *Daily States,* 22 May 1880. See also the review of the Southern Art Union's first exhibition, "The Art Exposition. Opening of the Rooms of the Southern Art Union and Woman's Industrial Association," *New Orleans Daily Picayune,* 26 May 1881. Courtesy of the Historic New Orleans Collection. I have found no evidence to suggest that Walker was a participant in this exhibition. The review includes a list of the names of participating artists together with their works, which the anonymous writer describes as "a tolerably accurate list of contributions." Walker's name does not appear on this roll. A search of libraries in New Orleans has failed to produce a catalogue of this exhibition.

[5] Mahe and McCaffrey, 397. Wagener's relationship to the Southern Art Union is found in the newspaper reference, "Mr. Wagener is the efficient and popular custodian of the pictures." "Art Subjects. Works of New Orleans Painters on Exhibition," *New Orleans Daily Picayune,* 28 May 1881.

[6] Mahe and McCaffrey, 237-238.

[7] Ibid., 346.

[8] "Seebold's Art Gallery. A New Orleans Exhibition of Oil Paintings, Engravings and Etchings," *New Orleans Daily Picayune,* 30 November 1884. Courtesy of the Historic New Orleans Collection.

[9] William Aiken Walker, New Orleans, to Dr. C. Louis Diehl, Louisville, 18 April 1905. Robert M. Hicklin Jr., Inc., Spartanburg, South Carolina. Although this letter was written on Walker's last visit to New Orleans, a full twenty-five years after the period under discussion, it is significant that Walker refers to his *old* landlady, which I feel refers not to the woman's age, but to the fact that Walker had boarded with her in the past.

[10] *Collection of Paintings by Leading New Orleans Artists and others of the United States and Europe, on Free Exhibition and Sale at Lilienthal's Art Gallery* (New Orleans: 1883). Courtesy of the Historic New Orleans Collection.

[11] "Pictures in New Orleans," *New Orleans Times-Democrat,* 17 July 1883. Courtesy of the Historic New Orleans Collection.

[12] Telephone interview by the author with Anna Wells Rutledge, 9 August 1990.

[13] "The South Carolina Problem: The Epoch of Transition," *Scribner's Monthly* 8, no. 2 (June 1874): 138.

[14] Eric Foner, *Reconstruction: America's Unfinished Revolution 1863-1877* (New York: Harper and Row, Publishers, 1988), 399.

[15] Philip A. Bruce, "A Tobacco Plantation," *Lippincott's Magazine*, old series, 36, no. 216; new series, 10, no. 60 (December 1885): 533.

[16] *New Orleans Daily Crescent*, 26 January 1859. Courtesy of the Historic New Orleans Collection.

[17] *Frank Leslie's Illustrated Newspaper*, 31 December 1887.

[18] William Makepeace Thackeray to Mrs. Baxter, 12 March 1853, as quoted in Rutledge, 152.

[19] Although no Walker paintings were hung in the art gallery of the Cotton Centennial Exposition, *Cotton Plantation* by Walker was lent by W. J. Warrington of New Orleans to the North, Central, and South American Exposition, a fair that opened in New Orleans on November 10, 1885 and closed April 1, 1886, the purpose of which was to recoup financial losses of the earlier fair. See *Official Catalogue of the Creole Exhibition, Art Gallery, American Exposition* (New Orleans: W. B. Stansbury, 1886). *Cotton Plantation* was number 344 in the catalogue.

[20] "Seebold's Art Gallery. A New Orleans Exhibition of Oil Paintings," *New Orleans Daily Picayune*, 30 November 1884. Courtesy of the Historic New Orleans Collection.

[21] *New Orleans Daily Picayune*, 3 December 1884. Courtesy of the Historic New Orleans Collection.

[22] "Art Talk. The Brush and Pencil in New Orleans," *New Orleans Daily Picayune*, 26 July 1885. Courtesy of the Historic New Orleans Collection.

[23] Foner, 79.

[24] "Art Talk. The Pencil and Brush in New Orleans," *New Orleans Daily Picayune*, 25 October 1885. Courtesy of the Historic New Orleans Collection.

[25] Dawson Blanchard, Washington, D.C., to Mrs. H. Blanchard, New Orleans, 16 March 1888. In this letter Blanchard refers to the death of "Mr. Giroux," writing to his wife of "you aiding the poor man in his last few days on earth." Blanchard-Williams Family Papers, Manuscripts Division, Howard Tilton Memorial Library, Tulane University, New Orleans, Louisiana.

[26] This painting is in the collection of Jay P. Altmayer.

[27] "The Artists' Association. A Flourishing Institution to Encourage a School of Art." *New Orleans Daily States*, 5 November 1886.

[28] *Catalogue/First Annual Exhibition/Artists' Association of New Orleans.* (New Orleans: 1886), nos. 53-61. Also see "The Art Exhibit. The Doors Thrown Open to the Public—Proficiency of the Student Class," *New Orleans Daily Picayune*, 7 November 1886. This review does not discuss Walker's paintings. Courtesy of the Historic New Orleans Collection.

[29] There is some question about when Walker started spending his summers in the Asheville area. His earliest picture of a North Carolina subject, *View from the Reverend D. C. Howell's Farm, N.C.*, which will be discussed shortly, is dated 1881. However, in a letter to his friend Dr. C. Louis Diehl dated April 7, 1899, Walker refers to Asheville as "that beautiful mountain region that I have looked upon for fourteen summers," from which we may infer that he had only spent his summers in the Asheville area since 1885.

[30] "Artists' Association. The Fourth Annual Exhibition. Creditable Work of Local Character— Home Scenes on Canvas. New Orleans Amateurs Skillful with the Brush," *New Orleans Daily Picayune*, 17 December 1889. Courtesy of the Historic New Orleans Collection.

[31] Walker exhibited the following paintings at the fifth annual exhibition of the Artists' Association of New Orleans: No. 56. *The Placa* [sic] and *Hotel Ponce de Leou* [sic], *St. Augustine, Fla.*; No. 57. *On the Way to Knowledge*; Nos. 58-62. *Sketches from Ediston* [sic] *Island*; and Nos. 63-69. *Sketches near Arden Park, N.C. Catalogue, Fifth Annual Exhibition, Artists' Association of New Orleans, Saturday, December 20, 1890* (New Orleans: 1890). Courtesy of the Historic New Orleans Collection.

[32] "Second Annual Exhibition of Artists' Association of New Orleans," *Art and Letters* I, no. 6 (December 1887): 228. One reviewer made only a general reference to pictures exhibited by Walker: "Walker contributes three watercolors and a landscape in oil. He has not furnished any of his negro creations this time, but the irrepressible colored man comes in somewhere in the landscape." "Home Artists. The Annual Exhibition of the Artists' Association," *New Orleans Daily Picayune*, 17 December 1887. Courtesy of the Historic New Orleans Collection.

[33] Foner, 405.

[34] Standard Photo Company sold Walker's paintings. When he died, thirty-six of his paintings were in the company's possession according to the inventory of the estate of William Aiken Walker completed by Probate Court, Charleston, South Carolina. Standard Photo Company also sold art supplies, so it is likely that Walker purchased supplies there.

[35] "Second Annual Exhibition of Artists' Association of New Orleans," *Art and Letters* I, no. 6 (December 1887): 227-228. Courtesy of the Historic New Orleans Collection.

[36] *Catalogue. Sixth Annual Exhibition of the Artists' Association of New Orleans, 1891* (New Orleans: 1891). Courtesy of the Historic New Orleans Collection.

[37] "Mrs. Walter Saxon, one of the most successful amateur artists in Louisiana, exhibits some excellent work. 'Shanties' is a reduced copy of the work which won for her the gold medal at last year's exhibition." "Artists' Association. The Fourth Annual Exhibition. Creditable Work of

Local Character—Home Scenes on Canvas. New Orleans Amateurs Skillful with the Brush," *New Orleans Daily Picayune*, 17 December 1889. Courtesy of the Historic New Orleans Collection.

[38] Ibid. The reviewer continued about Walker, writing, "His name is also upon four views of North Carolina scenery."

[39] Foner, 85.

[40] Thomas B. Alexander, "The Dimensions of Continuity Across the Civil War." In *The Old South in the Crucible of War*, edited by Harry P. Owens and James J. Cooke (Jackson: University Press of Mississippi, 1983).

CHAPTER FIVE • A MORE TRANQUIL LIFE

[1] Walker remained an active member of the Artists' Association at least until 1894. He participated in the Association's annual exhibitions of 1886, 1887, 1889, 1890, 1891, 1892, and 1894. I have not been able to locate a catalogue of the final exhibition in which he participated, but the following quote suggests that he only contributed one painting: "Mr. W. A. Walker was represented by one of his familiar Negro studies." "Artists' Annual. Ninth Annual Exhibit of the Local Association. A Number of Oil and Water Colors of Decided Merit and Others of Varying Degree of Excellence," *New Orleans Times-Democrat*, 14 December 1894. Courtesy of the Historic New Orleans Collection.

[2] In 1892 Walker exhibited a large plantation scene in the seventh annual exhibition of the Artists' Association of New Orleans. It was exhibited again at the World's Columbian Exposition in Chicago in 1893, where it was included in the Louisiana gallery. "Mr. William Walker is always alive in his subjects. 'Way Down South, in the Land of Cotton,' is a magnificent piece of art, and this gentleman is to be congratulated on his selection for the world's fair. Mr. Walker also exhibits a charming rural scene, quite striking to the beholder." "Artists' Reception. A Gala Evening at the Studio of the Art School. . . ." *New Orleans Daily Picayune*, 13 December 1892. Courtesy of the Historic New Orleans Collection.

[3] Evelyn Saffold Taber, "Mr. Walker as I Knew Him," *Sandlapper* 10 (August 1977): 18.

[4] "Fifth Annual Exhibition Artists' Association of New Orleans," *Current Topics* 1, no. 4 (December 1890): 25. Courtesy of the Historic New Orleans Collection. *The Plaza and Hotel Ponce de Leon* is probably the painting known today as *View of St. Augustine*. (Collection of J. Cornelius Rathborne, New Orleans, Louisiana). The view is taken from the basin of the Matanzas River looking towards the Plaza of the Constitution. Boats at anchor dominate the foreground. Between them

one sees sections of St. Augustine's sea wall. Steps lead up the sea wall and into the plaza. In the center of the plaza is a one-story, white, open-sided building which was known in the 1890s as the "old slave market." To the left of it is an obelisk, a monument to the Spanish Constitution erected 1812-1813. To the right is the Roman Catholic Cathedral. The cathedral was partially destroyed by fire in 1887. When it was rebuilt the bell tower visible in Walker's painting was added. A dense bank of trees forms the background to the painting. Above them appear the twin towers of the Ponce de Leon Hotel. Walker's residence, the Magnolia Hotel, though not visible in the painting, would have been two-and-one-half blocks behind the cathedral.

[5] *St. Augustine Tatler*, 6 January 1895. Walker's visits to St. Augustine the winters of 1896, 1899, and 1900 are also noted in the *Tatler*. "Mr. William F. [*sic*] Walker, the famous painter of the old-time negro slave, is at the Magnolia, and has his studio as usual at Tugby's." (*St. Augustine Tatler*, 18 January 1896.) "Wm. A. Walker, the New Orleans artist, who has reproduced scenes of every day life in the South in most natural fashion, has returned to his old quarters at the Magnolia." (*St. Augustine Tatler*, 4 February 1899.) "Mr. William A. Walker, famous as a painter of the old-time plantations of by-gone days, has returned to the Magnolia, S. C. [?]" (*St. Augustine Tatler*, 30 December 1899.) Courtesy of the Saint Augustine Historical Society.

[6] Advertisement for the Magnolia Hotel, in *The Standard Guide to St. Augustine* (St. Augustine: E. H. Reynolds; New York: C. B. Reynolds, 1892); and *Florida: Winter Pleasure Tours under the Personally-Conducted System of the Pennsylvania Railroad. Season of 1892* (The Parr Company, 1891), 17.

[7] Martha Pacetti is referred to repeatedly in Walker's letters as either Mrs. Pacetti or "the old lady." She died September 3, 1917. As early as 1899, shortly after her husband's death, their son Gomecinda Pacetti was manager of Pacetti House. This information appears on the letterhead of Pacetti House stationery. (Walker to Diehl, 17 April 1899, Pacetti House, Ponce Park, Florida. Robert M. Hicklin Jr., Inc., Spartanburg, South Carolina.) In 1919, Mrs. Bartola John Pacetti (Bertha Rowlinski Pacetti), Bartola and Martha's daughter-in-law, was in charge. Walker wrote to her as he was preparing to leave Ponce Park for the summer, enclosing a check for forty dollars to cover "my table board for last 4 weeks." (Walker to Mrs. B. J. Pacetti, 4 June 1919, Ponce Park, Florida. Courtesy of Gail Rothrock Trozzo.) Pacetti House was sold to someone by the name of Long from Pennsylvania in the 1920s. In 1936 it was purchased by Miss Olivia Penrose Gamble (1875-1961), daughter of sportsman James Norris Gamble, a vice-president in the firm Procter and Gamble of Cincinnati, who had been a frequent guest at Pacetti House.

[8] In the collection of Jay P. Altmayer, is *Man Smoking a Pipe* (oil on academy board, 4 x 8 inches; signed lower left: *WAWalker*) that was a gift to Bartolo and Martha's son and daughter-in-law, Mr.

and Mrs. Gomecinda Pacetti. The following inscription, in Walker's hand, appears on the reverse: *4 X 8/each* [price has been crossed out]*/pair $15.00/Ponce Park/Fla./Christmas/1900/For Mr. and Mrs. G. A. Pacetti/Compliments of Wm. A. Walker.* A painting in the Sewell Family Collection, *Saunder's House, Indian Key, Florida,* also bears an inscription indicating that it was given by Walker to Mr. and Mrs. Gomecinda Pacetti. (See figure 86.)

9

> Next week Merry Christmas will greet us,
> But you will not be here to meet us.
> Now Colonel come down,
> Help my sorrows to drown.
> Say, Colonel, now when will you meet us?
>
> The Bass have agreed in Convention,
> The Colonel's name never to mention.
> They say that his rod
> Lays them all on the sod,
> For his line covers heap much extension!
>
> Now come soon and help me be jolly.
> I'll give you a "wee drop" by golly.
> Won't make your head hum,
> I promise by gum,
> But we'll feel fit to ride on a trolly [sic].
>
> Merry Christmas and Happy New Year,
> Warm fire, fine punch and good cheer.
> I hope that the day
> Will find you quite gay,
> But I'm sorry you will not be here.
>
> To my friends pray give a kind greeting.
> The days of this old year are fleeting,
> But this fair Land of Flowers
> Will hold many hours
> Of pleasure in store for our meeting.

From Walker's manuscript book of poems, "Mes Pensées." Collection of the Carolina Art Association/Gibbes Museum of Art, Charleston, South Carolina.

[10] Walker to Diehl, 20 April 1899, Yacht *Orian,* near Hillsboro Inlet, Florida. Robert M. Hicklin Jr., Inc., Spartanburg, South Carolina.

[11] Charles Ledyard Norton, *A Handbook of Florida,* 3rd ed. (New York: Longmans, Green & Co., 1892), 222-223.

[12] Formerly titled *The Pacetti House,* the painting has been retitled *Saunder's House, Indian Key, Florida* on the basis of Walker's inscription on the drawing.

[13] Walker to Diehl, 19 June 1904, Arden Park Lodge, Arden, North Carolina. Robert M. Hicklin Jr., Inc., Spartanburg, South Carolina.

[14] Walker's admission of his deafness reads:

> Here is news for you. Mrs. Pacetti informed me just before leaving [before Walker left Pacetti House for the summer] that she had purchased a Piano which was to arrive next day! Think of it! Know you what that means? Much noise in future, for I can fancy the sort of music that Nettie will extract all the time out of that instrument of torture! But deafness is sometimes a blessing my friend, and I will escape much of it in my far off den. . . . I am afraid that piano will be a great nuisance next season to one of my musical cultivation.

Walker to Diehl, 19 June 1904, Arden Park Lodge, Arden, North Carolina. Robert M. Hicklin Jr., Inc., Spartanburg, South Carolina.

[15] Walker to Diehl, 18 November 1904, Ponce Park, Florida. Robert M. Hicklin Jr., Inc., Spartanburg, South Carolina.

[16] Walker to Diehl, 28 December 1904, Ponce Park, Florida. Robert M. Hicklin Jr., Inc., Spartanburg, South Carolina. After the first of the year, the weather turned extremely cold, and in his next letter to Diehl, Walker was not so satisfied with his progress. (Walker to Diehl, 2 February 1905, Ponce Park, Florida. Robert M. Hicklin Jr., Inc., Spartanburg, South Carolina.)

> Today is grey & foggy, sour weather, but you are coming when the weather ought to be getting better. I have loafed for over a month, been too cold many days to go out sketching or fishing, and on the pleasant days the genius would not burn. I have done a little fishing along the shore, but caught but little, the water is too cold. . . . We play solitaire a good deal in the office and get some fun out of it.

[17] Walker to Diehl, 3 June 1905, Biloxi, Mississippi. Robert M. Hicklin Jr., Inc., Spartanburg, South Carolina.

18

> Come and see how a few days in Louisiana [?] and feel, get the warm blood to [once] again course in your veins and feel restored to your [usual] vigor. You are right my boy the mountains of North Carolina or any other mountains in or about the same latitude are not satisfactory abodes in December, and I was surprised to hear you had remained [?] in the season at those altitudes. Other [?] do not usually exhibit such eccentricities.

George Langtry to William Aiken Walker, 13 January 1900. Collection of Josephine Walker Martin, Ph.D., Columbia, South Carolina.

[19] Walker to Diehl, 18 April 1905, New Orleans. Robert M. Hicklin Jr., Inc., Spartanburg, South Carolina.

[20] Walker to Diehl, 3 June 1905, Biloxi, Mississippi. Robert M. Hicklin Jr., Inc., Spartanburg, South Carolina.

[21] Ibid.

[22] Walker to Diehl, 7 December 1905, St. Augustine, Florida. Robert M. Hicklin Jr., Inc., Spartanburg, South Carolina.

23

> I hear there is no one at Pacetti House now, had only I boarder for a while, Mr. Dewey, wonder if it was our old friend? . . . I have not written any of the P. [Pacetti] family yet. I will possibly remain here until end of this month, then go to P. Park, maybe later, can't say yet. I prefer meeting some people there for company and for better table. I hope to hear from the Col. soon as to his movements as I wrote him a few days ago. If it is not made pleasant for me at the P. House, why I can leave. I will keep you fully posted about it.

Walker to Diehl, 7 December 1905, St. Augustine, Florida. Robert M. Hicklin Jr., Inc., Spartanburg, South Carolina.

[24] From Walker's manuscript book of poems, "Mes Pensées." Collection of the Carolina Art Association/Gibbes Museum of Art, Charleston, South Carolina.

[25] Walker to Diehl, 17 February 1911, Ponce Park, Florida. Robert M. Hicklin Jr., Inc., Spartanburg, South Carolina.

[26] Interview by the author with Mrs. Josephine Walker Martin, Columbia, South Carolina, July 1988.

[27] Ibid.

[28] Interview by the author with Mrs. Julia Walker Bradley, Charleston, South Carolina, July 1988.

[29] Ibid.

[30] Walker to Diehl, 26 May 1912, Charleston, South Carolina. Collection of Josephine Walker Martin, Ph.D.

[31] Taber, 19.

[32] *Ruins, Arden Park Lodge*, 1919, oil on academy board, 12 1/4 x 6 1/8 inches, signed and dated lower left: *WAWalker/Oct. 1 1919*. The Warner Collection of Gulf States Paper Corporation, Tuscaloosa, Alabama.

[33] *Arden*, 1920, pencil on paper, inscribed and dated lower left: *Arden/Oct. 15. 1920*. Location unknown.

[34] Certificate of Death, Bureau of Vital Statistics, record no. N93516, Charleston County Health Department, Charleston, South Carolina.

[35] *Charleston News and Courier*, 4 January 1921.

[36] Inventory of estate of William Aiken Walker, Surrogate's Court, Charleston, South Carolina.

E P I L O G U E

[1] "William Aiken Walker Resurrected," *The Art News* 38 (March 1940): 18.

[2] Marie Louise D'Otrange Mastai, "The World of William Aiken Walker," *Apollo* 74 (June 1969): 213

Select Bibliography

American Art from Alumni Collections. New Haven: The Yale University Art Gallery, 1968.

Bilodeau, Francis W., and Mrs. Thomas J. Tobias, comps. and eds. *Art in South Carolina 1670-1970.* Charleston: The Carolina Art Association, 1970.

Coleman, William. "The Life and Works of William Aiken Walker." *Sandlapper* 10 (August 1977): 16-18.

Edwards, Lee M. *Domestic Bliss: Family Life in American Painting, 1840-1910.* Yonkers, New York: The Hudson River Museum of Westchester, Inc., 1986.

Exhibition of Southern Genre Paintings by William Aiken Walker, 1838-1921. New York: The Bland Gallery, Inc., 1940.

Falk, Peter Hastings. *Who Was Who in American Art.* Madison, Wisconsin: Sound View Press, 1985.

Fulton, W. Joseph, and Roulhac B. Toledano. "New Orleans Landscape Painting of the Nineteenth Century." *The Magazine Antiques* 93 (April 1968): 504-510.

Gerdts, William H. *Nineteenth Century American Paintings from the Collection of Mr. and Mrs. George J. Arden.* Easton, Pennsylvania: The Gallery, Morris R. Williams Center for the Arts, Lafayette College, 1983.

Groce, George C., and David H. Wallace. *The New-York Historical Society's Dictionary of Artists in America, 1564-1860.* New Haven: Yale University Press, 1979.

Heins, Lucia Cogswell. "A Note on William Aiken Walker." *South Carolina Historical Magazine* 79 (1978): 322-324.

Life in America: A Special Loan Exhibition of Paintings Held during the Period of the New York World's Fair. New York: The Metropolitan Museum of Art, 1939.

Louisiana Landscape and Genre Paintings of the Nineteenth Century. Shreveport: The R. W. Norton Art Gallery, 1981.

The M. and M. Karolik Collection of American Paintings, 1815 to 1865. Cambridge: Harvard University Press, 1949.

Mahe, John A. II, and Roseanne McCaffrey, eds. *Encyclopedia of New Orleans Artists, 1718-1918.* New Orleans: The Historic New Orleans Collection, 1987.

Mastai, M. L. D'Otrange. "William Aiken Walker, Painter of 'The Land of Cotton.' " In *The Connoisseur Year Book,* 74-79. London: The Connoisseur, 1964.

_____. "The World of William Aiken Walker." *Apollo* 74 (June 1961): 213-215.

McElroy, Guy C. *Facing History: The Black Image in American Art 1710-1940.* San Francisco: Bedford Arts, Publishers, in association with the Corcoran Gallery of Art, 1990.

The Old South: Selections from the Warner Collection of Gulf States Paper Corporation. Jackson: The Mississippi Museum of Art, 1986.

Painting in the South: 1564-1980. Richmond: The Virginia Museum of Fine Arts, 1983.

Parker, Barbara N. "American Paintings, 1815-1865, in the M. and M. Karolik Collection." *The Magazine Antiques* 60 (October 1951): 292-295.

Pennington, Estill Curtis. *Look Away: Reality and Sentiment in Southern Art.* Spartanburg, South Carolina: Saraland Press, 1989.

Pennington, Estill Curtis, and James C. Kelly. *The South on Paper: Line, Color, and Light.* Spartanburg, South Carolina: Robert M. Hicklin Jr., Inc., 1985.

Pinckney, Pauline A. *Painting in Texas, the Nineteenth Century.* Austin: University of Texas Press, 1967.

Porcher, Francis James. Catalogue of Paintings. The Carolina Art Association/Gibbes Museum of Art, Charleston, South Carolina.

Rathbone, Perry T., ed. *Mississippi Panorama*. New and rev. ed. St. Louis: The City Art Museum, 1950.

_____. "Mississippi Panorama." *Art News* 48 (October 1949): 38, 40, 53-54.

Reflections of the Old South. Thomasville: The Thomasville, Georgia Cultural Center, Inc., 1989.

Rogers, Dorian. "William Aiken Walker is Collectors' Favorite." *Antique Monthly* (June 1981): 16B-17B.

Rutledge, Anna Wells. *Artists in the Life of Charleston Through Colony and State from Restoration to Reconstruction*. 1949. Reprint with a new preface by John Morrill Bryan. Columbia: University of South Carolina Press, 1980.

Sacharow, Stanley. "North American View, Black Americana." *Antique Collector* (March 1982): 82.

Selections from the Collection of the Carolina Art Association. Charleston: The Carolina Art Association, 1977.

Taber, Evelyn Saffold. "Mr. Walker as I Knew Him." *Sandlapper* 10 (August 1977): 18-21.

Trovaioli, August P., and Roulhac B. Toledano. "William Aiken Walker, Chronicler of a Bygone Era." *New Orleans* 5 (March 1971): 26-27, 30, 40, 42, 47.

_____. *William Aiken Walker: Southern Genre Painter*. Baton Rouge: Louisiana State University Press, 1972.

Van Ravenswaay, Charles. "Old Man River: Life and Character of the Mississippi." *American Heritage* 2 (Autumn 1950): 49.

Walker, William Aiken. Cuban Diary. The Carolina Art Association/Gibbes Museum of Art, Charleston, South Carolina.

_____. Letters, 1899-1914. Robert M. Hicklin Jr., Inc., Spartanburg, South Carolina.

_____. "Mes Pensées." The Carolina Art Association/Gibbes Museum of Art, Charleston, South Carolina.

Waring, Thomas R. "The Old Southern Scene." *Charleston News and Courier,* 22 January 1973.

Wiesendanger, Martin, and Margaret Wiesendanger. *Nineteenth Century Louisiana Painters and Paintings from the Collection of W. E. Groves.* Gretna, Louisiana: Pelican Publishing Company, 1971.

William Aiken Walker from Southern Collections. Charleston: The Gibbes Museum of Art, 1988.

William Aiken Walker: Paintings, 1879-1918. Florence: University of North Alabama, 1990.

"William Aiken Walker Resurrected." *The Art News* 38 (March 1940): 18.

Williams, Herman Warner, Jr. *Mirror to the American Past: A Survey of American Genre Painting, 1750-1900.* Greenwich: The New York Graphic Society, 1973.

Williams, Mary Frances. *Catalogue of the Collection of American Art at Randolph-Macon Woman's College: A Selection of Paintings, Drawings, and Prints.* Second Edition. Charlottesville: University Press of Virginia, 1977.

The World of William Aiken Walker. New Orleans: The Louisiana State Museum, 1972.

Wright, R. Lewis. *Artists in Virginia Before 1900.* Charlottesville: University Press of Virginia, in association with the Virginia Historical Society, 1983.

In Appreciation

The author and publisher wish to thank the following collectors and friends for their generous assistance in creating this volume, and, where applicable, for granting us permission to reproduce their works of art.

Mr. and Mrs. Jay P. Altmayer
Mrs. George Arden/The Arden Collection
Mrs. Agnes Baldwin
Berry-Hill Galleries, Inc.
Mrs. Claudia Cogswell Bolduc
Mr. and Mrs. George Brandt III
Mr. and Mrs. Donald Bush
Christie's, New York, New York
Mrs. George Walker Cogswell
Mr. and Mrs. Stephen Cogswell
Mrs. William H. Cogswell III
The Columbia Museum of Art, Columbia, South Carolina
Mrs. Virgil Cooper
Miss Louise Crane
The Filson Club, Louisville, Kentucky
Mr. John Fowler
The Gibbes Museum of Art/Carolina Art Association, Charleston, South Carolina
The Gilcrease Museum, Tulsa, Oklahoma
Mr. and Mrs. Henry C. Goodrich
Mr. and Mrs. Bill Graham
The Greenville County Museum of Art, Greenville, South Carolina
Mrs. Lucia Cogswell Heins
The High Museum of Art, Atlanta, Georgia

The Historic Charleston Foundation, Charleston, South Carolina

The Historic New Orleans Collection, New Orleans, Louisiana

Mr. and Mrs. Robert J. Hussey, Jr.

Mrs. Lisa Cogswell Kirk

The Lagakos-Turak Gallery, Philadelphia, Pennsylvania

Dr. and Mrs. Ron Lawson

The Library of Congress, Washington, D.C.

The Louisiana State Museum, New Orleans, Louisiana

Louisiana State University, Baton Rouge, Louisiana

Mr. and Mrs. G. Thomas Ludwig

The Mariners' Museum, Newport News, Virginia

Dr. A. McLeish Martin

Ms. Helen S. Martin

Ms. Josephine Martin, Ph.D.

Mr. G. Simms McDowell, Jr.

Dr. and Mrs. Oscar Maxwell

Mr. and Mrs. Charles C. Mickel

Ms. Constance Cogswell Miller

Dr. Robert L. Moore, Jr.

Mr. Malcolm W. Monroe

Mr. William S. Morris III/The Morris Museum of Art, Augusta, Georgia

The Museum of Fine Arts, Boston, Massachusetts

The Museum of the Confederacy, Richmond, Virginia

The New York Public Library, New York, New York

The Roger Houston Ogden Collection, New Orleans, Louisiana

The Old Court House Museum, Vicksburg, Mississippi

The Parrish Art Museum, Southampton, New York

Mr. Ted Phillips

Mr. and Mrs. Francis M. Pinckney

Mr. Remak Ramsey

Mr. J. Cornelius Rathborne

Ms. Tina Rathborne

The Rosenberg Library, Galveston, Texas

Mr. and Mrs. Walter H. Rubin

Mrs. J. Raymond Samuel

The San Antonio Museum Association, San Antonio, Texas

Mr. and Mrs. Quincy Scarborough

Mr. and Mrs. Guy B. Scoggin

Mr. and Mrs. Logan Sewell/The Sewell Family Collection

Mr. and Mrs. Edward McIlhenny Simmons, Jr.

Mrs. Cooper Smith

The South Carolina State Museum, Columbia, South Carolina

Mr. Thomas Styron

Ms. Theresa Thompson

Ms. Roulhac Toledano

Mrs. Judith S. Vane

Mr. and Mrs. Samuel H. Vickers

Mrs. Edward Hall Walker

Mr. Philip L. Walker

Mr. and Mrs. William E. Walker, Jr.

Mr. James Wallis

Dr. and Mrs. John Ward

Mr. Jack Warner/The Warner Collection of Gulf States Paper Corporation,
    Tuscaloosa, Alabama

Mr. and Mrs. Hunter White

Mrs. Derita Coleman Williams

Dr. Ted Wingard

The Witte Museum, San Antonio, Texas

Gerold Wunderlich

The Yale University Art Gallery, New Haven, Connecticut

Photography Credits

Larry Amato, *pp. 156, 197*

Jeff Barnes, *p. 140*

Jim Carpenter, *p. 77*

Mark Coffee, *pp. 19, 190*

Pat Crawford, *frontispiece*

Judy Davis, *p.184*

Art Downs, *pp. 169, 179*

Rick Echelmeyer, *p. 143*

Hans Lorenz, *p. 152*

Blake Praytor, *pp. vi, 14, 15, 42, 52, 61, 79, 93, 99, 104, 112, 115, 116, 119, 128, 129, 130, 133, 135, 136, 145, 147, 151, 165, 167, 168, 173, 181, 182, 193*

Rick Rhodes, *pp. 26, 142, 166, 189, 195*

David Richmond, *p. 85*

Howard Smith, *pp. 23, 131*

List of Illustrations

Index